DATA MINING FOR THE SOCIAL SCIENCES

DATA MINING FOR THE SOCIAL SCIENCES

An Introduction

Paul Attewell and David B. Monaghan
with Darren Kwong

 UNIVERSITY OF CALIFORNIA PRESS

University of California Press, one of the most distinguished university presses in the United States, enriches lives around the world by advancing scholarship in the humanities, social sciences, and natural sciences. Its activities are supported by the UC Press Foundation and by philanthropic contributions from individuals and institutions. For more information, visit www.ucpress.edu.

University of California Press
Oakland, California

Library of Congress Cataloging-in-Publication Data
Attewell, Paul A., 1949- author.
 Data mining for the social sciences : an introduction / Paul Attewell and David B. Monaghan. -- First edition.
     pages cm
  Includes bibliographical references and index.
   ISBN 978-0-520-28097-7 (cloth : alk. paper)—ISBN 0-520-28097-0 (cloth : alk. paper)—ISBN 978-0-520-28098-4 (pbk. : alk. paper)—ISBN 0-520-28098-9 (pbk. : alk. paper)—ISBN 978-0-520-96059-6 (ebook)—ISBN 0-520-96059-9 (ebook)
   1. Social sciences--Data processing.   2. Social sciences--Statistical methods.   3. Data mining.   I. Monaghan, David B., 1988- author.   II. Title.
   H61.3.A88 2015
   006.3'12—dc23
                                                  2014035276

Manufactured in the United States of America
24 23 22 21 20 19 18 17 16 15
10 9 8 7 6 5 4 3 2 1

To my family, Kathy, Steven, and David, whose support
and affection motivate all that I do.
PAA

To my wonderful wife, Melinda, for her love, support, and
encouragement. And to my parents, for their love
and guidance.
DBM

CONTENTS

ACKNOWLEDGMENTS

Data mining, especially as applied to social science data, is a rapidly changing field, and our understanding of these new methods has benefited enormously from the teaching and advice of others, most especially Professors Robert Stine, Robert Haralick, and Andrew Rosenberg. Several students who are using these techniques in their doctoral research projects have contributed their wisdom. First and foremost, Darren Kwong prepared several of the worked examples reported in this book, sometimes struggling with obdurate software in the process. Darren also organized an invaluable public seminar series on data mining methods at the CUNY Graduate Center in New York, which kept us informed about emerging quantitative methods. Dirk Witteveen and Andrew Wallace shared their insights and skills about various computational techniques that they have been mastering. Wenjuan Zheng contributed her hard work to completing a particularly thankless task. Other graduate students too numerous to name enrolled in doctoral courses in data mining and gave us the opportunity to test our ideas and explanations of these methods. Not least, we owe many thanks to the National Science Foundation, whose grant no. DRL1243785 has funded our research and other related activities involving data mining in the social and behavioral sciences and in education.

PART 1

CONCEPTS

1

WHAT IS DATA MINING?

Data mining (DM) is the name given to a variety of computer-intensive techniques for discovering structure and for analyzing patterns in data. Using those patterns, DM can create predictive models, or classify things, or identify different groups or clusters of cases within data. Data mining and its close cousins *machine learning* and *predictive analytics* are already widely used in business and are starting to spread into social science and other areas of research.

A partial list of current data mining methods includes:

- association rules
- recursive partitioning or decision trees, including CART (classification and regression trees) and CHAID (chi-squared automatic interaction detection), boosted trees, forests, and bootstrap forests
- multi-layer neural network models and "deep learning" methods
- naive Bayes classifiers and Bayesian networks
- clustering methods, including hierarchical, k-means, nearest neighbor, linear and nonlinear manifold clustering
- support vector machines
- "soft modeling" or partial least squares latent variable modeling

DM is a young area of scholarship, but it is growing very rapidly. As we speak, new methods are appearing, old ones are being modified, and strategies and skills in using these methods are accumulating. The potential and importance of DM are becoming widely recognized. In just the last two years the National Science Foundation has poured millions of dollars into new research initiatives in this area.

DM methods can be applied to quite different domains, for example to visual data, in reading handwriting or recognizing faces within digital pictures. DM is also being used to analyze texts—for example to classify the content of scientific papers or other documents—hence the term *text mining*. In addition, DM analytics can be applied to digitized sound, to recognize words in phone conversations, for example. In this book, however, we focus on the most common domain: the use of DM methods to analyze quantitative or numerical data.

Miners look for veins of ore and extract these valuable parts from the surrounding rock. By analogy, data mining looks for patterns or structure in data. But what does it mean to say that we look for structure in data? Think of a computer screen that displays thousands of pixels, points of light or dark. Those points are raw data. But if you scan those pixels by eye and recognize in them the shapes of letters and words, then you are finding structures in the data—or, to use another metaphor, you are turning *data* into *information*.

The equivalent to the computer screen for numerical data is a spreadsheet or matrix, where each column represents a single variable and each row contains data for a different case or person. Each cell within the spreadsheet contains a specific value for one person on one particular variable.

How do you recognize patterns or regularities or structures in this kind of raw numerical data? Statistics provides various ways of expressing the relations between the columns and rows of data in a spreadsheet. The most familiar one is a *correlation matrix*. Instead of repeating the raw data, with its thousands of observations and dozens of variables, a correlation matrix represents just the relations between each variable and each other variable. It is a summary, a simplification of the raw data.

Few of us can read a correlation matrix easily, or recognize a meaningful pattern in it, so we typically go through a second step in looking for structures in numerical data. We create a model that summarizes the relations in the correlation matrix. An ordinary least squares (OLS) regression model is one common example. It translates a correlation matrix into a much smaller regression equation that we can more easily understand and interpret.

A statistical model is more than just a summary derived from raw data, though. It is also a tool for prediction, and it is this second property that makes DM especially useful. Banks accumulate huge databases about customers, including records of who defaulted on loans. If bank analysts can turn those data into a model to accurately predict who will default on a loan, then they can reject the riskiest new loan applications and avoid losses. If Amazon.com can accurately assess your tastes in books, based on your previous purchases and your similarity to other customers, and then tempt you with a well-chosen book recommendation, then the company will make more profit. If a physician can obtain an NMR scan of cell tissue and predict from that data whether a tumor is likely to be malignant or benign, then the doctor has a powerful tool at her disposal.

Our world is awash with digital data. By finding patterns in data, especially patterns that can accurately predict important outcomes, DM is providing a very valuable service. Accurate prediction can inform a decision and lead to an action. If that cell tissue is most likely malignant, then one should schedule surgery. If that person's predicted risk of default is high, then don't approve the loan.

But why do we need DM for this? Wouldn't traditional statistical methods fulfill the same function just as well?

Conventional statistical methods do provide predictive models, but they have significant weaknesses. DM methods offer an alternative to conventional methods, in some cases a superior alternative that is less subject to those problems. We will later enumerate several advantages of DM, but for now we point out just the most obvious one. DM is especially well suited to analyzing very large datasets with many variables and/or many cases—what's known as Big Data.

Conventional statistical methods sometimes break down when applied to very large datasets, either because they cannot handle the computational aspects, or because they face more fundamental barriers to estimation. An example of the latter is when a dataset contains more variables than observations, a combination that conventional regression models cannot handle, but that several DM methods can.

DM not only overcomes certain limitations of conventional statistical methods, it also helps transcend some human limitations. A researcher faced with a dataset containing hundreds of variables and many thousands of cases is likely to overlook important features of the data because of limited time and attention. It is relatively easy, for example, to inspect a half-dozen variables to decide whether to transform any of them, to make them more closely resemble a bell curve or normal distribution. However, a human analyst will quickly become overwhelmed trying to decide the same thing for hundreds of variables. Similarly, a researcher may wish to examine statistical interactions between predictors in a dataset, but what happens when that person has to consider interactions between dozens of predictors? The number of potential combinations grows so large that any human analyst would be stymied.

DM techniques help in this situation because they partly "automate" data analysis by identifying the most important predictors among a large number of independent variables, or by transforming variables automatically into more useful distributions, or by detecting complex interactions among variables, or by discovering what forms of heterogeneity are prevalent in a dataset. The human researcher still makes critical decisions, but DM methods leverage the power of computers to compare numerous alternatives and identify patterns that human analysts might easily overlook (Larose 2005; McKinsey Global Institute 2011; Nisbet, Elder, and Miner 2009).

It follows that DM is very computationally intensive. It uses computer power to scour data for patterns, to search for "hidden" interactions among variables, and to try out alternative methods or combine models to maximize its accuracy in prediction.

THE GOALS OF THIS BOOK

There are many books on DM, so what's special about this one? One can think of the literature on DM as a layer cake. The bottom layer deals with the mathematical concepts and theorems that underlie DM. These are fundamental but are difficult to understand. This book doesn't try to operate at that technically demanding level, but interested readers can get a taste by looking at the online version of the classic text by Hastie, Tibshirani, and Friedman (2009): *The Elements of Statistical Learning: Data Mining, Inference, and Prediction* (there is a free version at www.stanford.edu/~hastie/local.ftp/Springer/OLD// ESLII_print4.pdf).

Moving upward, the next layer of the DM literature covers computer algorithms that apply those mathematical concepts to data. Critical issues here are how to minimize the time needed to perform various mathematical and matrix operations and choosing efficient computational strategies that can analyze data one case at a time or make the minimum number of passes through a large dataset. Fast, efficient computer strategies are especially critical when analyzing big data containing hundreds of thousands of observations. An inefficient computer program might run for days to accomplish a single analysis. This book doesn't go into the algorithmic level either. Interested readers can consult the books by Tan, Steinbach, and Kumar (2005) and Witten, Eibe, and Hall (2011) listed in the bibliography.

At the top layer of the DM literature one finds books about the *use* of DM. Several are exhortations to managers and employees to revolutionize their firms by embracing DM or "business analytics" as a business strategy. That's not our goal, however. What this book provides is a brief, nontechnical introduction to DM for people who are interested in using it to analyze quantitative data but who don't yet know much about these methods. Our primary goal is to explain what DM does and how it differs from more familiar or established kinds of statistical analysis and modeling, and to provide a sense of DM's strengths and weaknesses. To communicate those ideas, this book begins by discussing DM in general, especially its distinctive perspective on data analysis. Later, it introduces the main methods or tools within DM.

This book mostly avoids math. It does presume a basic knowledge of conventional statistics; at a minimum you should know a little about multiple regression and logistic regression. The second half of this book provides examples of data analyses for each application or DM tool, walks the reader through the interpretation of the software output, and discusses what each example has taught us. It covers several "tricks" that data miners use in analyses, and it highlights some pitfalls to avoid, or suggests ways to get round them.

After reading this book you should understand in general terms what DM is and what a data analyst might use it for. You should be able to pick out appropriate DM tools for particular tasks and be able to interpret their output. After that, using DM tools is mainly a matter of practice, and of keeping up with a field that is advancing at an extraordinarily rapid pace.

SOFTWARE AND HARDWARE FOR DATA MINING

Large corporations use custom-written computer programs for their DM applications, and they run them on fast mainframes or powerful computer clusters. Those are probably the best computer environments for analyzing big data, but they are out of reach for most of us. Fortunately, there are several products that combine multiple DM tools into a single package or software suite that runs under Windows on a personal computer.

JMP Pro (pronounced "jump pro") was developed by the company that sells the SAS suite of statistical software. You can download a free trial version, and the company provides online tutorials and other learning tools. JMP is relatively easy to use, employing a point-and-click approach. However, it lacks some of the more recent DM analytical tools.

SPSS (Statistical Package for the Social Sciences), now owned by IBM, is one of the oldest and most established software products for analyzing data using conventional statistical methods such as regression, cross-tabulation, t-tests, factor analysis, and so on. In its more recent versions (20 and above), the "professional" version of SPSS includes several data mining methods, including neural network models, automated linear models, and clustering. These are easy to use because they are point-and-click programs and their inputs and outputs are well designed. This may be the best place for a beginner to get a taste of some DM methods.

A more advanced data mining package called IBM SPSS Modeler includes a much larger choice of DM methods. This program is more complicated to learn than regular SPSS: one has to arrange various icons into a process and set various options or parameters. However, Modeler provides a full range of DM tools.

There are other commercial software products for PCs that include some DM tools within their general statistics software. Among these, MathWorks MATLAB offers data mining within two specialized "toolboxes": Statistics and Neural Networks. StatSoft's Statistica package includes an array of DM programs; and XLMiner is a commercial add-on for data mining that works with Microsoft's Excel spreadsheet program.

Beyond the commercial software, there are several free data mining packages for PCs.

RapidMiner is an extensive suite of DM programs developed in Germany. It has recently incorporated programs from the Weka DM suite (see below), and also many DM programs written in the R language. As a result, RapidMiner offers by far the largest variety of DM programs currently available in any single software product. It is also free (see http://rapid-i.com for information). The software takes considerable time to master; it uses a flowchart approach that involves dragging icons onto a workspace and linking them into a program or sequence. This idea is familiar to computer programmers, but may take others some time to learn. However, the user does not write commands or code. There is good online documentation, and North (2012) has written an introductory text-book for RapidMiner that has a free online version (http://dl.dropbox.com/u/31779972/DataMiningForTheMasses.pdf).

Weka is one of the oldest DM suites, and it is also free (see www.cs.waikato.ac.nz/ml/weka/). Developed in New Zealand, it is exceptionally well documented, including an encyclopedic textbook (Witten, Eibe, and Hall 2011) and online tutorials (www.cs.ccsu.edu/~markov/weka-tutorial.pdf).

Rattle (http://rattle.togaware.com) is a free graphical user interface for a large collection of DM tools available in the R language. (R itself is also a free download.) Rattle is well documented, including a textbook (G. Williams 2011).

TraMineR (http://mephisto.unige.ch/traminer/) is a free suite of specialized programs developed in Switzerland to analyze sequences and longitudinal data. This is not an alternative but a supplement to more general DM software.

No one knows which of these competing software packages will dominate in the years to come, so it is difficult to recommend one that you should invest your time and energy in learning. If ease of use matters most to you, then you might start with SPSS Professional or JMP. On the other hand, if you want access to the full palette of DM techniques, then Modeler or RapidMiner might be a good choice.

A CAUTIONARY NOTE ABOUT HARDWARE

Makers of DM software for PCs tend to understate the hardware configuration needed to use their products effectively. DM software pushes Windows-based PCs to their limits. When using ordinary desktop computers to run DM software, one discovers that some analyses run very slowly, and a few "crash" or "hang up," even when datasets are not large. To avoid those frustrations, it is best to use as powerful a PC as possible, one with at least 8 GB of RAM (more than that is even better) and a fast multicore processor (for example an Intel i7). Even then, you may need to go for a coffee break while some programs are left running.

Big data requires large hard drives, but 1- or 2-terabyte drives have become inexpensive options when buying a new PC. For most datasets, smaller drives will suffice. Reading data does not seem to be a bottleneck when data mining on a PC; memory and CPU processing speed appear to be the limiting factors.

BASIC TERMINOLOGY

Data mining is an interdisciplinary field to which computer scientists, mathematicians, and applied social scientists have all made contributions. DM terminology reflects these diverse origins. Here are a few basic terms and concepts that the reader should know from the start.

- What statisticians refer to as *variables*—for example a person's height, weight, and eye color, or a customer's address, phone number, and Zip code—are usually called *features* or *attributes* by data miners and computer scientists.

- Statisticians distinguish between *independent variables* (which are predictors) and the *dependent variable* (which is the measure being predicted). When talking about the same thing, data miners will refer to *features* or *attributes* predicting a *target*. In certain contexts, they also use the term *class* or *label* (instead of *target*) to mean the dependent variable that is being predicted.

- A *model* consists of numerical features or attributes that are combined in some mathematical fashion into a prediction of a target variable. In many situations, a DM model is an equation that links the values of several observed features to a predicted value for the target variable. That prediction is often achieved by multiplying the observed value of each variable or feature by some number (a *weight* or *coefficient*) specific to that variable, and then adding those components together. The appropriate values of those weights or coefficients are what the program decides upon (or discovers or learns) when building a model.

- Data miners talk about *fitting a model*. Sometimes this phrase refers to the selection of a particular modeling technique; sometimes it refers to the choice and form of variables being entered into a model and their modification; and at other times it refers to the process of successive approximation by which a model comes incrementally closer to accurately describing the data.

- Certain measures (listed in a later section) are called *fit statistics* or *score functions*. They describe how well a DM model *fits the data*, meaning how closely the predicted value of a target for each case or person—a number provided by the model—matches the actual observed value of the target for that person. The goal of a DM analysis is to create a model that predicts accurately, or as we say, fits the data well. Fit statistics can be compared to decide which model or method performs best with a specific dataset.

- The term *machine learning* refers to computer analyses that produce a model that predicts or classifies or identifies patterns in data. Many DM methods are *iterative*. They first go through a sequence of steps that yields an initial estimate or answer. Next, some methods obtain a better estimate by adding more evidence (more cases or data) to change the initial estimate. Other methods work by trial and error: they make small changes to initial estimates and see whether the resulting prediction is better than the previous one. In either approach, the DM program repeats a sequence of steps multiple times—it *iterates*—so that estimates or solutions get more accurate with each additional cycle. This incremental process, involving successively better approximations, leads to the metaphor of *machine learning*.

- Data miners distinguish between *supervised* and *unsupervised* machine learning. Supervised machine learning refers to those DM methods where there are both independent and dependent variables (that is, *features* and a *target* or *label*). In the model-building phase, the analyst already knows for each case what its actual value for the target or dependent variable is. Hence, the modeling consists of discovering or learning a formula that accurately predicts the observed value of the target using the observed values of the features. This is also called *training* the model. In a sense, the target data are "supervising" a learning process. In subsequent phases of research, that formula or model may be used to predict the values of the target for new data where the real values are not yet known (sometimes called *out-of-sample* data). In contrast, there are other DM methods or tools where there is no target (or label or class) variable to be predicted. In statistical language, there is no "dependent variable." This second kind of DM, without a target, is termed *unsupervised* learning. The computer program or model is still learning (finding structure), but it is not using a target variable as its guide. Finding clusters of similar cases within a dataset is one example of unsupervised learning.

· In DM, the term *feature selection* refers to reducing the number of variables or features to be included in a model by identifying the important ones and dropping the rest, in such a way that those remaining can still accurately predict the target.

· *Feature extraction* has the same goal of ending up with fewer variables, but in feature extraction a new reduced set of variables is created by mathematically collapsing original variables into fewer new ones, for example by combining some of them into scales.

· The pattern or the structure in data is sometimes called the *signal*. Because of measurement error or random fluctuations, in any real dataset this signal is combined with (or polluted by) *noise*. Noise can come from imprecision in measurement or from unique contextual factors that affect particular cases or persons in the dataset differently from otherwise similar cases. Noise is usually conceived as random, since it is conceptually the antithesis of patterns or structures in the data. The analogy comes from the early days of radio, when a broadcaster's voice (the signal) could become obscured by the crackling and other background noise that sometimes made it difficult to make out the signal. Raw data will always contain a mixture of signal and noise, and all DM analyses seek to distinguish the signal from the noise.

· Historian of science Thomas S. Kuhn (1962) popularized the term *paradigm* to refer to schools of scientific thought. Kuhn pictured the progress of science as a competitive process where one school of thought (one paradigm), with its own researchers and particular methods of inquiry, sometimes clashed with a newer school or paradigm that had different adherents, concepts, and research methods. If and when a newer paradigm beat out an older paradigm, Kuhn termed this a *paradigm shift*. Throughout this book we will contrast what we call the conventional or established paradigm of quantitative data analysis with data mining, which we view as an emerging new paradigm. Perhaps DM will result in a paradigm shift, but it is equally possible that DM techniques will simply be absorbed into the older data analysis paradigm in the future.

· Data miners refer to the *dimensionality* of data, for example talking about a problem as being of *high dimension*, or referring to *dimension reduction* or the *measurement space*. These terms all use a spatial metaphor to think about data, so let's explain this metaphor.

In the physical space in which we humans live there are only three dimensions—length, height, and depth—with coordinates on the *x*, *y*, and *z* axes. Each of these dimensions in space can represent a single variable in a dataset. So if we had data about three variables— say people's height, weight, and income—we could treat height as *x*, weight as *y*, and income as *z*. We could then plot each observation in this three-dimensional space, locating the values on the *x*, *y*, and *z* axes to represent each person's height, weight, and income, and placing a dot at that point in space that corresponds to that person's *x*, *y*, and *z* values.

If we continued and plotted a whole dataset, we would see thousands of dots in space, some in dense clusters and some dots sitting out on their own. The dots for people who had similar values on these three variables or dimensions would be close together, while people who were unlike others on the three dimensions would be off on their own.

Mathematicians can conceptualize spaces with hundreds of dimensions, which they term *high-dimensional spaces*. In our three-dimensional world, we cannot draw or build high-dimensional spaces, but we can imagine a world that has many dimensions. This is useful because datasets typically contain far more than three variables, and a dataset with many variables corresponds to a high-dimensional space.

Each observation in a dataset could (in our imagination) be plotted in a coordinate system of not just three but hundreds of dimensions, with each dimension representing one variable. Using this spatial metaphor, data miners talk about a *measurement space*, meaning the multidimensional space containing their data, and they also think about the structure in their data or the relations between variables in the data in terms of patterns or shapes in this notional high-dimensional space.

Continuing the metaphor, some structures consist of dense clouds of data points or dots that are located close together in this multidimensional space because their values on several variables or dimensions are similar. Other structures are imagined as data points strung together in long lines. Yet other structures (or relations between variables) are represented as flat planes, or as curved or strangely shaped surfaces. (Mathematicians call these shapes *manifolds*.) Each shape represents some kind of mathematical relation between some variables in the dataset.

Operating in this conceptual world of many dimensions, some DM methods work by *projecting*, that is mathematically translating data from a higher-dimensional space to a lower-dimensional space, because it is easier to handle the math problem in fewer dimensions. This projection is possible because structures or relations apparent in higher-dimensional spaces are often preserved when projected into lower-dimensional spaces. This is equivalent to reducing many variables to fewer variables and discovering that the basic relations are preserved.

Other DM methods work in the opposite direction: a problem that cannot easily be solved in a lower-dimensional space, when projected into a higher-dimensional space, may become easier to handle mathematically, using a *kernel trick*. Several DM methods for classifying observations use this strategy, as later examples will show.

2

CONTRASTS WITH THE CONVENTIONAL STATISTICAL APPROACH

Data mining (DM) offers an approach to data analysis that differs in important ways from the conventional statistical methods that have dominated over the last several decades. In this section we highlight some key contrasts between the emerging DM paradigm and the older statistical approach to data analysis, before detailing in later chapters the individual methods or tools that constitute DM. In illustrating these contrasts, we will use multiple regression to stand for the conventional approach, since this statistical method— along with its many extensions and offshoots, including logistic regression, event-history analysis, multilevel models, log-linear models, and structural equation modeling—has been the mainstay of conventional data analysis in recent decades.

This comparison will highlight some weaknesses and difficulties within the conventional paradigm that cease to be as problematic in the DM approach. However, just because we emphasize pitfalls in conventional modeling does not imply that DM itself is problem-free. On the contrary, DM has its own limitations, some of which will be identified in later sections.

PREDICTIVE POWER IN CONVENTIONAL STATISTICAL MODELING

In conventional statistical analyses, such as regression, most of an analyst's attention is usually focused on the numerical values or coefficients of important predictors in a model; the predictive power or "fit" of that model is usually of secondary importance (Breiman

2001). That is because the primary goal for many researchers using conventional methods is to test hypotheses about particular predictors or to understand how individual predictors are associated with the dependent variable. Those relations are represented by the coefficients for each variable in a regression or other predictive model.

Nevertheless, measures of model fit are always reported in conventional data analyses. The most common measures are R^2 and adjusted R^2, usually interpreted as the percentage of variance of the dependent variable that is explained by the combination of predictors in the model. More complex measures of fit are found in other contexts, and a whole raft of other fit statistics are available, including A′ (A prime), kappa, AIC, BIC, RIC, EBIC, pseudo-R^2 measures, and −2 log-likelihood. But the general point we are about to make applies to them all.

In articles that use conventional methods and are published in leading research journals in the social sciences, it is common to find predictive models where the percentage of variance explained is quite modest, for example 25% or less, *but this low level of explanatory power is rarely viewed as detracting from a study's validity or treated as an indictment of model quality.*

Authors of journal articles seldom dwell on how much of the variance in their dependent variable is explained by their particular model; more rarely still is any substantive interpretation offered about the unexplained variance of a model. One exception occurred decades ago when Christopher Jencks and his colleagues diverged from common practice in their path-breaking book, *Inequality* (1972), and interpreted the unexplained variance of their particular model of social mobility as the influence of "luck." A storm of criticism followed (Coleman et al. 1973).

The outcome of that controversy seems to have been a consensus within the conventional paradigm that unexplained variance should be viewed as stemming from a mix of measurement error and omitted causal factors. So long as a regression or other model is statistically significant as a whole and there are also individual statistically significant predictors within the model, reporting a model where the large majority of variance remains unexplained is accepted as normal and appropriate by many researchers and by major journals in the social and behavioral sciences.

In contrast, DM places a much stronger emphasis on maximizing the predictive power of a model, which means reducing the amount of unexplained variance as far as possible. Explaining only 25% of the variance of the dependent variable would be viewed as inadequate by many data miners. As we shall see, a data miner will explore different methods, and sometimes combine several, precisely to maximize the overall predictive power. Data miners do this because accurate prediction is often their primary purpose in modeling, since the predicted values will be used in real-world situations to inform decisions and actions.

To recap, the conventional statistical approach focuses on the individual coefficients for the predictors, and doesn't care as much about predictive power. DM does the reverse. This difference in goals is the first major point of contrast between DM and the conventional paradigm.

What can DM and conventional statistics have to say to one another if they have such very different goals? Because of its emphasis on predictive power, DM has developed some powerful new analytical tools, but it is not always obvious how DM's strengths in predicting can be integrated into a conventional social science framework which prioritizes the assessment of hypotheses about particular predictors and their estimated effects. Our view is that DM is likely to bring about big changes in social and behavioral research, and to the statistical end of biomedical research. In many cases, DM tools provide so much more explanatory strength than conventional statistical models that researchers are likely to be drawn into using them. However, the emphasis that social and behavioral scientists and other researchers place on understanding causal mechanisms, and the importance they place on estimates of effects for individual predictors (measured as coefficients of specific variables), are not likely to disappear. One compromise is seen in the development of some new DM tools that provide information about mechanisms, in addition to DM's older preoccupation with maximizing accuracy in prediction (see e.g. Pearl 2000).

HYPOTHESIS TESTING IN THE CONVENTIONAL APPROACH

Within the conventional statistical paradigm that has dominated quantitative methods, linkages are made between theory and data analysis by testing hypotheses about the coefficients of one or more independent variables in a predictive model. For example, a researcher or data analyst may focus on whether a regression coefficient for a particular theoretically important predictor is statistically significant. In regression output, the coefficient for each predictor is reported along with a test statistic (a t- or z-test) and its associated p-value or significance level. The p-value associated with each predictor is the probability of obtaining a value of the test statistic as large as the one observed, conditional on the null hypothesis being true.

Less often, within the conventional approach, a hypothesis is tested that examines whether the joint effect of several variables is statistically significant, and occasionally a hypothesis is tested about whether one model as a whole is significantly different from or superior to some alternative model.

Stepping back from these details, what significance testing provides inside the conventional approach is a way of judging whether a finding is *representative*: whether an estimate derived from one sample or set of observations will prove to be accurate when applied to the larger population from which the sample was drawn. When we find that a regression coefficient is "statistically significant," we conclude that it is unlikely that the particular value we observed in our sample would have occurred by chance, through sampling error. So, significance testing is a way of assessing whether a finding in one's sample is likely to hold for the larger population from which the sample was drawn.

However, many statisticians have raised serious criticisms regarding commonly accepted practices in the social and behavioral sciences and in medical research involving significance testing, in what has become known as the "significance test controversy" (Morrison and Henkel 1970). These critics argue that many researchers misuse significance tests in ways that undermine the validity of their reported findings. We'll summarize some of their criticisms, and then show that data mining usually takes an alternative approach to assessing findings, one that does not depend as heavily on conventional significance testing. Consequently, DM avoids several of these long-standing misuses of significance testing.

One criticism asserts that deciding that a predictor with a *p*-value (significance) of .051 should be ignored while a predictor with a *p*-value of .049 should be treated as significant is misleading. One implication is that result or effect sizes—the magnitude of a coefficient or effect—ought to be the focus of analytical and interpretive attention, rather than just whether or not that predictor's coefficient is statistically significant (Nickerson 2000).

A second charge of misuse of significance testing argues that the critical value commonly used by researchers to decide whether a coefficient is statistically significant is too small in many contexts and leads to a proliferation of type I errors (false-positive findings). This argument involves the perils of *multiplicity*—when regression or other models contain many predictors (Benjamini 2010; Hsu 1996; Saville 1990; Shaffer 1995; Tukey 1991). In models containing many predictors, the critics consider it inappropriate to use the conventional critical value (*t* or *z* = 1.96) for assessing the statistical significance of each predictor, since that particular critical value properly applies to a single comparison, not to multiple predictors each with its own significance test (Larzelere and Mulaik 1977). The likelihood of finding a statistically significant result increases as more predictors are entered into any model, simply because one is repeating a significance test so many times. One in twenty predictors will be significant at $p \leq 0.05$ through chance alone. This dispute also revolves around the question of whether the tests for the different predictors in a model are truly independent of one another.

The problem of multiplicity or testing many effects or coefficients in one model can easily be avoided by adjusting the critical value used to decide which predictors are statistically significant to allow for the number of multiple comparisons. One statistically conservative solution is to use a Bonferroni correction for multiple comparisons. If there are five predictors, for example, instead of accepting any predictor with $p < .05$ as significant, one accepts only a predictor with $p < .01$ (i.e., dividing the conventional value of 0.05 by the number of predictors). This is equivalent to using a critical value of 2.58 instead of 1.96 for a regression model containing five predictors, or a value of 3.48 for a model with a hundred predictors.

The Bonferroni adjustment is just one possible multiplicity correction that can be applied to the significance tests reported by ordinary statistical software. More sophisticated approaches to multiplicity include calculation of false discovery rates and family-wise error rates (Benjamini 2010). If research journals required such adjustments for predictive models containing multiple predictors, the incidence of type I errors (false positives) would be greatly reduced. However, despite decades of criticisms along these lines, prestigious research journals continue to accept the use of a critical value of 1.96 in models with multiple predictors, leading to exposés about the lack of reproducibility of research (Ioannidis 2005).

This issue regarding significance testing in the context of multiple predictors is compounded when some researchers actively *search for* statistically significant effects by analyzing numerous predictors until they happen across a finding with a *t*- or *z*-value of 1.96 or greater, which they then include in a final model and report as significant. A 1.96 critical value for significance testing is very misleading if hundreds of predictors are assessed first, before reporting just the ones that prove to be statistically significant.

This problem has grown ever more acute in medical research and in analyses of gene sequences, where it is increasingly common for thousands of significance tests be tried before reporting the significant ones (Benjamini 2010). Methods textbooks warn against this search for significant predictors, which is informally known as *fishing* or *data dredging*. Textbooks recommend that researchers make their hypotheses in advance, before analyzing data, in order to avoid the temptation to search after the fact through numerous possible predictors. Unfortunately, many researchers still "fish" for significant results, using a low critical value ($t = 1.96$, or $p < .05$) for statistical significance.

As we have noted, there are effective remedies to deal with multiplicity within the conventional paradigm; but, as we detail below, most DM methods take a different approach to evaluating the representativeness of a model (using a form of replication known as *cross-validation*) which avoids the multiplicity problem entirely and is not based on significance testing. This is the second major point where DM and the conventional paradigm diverge.

HETEROSCEDASTICITY AS A THREAT TO VALIDITY IN CONVENTIONAL MODELING

Beyond the issue of multiplicity, the accuracy of significance tests in the conventional paradigm is also affected by certain theoretical statistical assumptions that form the foundation of multiple regression models and their statistical relatives (Berry 1993). We spell out some of these in order to set the groundwork for another contrast with DM.

For each case or observation in a dataset, a model estimates a predicted value for the target (dependent variable). Subtracting this predicted value from the observed value yields a number known as the *residual* which represents the prediction error for each individual observation; so the residual is a special kind of variable. Summed across all observations, the residuals (or errors) constitute the unexplained variance of a predictive model.

One set of assumptions underlying the statistical logic of multiple regression and related methods is that residuals should be normally distributed, with a constant variance and a mean of zero, and be independent of one another. When these assumptions are accurate, the errors are said to be *homoscedastic*—a Greek term meaning equal variances.

When these assumptions are inaccurate, errors are said to be *heteroscedastic*—having unequal variances. Heteroscedasticity often occurs when the residuals or prediction errors are more spread out (have a higher variance) at low or high values of a given predictor (or X) than at middling values of that X; or sometimes the residuals are more spread out at low or high values of Y (the dependent variable) than at middling values of Y. What this implies is that the predictive model is accurate (and has small residuals) across a certain range of values of X or Y but starts to break down (become less accurate) elsewhere, often at extreme values of X and/or Y.

There are statistical tests to determine whether errors are heteroscedastic, but researchers will often plot residuals against each X variable and/or against Y. In such plots, heteroscedasticity shows itself as a funnel shape: the wide part of the funnel is where the variance in the errors increases.

Why are we delving so deeply into what may seem to be a technical detail? First, heteroscedasticity is a problem that surfaces in many quantitative analyses. Second, it has serious consequences, causing biases that, in our opinion, undermine the accuracy of some research. Third, DM provides a number of avenues for remedying, or in some cases circumventing, the problem of heteroscedasticity.

There are multiple reasons that heteroscedasticity occurs, causing it to be a widespread problem.

· When the units of analysis in a dataset are aggregates of different sizes (e.g., schools containing differing numbers of students) and the variables for each unit are (say) average student SAT score, this often causes heteroscedasticity, because there will be more error in measurement for small schools where one averages test scores from a few students than in large schools where the mean SAT is based on many more students.

· Heteroscedasticity can also occur when a dataset includes subpopulations which manifest different relations between X and Y. An analysis predicting the effect of taking remedial courses in college upon dropping out would be heteroscedastic and also yield very misleading coefficients if, for example, the sample included undergraduates from both community and four-year colleges and it turned out that taking remedial courses in college had a very different impact on dropping out for community college students than for four-year college students.

· Heteroscedasticity can also happen when predictors are scaled inappropriately, for example when income rather than the log of income is used as a predictor.

· Finally, heteroscedasticity can occur when a relation is "necessary but not sufficient." For example, expenditures on vacation travel tend to increase with family income, since one needs sufficient income to afford to travel. But not every high-income family travels a lot for vacations. Consequently, when predicting expenditures on vacations from family income, there will be higher prediction errors (residuals) at higher incomes than at lower incomes. This will manifest itself as a positive correlation between income and the residual term.

Heteroscedasticity is widespread in all manner of data, and it has serious consequences for conventional models. In the case of ordinary least squares regression, heteroscedasticity does not bias the estimates of the regression coefficients or predictors, but it does bias the estimates of standard errors for those predictors, and hence it biases the significance tests reported for those regression coefficients. That may create type I error—leading researchers to mistakenly conclude that a coefficient for a predictor is statistically significant when it is not—or result in upward biases of standard errors, leading to type II error—that is, leading researchers to believe that certain coefficients are not significant when they actually are. Either problem is a threat for conventional modeling.

In the case of logistic regression, probit, and related techniques that predict binary or categorical dependent variables, heteroscedasticity has even worse consequences; it biases the regression coefficients as well as their standard errors (R. Williams 2010).

Not all researchers would agree with our contention that heteroscedasticity creates a serious problem for conventional models. Econometricians, for example, have developed special estimators of standard errors, known as *sandwich estimators* or *Huber-White estimators*, and *robust standard errors* that are said to reduce biases resulting from heteroscedasticity. However, other statisticians dispute the validity of these corrective measures (Freedman 2006), suggesting that they are not a quick fix.

DM provides several tools for identifying and/or remedying heterogeneity. One possible cause of heterogeneity is that a predictor is poorly scaled or has a nonlinear relation to the dependent variable. In a later section, we will present DM tools known as *binning* and *entropy discretization* that allow analysts to identify nonlinear effects; if these are correctly represented in a model, then that source of heteroscedasticity may be removed.

Heteroscedasticity is sometimes a consequence of important statistical interactions' being left out of a model. DM offers several tools, including data partitioning or *decision trees* that scour datasets for interactions and identify which interactions matter. If analysts identify and model those interactions, then heteroscedasticity will be reduced. Similarly, DM provides ways to identify subgroups in a dataset that have different relations between the predictors and the dependent variable. Once distinct subgroups are identified in a dataset using DM, researchers may decide to run separate analyses for each subgroup, or they may decide to add interaction terms for each subgroup (Melamed, Breiger, and Schoon 2013). In either case this should reduce heteroscedasticity.

In yet other situations, analysts find that the error term of their model is heteroscedastic but despite their best efforts they are unable to identify the reasons for the problem. In this case, as we explain in a later section, DM has a "trick" for calibrating models that are initially "uncalibrated" due to heteroscedasticity. This trick doesn't identify the causes for the problem in the first place, but it may provide an effective Band-Aid that removes the problem.

Finally, many DM methods are nonparametric: they do not require the kinds of statistical assumptions about the distribution of error terms that underlie many conventional modeling methods. In such cases, while DM methods cannot prevent heteroscedasticity from occurring in data, they can circumvent some of its more destructive or problematic effects.

THE CHALLENGE OF COMPLEX AND NONRANDOM SAMPLES

In the conventional paradigm, the significance tests accompanying each predictor in a regression model are typically calculated by statistical packages using formulae that assume that the data constitute a simple random sample (SRS) drawn from a larger population. That assumption is sometimes unwarranted. Many modern surveys involve complex or multistage sampling schemes: first randomly sampling among higher-level units such as cities or Zip codes, and then randomly sampling individuals within each of those higher-level units. Standard errors for multistage samples are much larger than the standard errors for simple random samples with the same number of observations or cases (N). Using the SRS kind of standard errors when the other kind is called for unjustifiably understates the standard error for each predictor and thereby produces false-positive results (Thomas and Heck 2001).

Several approaches within conventional research can be used to adjust standard errors for complex sample designs. The earliest correction factors were known as DEFF (design effects); more recent software uses Taylor linearization to estimate corrected standard errors. These are effective remedies, although not all researchers use them.

However, significance testing becomes even more problematic when researchers want to analyze data that are not systematically drawn random samples at all. Increasingly, scholars encounter datasets taken from organizational records, or derived from information taken from the web, or from other large data sources. Although such datasets may be very large, they are not drawn randomly from a known population. The technical term for this kind of dataset is a *convenience sample*. For convenience samples, conventional tests of statistical significance that assume that the researcher is analyzing an SRS drawn from a population are completely inappropriate.

BOOTSTRAPPING AND PERMUTATION TESTS

DM has several procedures that can avoid pitfalls associated with significance testing in the conventional paradigm. One of these DM solutions involves testing the accuracy of inferences through replication and cross-validation. We explain those ideas in detail in a later section. But a second solution—*bootstrapping*—is now widely applied to significance tests

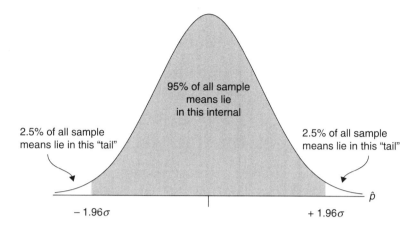

FIGURE 2.1
Distribution of a sample mean.

in conventional statistical models, as well as within DM itself, so we will discuss this technique first (Mooney and Duval 1993).

The conventional approach to significance testing (predating bootstrapping) uses a *sampling distribution* in order to estimate the standard error and then the statistical significance or *p*-value of an estimate. A sampling distribution is a theoretically obtained distribution (represented as a mathematical formula or visually as a graph, as in figure 2.1) that describes the way that estimates from random samples drawn from a population are related to the true value of that parameter in the population.

An *assumption* (also called a *parametric assumption*) is made about the validity of a theoretical sampling distribution when it is used in a specific analysis in order to obtain confidence intervals or *p*-values for a particular regression or other model. Unfortunately, if data happen to violate that assumption, then the inferences made about statistical significance are flawed.

One way around this difficulty is to use a *nonparametric* technique known as *bootstrapping*. Instead of making an assumption about the shape of a sampling distribution, bootstrapping uses an empirical strategy to determine standard errors and to obtain the statistical significance or *p*-values for the specific dataset or analysis being undertaken.

In its simplest form, bootstrapping uses the single sample of data that a researcher is analyzing *as if it were an entire population*. Bootstrapping draws many random subsamples from this single sample. After drawing the first observation to be included in a subsample, it replaces that case back into the sample, and then randomly selects another observation and replaces that into the pool, repeating until it has created a bootstrap sample equal in size to the original sample. This is known as *sampling with replacement*. This process is repeated to construct perhaps a thousand bootstrap samples.

For each of these numerous bootstrap samples, statistical software then estimates a statistic of interest, which might be a sample mean or a regression coefficient for a particular predictor in a certain model. The result is a thousand different estimates of that statistic. From those one thousand bootstrap estimates, a distribution is constructed, and that distribution is used to determine the statistical significance of any statistic from the original (nonbootstrapped) sample: one measures how many of the thousand estimates lie within various distances from the center of the distribution, and calculates p-values associated with those distances.

Bootstrapping (or a related technique called the *jackknife*) makes no assumptions about the shape of the sampling distribution. Both are purely empirical procedures that use brute computing power, repeating a whole regression or other analysis perhaps a thousand times. As a result, bootstrapping takes considerable processing time, even on fast computers.

Data miners sometimes use yet another "brute force" approach to significance testing—known as a *permutation test* or *exact test*—in contexts where conventional significance testing is impossible. Let's say your predictive model consists of five predictors and one dependent variable, Y. Each column in a spreadsheet or data matrix represents one of the predictor variables or the dependent variable. (The rows are people or cases.) Permutation test software shuffles the values within a column. For example, the values found within the column for Y—the dependent or target variable—might be randomly swapped with other values already in that column that belong to other cases or observations. This shuffling deliberately mixes up, in a random fashion, the values of Y across observations.

Shuffling destroys any structure (or relations) that previously existed between the X predictors and the now-shuffled Y. For example, before shuffling there might have been a strong positive correlation between X and Y: individuals who had a high value on X tended also to have a high value on Y, and mostly those with a low value on X had a low value on Y. But by shuffling values within the Y column, an individual with some value on X is now linked with someone else's value on Y. The previous structure of correlation has been erased and replaced by randomness. Note, however, that the mean value of the Y variable and the standard deviation of Y will have been preserved.

A statistical program then runs exactly the same predictive model that it previously ran for the real original data, but now on these scrambled or shuffled data. This will provide a measure of fit—R^2, for example—for the shuffled or scrambled dataset. (Or we might focus on some other statistic, for example a coefficient for a particular predictor. The same logic would still apply.)

This process of shuffling and then calculating a model is repeated many times, say a thousand. So now the researcher has the value of R^2 for the correct or real data and also for a thousand other values of the R^2 statistic, one for each of the samples with randomized or shuffled data. This obviously takes a lot of computational time. A researcher might only perform such a procedure at the very end of an analysis project, when she is very sure of the final model but wants a significance level for that model.

Next, the researcher compares the value of R^2 (or other statistic of interest) in the model with real data to the values in the shuffled models. Let's first imagine that the R^2 for the true model happens to be larger than the values for all 1,000 shuffled models. Then we can conclude that the probability of obtaining this R^2 by chance is below one in 1,000 ($p \leq .001$), given that we examined 1,000 samples and none had an R^2 that large. Our 1,000 models with shuffled data are a literal embodiment of chance: by scrambling the data, we just measured how often a certain size of R^2 occurred "just by chance."

Next, imagine that among the 1,000 randomized (shuffled) models, 10 have an R^2 equal to or larger than the R^2 for the model with real data. Then the probability of obtaining by chance the R^2 found for the true model is 10/1,000; that is, $p = .01$. Alternatively, if the shuffle process leads to 500 of the 1,000 runs having R^2 equal to or larger than the R^2 obtained for the real (non-shuffled) data sample, then the statistical significance for one's real data is .5, and the real model is not statistically significant at the .05 level. It could easily have occurred just by chance.

This permutation procedure is a kind of *exact test* in that it doesn't make any assumptions about the shape of the distribution of R^2 or any other statistic being examined. This procedure is also a form of Monte Carlo simulation.

.   .   .

To recap this section about hypothesis testing, the main points to be remembered are that significance testing plays a crucial role in the conventional statistical approach, where it is used to decide which coefficients or effects are likely to be different from zero in the larger population from which a sample was drawn. However, critics have complained that researchers' everyday practices in conventional modeling often misuse significance testing, resulting in erroneously small standard errors and many false-positive results. The most serious problems with significance testing occur when modelers add many predictors to models, and especially when they search through hundreds of predictors before deciding which to include in a model.

In reaction to these faults, some data miners and forecasters have argued for abandoning significance testing altogether (Armstrong 2007). Most data miners are not that extreme, and most have not totally rejected significance testing. However, they do place much more emphasis on replication and cross-validation as alternatives to significance testing when evaluating a predictive model.

Moreover, to the extent that DM applications do provide significance tests for individual predictors, they are more likely to employ significance tests based either on bootstrapping or on permutation tests, which avoid many of the pitfalls associated with the conventional approach.

In a typical regression model, several independent variables or predictors (call them X_1, X_2, and X_3) are used to predict a dependent variable (call it Y). Before creating a model, those predictors that represent nominal categories (such as Republican, Democrat, and independent) are usually turned into a set of dummy variables, each of which takes a value of zero or one.

Continuous independent variables, such as age, income, or years of education, called *interval* or *ratio* measurements, are usually entered into a regression in a simple form, for example age in years, or income in thousands of dollars, or education in years. The regression coefficient for those latter variables is conventionally interpreted as the change in Y associated with a one-unit increase in X, while controlling for the other independent variables.

This interpretation assumes that the relation between an X and Y is linear: that a one-unit increase of X at the low end of the X scale is associated with the same amount of change in Y as a one-unit increase of X at high values of X. In other words, plotting X against Y on a graph would produce a straight line. But what if we suspect that the relation may vary across different values of X? (That would produce some kind of curve or wiggly line, if X is plotted against Y.)

In some cases, it is relatively simple to replace a continuous interval or ratio predictor with a set of dummy variables (each taking a value of one or zero) that will allow us to see whether a nonlinear relation exists between an X and Y. A common example is when years of education are used as a predictor. Many researchers assume that the effect of years of education is not linear, and therefore recode years of education into a set of dummy variables—for example less than high school graduate; high school graduate; some college; BA degree; and MA or higher degree. Those variables, entered as a set into a conventional regression analysis, with one omitted category serving as the reference category, can then capture nonlinear relations between education and Y, at different levels of education.

For many other continuous predictors, however, a researcher doesn't know ahead of time whether the relation between a particular X variable and Y is linear. The usual practice in conventional quantitative research has been to assume linearity unless one has a strong reason to suspect otherwise. In part this is simply a matter of time and effort: it is extremely time-consuming to examine nonlinearity for many predictors.

However, there is something more basic going on than simply time and convenience. A large part of conventional statistics has been built upon the concept of correlation—the extent to which as one variable increases in value, the other also changes. A whole dataset can be represented by a *correlation matrix* or a *variance-covariance matrix* that summarizes the relations between variables.

Unfortunately, a correlation coefficient only measures the *linear* relation between any pair of variables; it overlooks any nonlinear aspect. It simplifies matters at the cost of sometimes forcing a square peg into a round hole. With the development of machine learning and other computationally intensive methods, however, this simplification is no longer necessary. We have new "automated" methods that can search for and model nonlinear relations, and in some cases these will result in more accurate prediction.

The simplest of these new DM tools just allow researchers to visualize their data: to see the nonlinear relations between two or more variables as pictures, from simple graphs or scatterplots to fancier visualizations that represent relations as curved surfaces that can be rotated and viewed from many angles. In JMP, for example, one of the most useful visualization tools is called the Profiler. After constructing a model one can use this tool to see how values of any one variable are affected when the values of other variables change.

Beyond visualization, other DM procedures can automatically generate breakpoints for continuous independent variables in order to capture a nonlinear effect of an X on Y. For example, a CART analysis (classification and regression tree—one kind of data-partitioning or tree model) might indicate nonlinear effects of income on Y, finding important income breakpoints at $20,000, $60,000, $90,000, and $150,000.

An alternative way of discovering nonlinear relations in data involves a process that data miners call *binning*. In general, binning involves transforming a continuous numerical variable such as income into a set of ordered categories or bins. So instead of representing income in dollars, ranging from zero to $1,000,000 plus, binning groups cases or people into categories such as zero to $5000; $5,001 to $15,000; $15,001 to $25,000; and so on. Another term that is used for this is *discretization*: making discrete categories out of something that was continuous.

A special kind of binning, called *optimal binning* or *entropy-based discretization*, is especially useful for handling nonlinear relations. It locates breaks between bins in such a way as to maximize the prediction of a dependent variable Y. In other words, the limits or boundaries for each bin are chosen by the software in such a way as to make the cases in each bin as different as possible from the other bins in terms of their values on Y (Witten, Eibe, and Hall 2011, 316). This is very helpful in identifying nonlinear relations between a predictor and a dependent variable.

We will provide examples in later sections. At this stage, the key idea to retain is that when using conventional statistical methods it is time-consuming and sometimes hit-or-miss to identify nonlinear relations between each of the many continuous independent variables and the dependent variable, and that as a result the default or common practice has been to treat relations as linear. DM now provides several tools that partly automate the search for nonlinear relations, and this is one reason why DM models tend to predict more accurately than conventional regression-like models.

STATISTICAL INTERACTIONS IN CONVENTIONAL MODELS

Often, conventional modeling seeks to estimate the simultaneous contributions of several covariates in predicting an outcome variable, Y. For example, an education researcher may theorize about the role of an undergraduate's high school academic preparation, family socioeconomic status, work demands, and financial support in a model predicting which undergraduates drop out of college. The researcher's goal might be to determine which of these predictors is most important or influential in affecting risk of dropping out of college (see e.g. Attewell, Heil, and Reisel 2011).

However, Charles Ragin (2008) has argued that many sociological problems call for a quite different logic from this one, with a different goal: understanding *combinations of factors* associated with different outcomes, rather than isolating the role of individual predictors. Ragin phrases this as "configurations of conditions versus independent variables." "Configurations of conditions" can be incorporated in conventional regression and similar models by including *interaction terms* between predictors (see Aiken and West 1991 and Jaccard and Turrisi 2003 for details).

But just because it is possible to include interaction terms in conventional models does not mean that researchers routinely do so. On the contrary, Elwert and Winship (2010) complain that the overwhelming majority of published quantitative studies in sociology report *main effects* only (i.e., a model with several predictors but without their interactions). In part, this omission of interactions from predictive models occurs because (according to these authors) many researchers misunderstand the meaning of main effect coefficients when other covariates are "controlled for." In addition, the absence of interaction effects in published papers stems from a practical problem: there are huge numbers of potential interactions between predictors. With 8 predictors there are 28 two-way interactions (combinations), plus additional higher-order interactions. How does a researcher identify which among the 28 potential interactions are the consequential ones? It would be very time-consuming to build every interaction variable and test whether each is important. In practice, Elwert and Winship suggest, most sociological modelers neglect this task and limit themselves to main effects models.

The implication of both Ragin's and Elwert and Winship's criticisms is that dependence on main effects in conventional statistical models is a serious weakness and that researchers should place more emphasis upon identifying complex interactions between multiple predictors.

Two data mining techniques detailed in later chapters (CART and CHAID) achieve this speedily by testing thousands of possible interactions or combinations among predictors to determine which are consequential for predicting a particular dependent variable and which are not. Once identified, the techniques then use those combinations of values or interactions to predict a dependent variable or target in a manner consistent with Ragin's recommendation to study "configurations of conditions" rather than "independent variables."

Other DM techniques achieve a similar effect by automatically generating the equivalent of interactions within their predictive models; neural network models are one instance which will be described later.

TABLE 2.1   Contrasts between Conventional Modeling and Data Mining

Issue	Conventional approach	Data mining
Increasing predictive power	· Prediction not the main focus · Low R^2 tolerated	· Prediction often the primary focus · High predictive power valued
Significance testing	· Basis for generalizability · Critical for evaluating hypotheses and interpreting mechanisms · Some testing practices flawed by multiplicity	· Generalizability by cross-validation instead of significance testing · Some techniques are "black boxes" (no meaningful internal parameters)
Sampling	· Significance testing tied to sampling assumptions · All samples expected to be simple random samples or complex random samples	· Bootstrapping and nonparametric techniques widespread · Convenience samples OK
Nonlinear relations between X and Y	· Often overlooked or skipped	· Partly automated identification
Interactions between predictors	· Often overlooked or skipped · Predominance of main effects	· Partly automated identification of interactions and heterogeneous effects

DM models can often outperform conventional statistical models in terms of prediction, or in the percentage of variance explained, because so many conventional models neglect interactions between predictors (either omitting them entirely or including only a few out of many potential interactions) while DM methods are more thorough in their assessment and use of interactions among predictors.

·   ·   ·

Table 2.1 summarizes the various contrasts we have drawn between conventional statistical modeling and DM. In the following chapters we explain how DM methods perform differently and arguably better than the conventional approach, and therefore are superior at prediction.

CONCLUSION

In this chapter we have described several areas of contrast between data mining approaches to quantitative analysis on the one hand and conventional statistical modeling on the other, and we have emphasized the ways that a data mining perspective entails certain criticisms of more established approaches to data analysis. So, what does this imply for the future relationship between data mining and conventional statistical research? In our view, it is highly unlikely that data mining will displace conventional statistical approaches. A much more likely development is a process of hybridization, where quantitative analysts increasingly make use of certain data mining tools in their work and where certain more general perspectives originating in data mining make inroads into the execution and reporting of quantitative analysis in the social and behavioral sciences. We anticipate the following kinds of short-term changes.

- Increasingly, researchers will pay attention to the possibility of nonlinear relations between predictors and outcomes, by taking advantage of DM tools such as optimal binning and trees to create new predictors that better represent nonlinearities. These modified predictors will be added to models and in some cases will help raise the predictive accuracy of models. We provide examples in the coming chapters.

- The search for statistical interactions between predictors will become more systematic or thorough, drawing on automated searches for statistical interactions of the kind already provided in JMP Pro's modeling tools, and/or using decision trees or partitioning methods like CHAID and CART that identify interactions. We therefore expect that it will become more common to see several interaction terms included in conventional predictive models, which again will enhance model accuracy, R^2, or fit.

- Researchers will be more likely to examine their data for *effect heterogeneity*, the possibility that the coefficients for predictors in their predictive model differ substantially for different subgroups within the sample or population. Cluster methods provided by DM, and tools featured below like mixture models and latent class regression, facilitate the search for heterogeneous effects and tend to provide a more complex or nuanced view of social or causal processes, moving away from a "one size fits all" vision.

- To the extent that they are influenced by data mining in the coming years, quantitative researchers may shift their mindset away from the goal of constructing a single predictive model, viewed as their best effort, and instead adopt an approach from DM which constructs several different predictive models, often using quite different methods, and then optimally combines the predictions from these several methods to yield a final prediction that is more accurate than that obtained from any single model. DM tools known as *boosting* and *ensemble methods*, which we discuss in later chapters, accomplish this. Again, this improves predictive accuracy relative to conventional practices.

- We expect that statistical significance testing is here to stay, in the social and behavioral sciences, as well as in educational and biomedical research, despite periodic efforts to persuade journal editors to abolish it in favor of an emphasis on effect sizes. However, we expect that data mining practices will increasingly influence and modify current conventional practices concerning the calculation and reporting of significance levels or p-values. We can already see that resampling techniques such as bootstrapping and permutation tests are growing in popularity, in part because modern software and faster computers make them easier to calculate and in part because these nonparametric methods for calculating standard errors of estimates do not depend on making implausible statistical assumptions. These newer methods for calculating p-values tend to be more conservative than the older approaches—often yielding larger standard errors and therefore fewer significant coefficients. They seem likely to reduce the amount of type I error, and that will begin the process of reducing the amount of nonreproducible research reported in journals.

An even bigger step toward that goal would occur if journal editors began requiring quantitative research articles to use the cross-validation methods that are commonplace in data mining. We have briefly introduced the logic of cross-validation above, and we will provide examples in the worked-examples chapters to follow, but the core idea is that every study would randomly partition its data and test whether a predictive model developed from one part of the data can accurately predict using a second set of observations which were not used in creating the predictive model. Cross-validation is a form of replication that "raises the bar" for evaluating empirical evidence. In our opinion, the adoption of cross-validation would have an important salutary effect on quantitative social science.

3

SOME GENERAL STRATEGIES
USED IN DATA MINING

CROSS-VALIDATION

Data dredging—searching through data until one finds statistically significant relations—is deplored by conventional methods textbooks, which instruct students to generate hypotheses before beginning their statistical analyses. The DM approach raises data dredging to new heights—but to its credit DM does not follow the conventional paradigm's bad example regarding significance testing when there are multiple predictors. It focuses instead on an alternative way of avoiding false-positive results or type I error: it emphasizes replication rather than significance testing, through a procedure known as *cross-validation*.

Prior to beginning an analysis involving cross-validation, DM software separates the cases within a dataset into different groups, randomly assigning each case or observation to one group or another. (*Random* assignment is critical here.) DM software typically allows the user to choose what proportion of cases from the original dataset should go into each group.

- One group or random subset of cases or observations is known as the *training sample* or *estimation sample*. This is the group of cases that will be analyzed first, to create a predictive model.

- In some but not all DM methods a second random sample is created, known as the *tuning sample* (it is sometimes called the *validation sample*). It is used to estimate certain modeling parameters that will yield an optimal prediction. For example, some DM techniques combine separate predictive models into one final best effort at prediction. This requires a decision about how to weight the prediction from each of the models when they are combined. In this context, this second random sample of cases, the tuning-sample data, would be used to calculate alternative weights so that the final weighting scheme yields the most accurate prediction. (This is known as *optimization*.) In other DM contexts, the tuning sample is instead used to decide how many predictors ought to be entered into a model.

- A third randomly selected group of observations is central to cross-validation. This is the *test sample,* sometimes called the *holdout sample.* The test sample is not used in any way during the creation of the predictive model; it is deliberately kept completely separate (held back).

During the last step in a DM analysis, a predictive model that has been generated using the data in the training sample (and sometimes involving the tuning sample data too) is applied to the new test sample data. The model generates predicted values of the target for these new test cases and those predicted values are compared to the actual observed values of the target in the test data. Fit statistics are calculated for this test sample, documenting how accurately the previously estimated model predicts this fresh set of observations.

Cross-validation fulfills a function in DM analogous to that provided by significance testing in the conventional approach: it is a way of assessing the generalizability of research findings. You might also think of cross-validation as a kind of quality control for data mining models.

The difference between the two approaches to generalization is that, in the conventional paradigm, tests for statistical significance speak to whether findings from one particular sample generalize to the *population* from which the sample was randomly drawn. Moreover, the assessment of generalizability is a theoretical or hypothetical one: the researcher doesn't have actual data for that entire population. In contrast, the test of generalizability in DM is an empirical one. A model that was developed and performed well for the training or estimation sample is applied to a different sample *of real data* (the test sample) and the goodness of that fit informs the researcher's judgment as to how well the model generalizes to the new data. In the DM case, generalizability is not from one sample to a population but rather from one random sample to another random sample (i.e., from the training to the test sample).

There are several variants of cross-validation. The simplest is known as the *holdout method* and is ideally suited to analyzing big data with many observations. It randomly divides a dataset into two or three subsamples (the training, tuning, and testing samples). The test sample is held out and is not used in training the predictive model. If the original dataset is very large, this random division of the original sample into two or three parts does not result in a problematic loss of statistical power when estimating predictive models; there will be lots of cases left in the training subsample. Note that in this holdout method, each observation is randomly assigned to either the training, the tuning, or the test subsample. Each subsample therefore contains completely separate cases or observations.

Cross-validation does not *require* a very large dataset, however. A different kind of cross-validation procedure known as k-*fold cross-validation* works with small as well as large datasets. The procedure begins by creating a chosen number (k) of random sub-samples; often 10 are created. Cases or observations are drawn at random from the original sample and are assigned to each subsample, until one has k randomly selected subsamples in all. Each contains one-kth of the original sample.

One of those k subsamples will initially function as the test dataset, while the other k − 1 subsamples are pooled together to form a training set. A model is estimated for that pooled training set, and afterwards this predictive model is tested on the single test set subsample, yielding a fit statistic or a measure of error.

This procedure is then repeated k times in all, such that each of the k subsamples serves just once as the test dataset, while the remaining folds combined are the training data. The final fit statistic that the software reports is the average of the fit statistics for the test samples across all k runs.

Whichever of these forms of cross-validation is chosen (and there are additional variants), the crucial point to remember is that when assessing the predictive accuracy of a model you should always look at the fit statistics for the *holdout* or *test* sample. Some software reports fit statistics for the training sample as well, but *the fit statistic for the holdout or test sample is always the important one.*

To understand why data miners depend solely upon the fit statistics for the test sample requires a digression into another important phenomenon, known as *overfitting*.

OVERFITTING

DM has its own weak spots, and overfitting is one of those. Some DM applications are *too* effective at building a predictive model; they construct something too complicated, that will not generalize to other samples. This is easiest to appreciate graphically (see figure 3.1).

A simple model would explain the relation between X and Y in this diagram by fitting a straight line. This line represents the predicted value of Y for various values of X. The vertical distance from each data point to the straight line represents the error of estimation for each data point in that simple model, the difference between the predicted value of Y and the observed value of Y for each value of X.

A much more complicated model might reduce the amount of prediction error. The wavy line represents an equation such as $Y = a + bX + cX^2 + dX^3 + eX^4 + fX^5$ . . . . As you can see in the diagram, this more complex line passes right through all the data points, implying no prediction error.

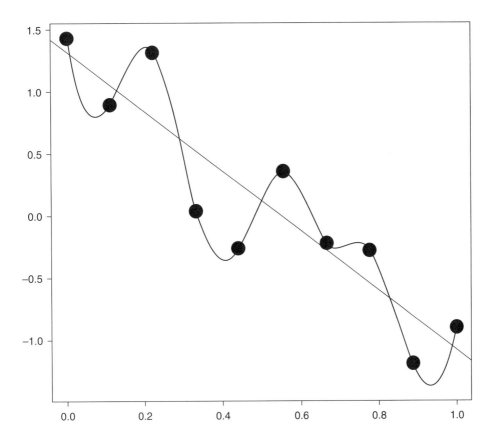

FIGURE 3.1
Overfitting data.

What could be wrong with choosing a more complex model if that reduces error and yields a stronger prediction? Data miners would caution that some of the distance from each data point to the straight line is probably due to measurement error, that is, to *noise*. Using a highly complicated model, like the wavy line, to fit those data points exactly is not just fitting the signal; it is also fitting the noise. The complex wavy model is, in DM jargon, *overfitting* the data. Overfitting is undesirable because it means that the complex model will not perform very well once it is applied to other data, such as the test data. The model has been tailored to the noisy training data and as a result won't fit other data very well.

How can one know whether any given model or equation is overfitted or not? When the predictive model (usually in the form of an equation) derived from a particular training sample is applied to a completely separate test sample, containing different observations or cases, then one can compare the predicted values obtained from the model to the observed values in the new dataset and determine how well they fit. This second step provides a trustworthy assessment of how well the predictive model works for data which were not used before.

The overfitting will "drop out" or fail to help in prediction of the test or holdout data because the part of the model that described chance patterns in the training data (the overfitted part) will fail to predict anything useful in the second or test dataset. There will be random noise in the second random test sample too, but by definition if it is random it isn't going to be the same noise as in the first dataset. So it won't have the same pattern; in fact it won't have any pattern.

Typically, therefore, a fit statistic for a model calculated for a training sample will be better than the fit of the same model applied to a test sample (because the test data will not overfit). If there is a large difference in the fit statistic between a training sample and a test sample, that is a strong indication that there was considerable overfitting in the former case. Conversely, if the fit of a model in a training sample and the fit of the same model applied to a test sample are pretty close, then this suggests that there was not much overfitting in the former: the model generalizes well.

To conclude, data mining's use of cross-validation appears to be a more rigorous approach to avoiding type I error (false-positive findings) than the significance-testing strategy common in conventional social research. *One evaluates the accuracy of a DM model by examining fit statistics obtained for a randomly selected test or holdout sample, and this provides a trustworthy measure of the generalizability of the findings.*

Figure 3.2 gives a visual illustration of how cross-validation can be used to avoid over-fitting. The two top quadrants in the diagram are analyses of the same data points. The top-left quadrant of the diagram shows a complex model fitted to these data, a curve with many inflection points where the model (represented by the line) closely fits all the data points, so it will yield a very good prediction for the *training data*. However, we are told in that quadrant that cross-validation (CV) informs us that this is a very bad model because its fit statistics when applied to *test data* were greatly reduced. The original model must have been overfitted.

The top right of the diagram shows a much simpler model fitted to the same data points. The fit is not as good as previously, since the line does not go right through each of the points. However, when applied to test data, via cross-validation, we are told this simpler model fits quite well. There is not much of a reduction in the fit statistics when comparing the model applied to the test data with the training data. So a data miner would opt for the top-right model.

The two bottom quadrants also refer to a single dataset, but it's a different dataset from the top half of the diagram. On the left, a complex DM model is fitted to the data; however, we are told that the cross-validation fit statistics for this model are nearly as good for the test sample as for the training sample. So we conclude that, although it is complicated, this is a generalizable model; it is not overfitted. Just to be prudent, we also try a simpler model on the same data. The bottom-right quadrant shows this. With this new model we find that the fit statistics for the test sample are not as good as for the training sample.

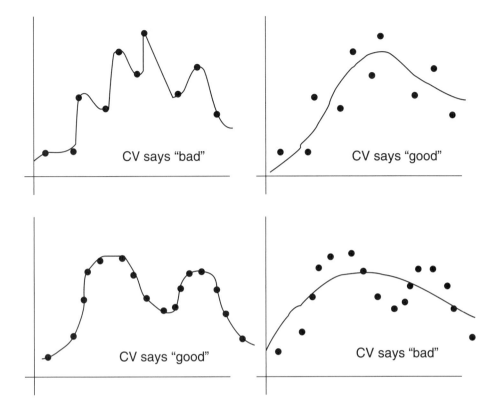

FIGURE 3.2
Cross-validation (from www.cs.cmu.edu/~schneide/tut5/node42.html#figcvo).

Three lessons can be drawn from these illustrations.

· Simplicity in a model is not always good (though we usually favor it); and
· complexity in a model is not always evidence of overfitting. However,
· cross-validation is an objective procedure that prevents one from accepting overfitted models.

BOOSTING

We have claimed that DM emphasizes the importance of accurate prediction and, compared to the conventional paradigm, is less accepting of models that can explain only a small percentage of the variance in a dependent variable. Because enhanced prediction is such a strong motive for data miners, they have developed novel strategies that improve prediction. Some of these seem quite strange when viewed from the perspective of conventional social science modeling. But, as we shall demonstrate, these strategies often outperform conventional models when it comes to prediction.

Boosting is one such strategy. It treats model creation as a series of steps. One might begin, for example, by estimating a regression model to predict an observed target variable, Y. The model fit is not perfect, so for each observation there will be a residual or prediction error, the difference between the observed and predicted value on Y for each case, or $Y - \hat{Y}$.

In a second step, another predictive model is estimated, using a different modeling method, but this time predicting the *residuals* from the first model, rather than predicting the original dependent variable, Y. This second model also yields predicted values, but some errors of prediction remain. So the residuals from this second model can, in turn, be predicted by a third model, and so on for many iterations.

The final stage in a boosted analysis is to combine the prediction equations obtained from each step (Ridgeway 1999). This is sometimes accomplished by providing diminishing weights to successive models, and then aggregating the predictions to get a single best prediction of Y.

Boosting can produce a substantial improvement in the final fit or predictive accuracy of a DM model, compared to a conventional single-step approach. Matthias Schonlau (2005) has written a Stata program called boost that applies a popular boosting algorithm. He reports its performance for two examples: a conventional linear regression and a stepwise logistic regression. In the former context, the conventional ordinary least squares (OLS) regression model predicted 21.3% of the variance (the R^2), while the identical predictors and data in a boosted regression explained 93.8% of the variance. For a stepwise logistic regression, the conventional Stata program correctly classified 54.1% of cases in test data, but boosting correctly predicted 76.0% of cases in a test sample. These are huge increases in predictive power thanks to boosting.

You will recall that a common explanation given for why conventional (non-DM) statistical models often explain only a small percentage of the variance is the presence of measurement error and/or the notion that some important factors have not been measured and are therefore omitted from the model. However, here we see that a single DM technique—boosting—can dramatically raise the percentage of variance explained, compared to a conventional model, while using exactly the same predictors and data as the conventional model. In this case, the claim that measurement error and omitted variables are what reduce explained variance rings hollow.

Evidently, there is something about the predictive performance of these conventional models that is inferior to the DM approach. Boosting was able to find much more structure in the data than the conventional approach could. This was *not* due to overfitting, because these impressive fit statistics are not for the original random sample of *training* data that created the predictive model but for a completely separate random sample of data, the *test* data.

Schonlau's paper used artificially constructed data. We performed a similar analysis to see whether boosting performed as well with real-world data. A conventional OLS

Total personal income (log)	Estimate	SE	p
Age	0.0674	0.0007	<.0001
Age squared (centered)	−0.0006	<0.0001	<.0001
Female	−0.5387	0.0021	<.0001
Occupational prestige	0.0211	<0.0001	<.0001
Black	−0.0626	0.0037	<.0001
Native American	−0.1804	0.0135	<.0001
Asian	−0.0489	0.0056	<.0001
Other race (ref = white)	−0.0162	0.0042	<.0001
Widowed	0.0707	0.0063	<.0001
Divorced	−0.0522	0.0028	<.0001
Separated	−0.1544	0.0061	<.0001
Married, spouse absent (ref = married, spouse present)	−0.1833	0.0070	<.0001
Non-citizen	−0.1609	0.0045	<.0001
Naturalized citizen (ref = citizen by birth)	0.0213	0.0042	<.0001
Less than HS	−0.2350	0.0041	<.0001
Some college, no degree	0.1019	0.0030	<.0001
Associate's	0.1528	0.0039	<.0001
Bachelor's	0.2913	0.0035	<.0001
More than bachelor's	0.4460	0.0042	<.0001
New England	0.0971	0.0051	<.0001
Mid-Atlantic	0.0951	0.0036	<.0001
East North Central	−0.0090	0.0034	<.0001
West North Central	−0.0172	0.0047	<.0001
East South Central	−0.0827	0.0047	<.0001
West South Central	−0.0050	0.0038	0.1820
Mountain	−0.0460	0.0047	<.0001
Pacific (ref = South Atlantic)	0.0712	0.0036	<.0001

NOTE: N of observations = 1,226,925; constant = 8.077; R^2 = 0.2882

regression is reported in table 3.1 above, in which the logarithm of personal income is predicted by several sociodemographic variables, using data from the U.S. Census Bureau's 2010 American Community Survey. Despite a large sample, numerous predictors, and technically high-quality data collection, the explained variance as represented by the regression R^2 is only 29%.

In table 3.2, this conventional model is compared with several DM models that used the same data. The first row reiterates the R^2 for the conventional OLS regression above, while the other rows report R^2 statistics for four different data mining models using the identical

TABLE 3.2   Performance of Standard OLS
Regression versus Data Mining Models

Model type	Test sample R^2
OLS	.288
Partition tree	.442
Bootstrap forest	.438
Boosted tree	.436
Neural network	.481

data and variables. In each case, the DM approach explains considerably more variance than the conventional regression: it has much better predictive power (though we did not see as large an improvement as in Schonlau's example). These results use real data, but are presented here solely for illustrative purposes. If we had "tweaked" the DM models further, by adjusting various parameters, we could probably have increased the R^2 even further.

CALIBRATING

Calibrating is yet another DM strategy for improving model prediction that also diverges from conventional practices. One of the statistical assumptions underlying conventional regression modeling is that, across the spectrum of values of the dependent variable Y, the best estimate of Y is always the prediction (called $\hat{Y}$ or Y-hat) provided by the regression equation. Consequently, a plot of the predicted values of Y against the observed values of Y should be a straight line. If so, the model is said to be *calibrated*.

Unfortunately, in real-world data analyses, a plot or graph of the relation between Y and $\hat{Y}$ is often linear across much of the range of values of Y but diverges from a straight line at either high or low values of Y or both. The line curves. In this case, the regression model is *uncalibrated*—the model does not predict as accurately at extreme values of Y as it does in the midrange. In the conventional approach, a researcher would try to identify variables producing this curved pattern and add those to the regression model, hopefully causing the curvature to disappear.

DM sometimes uses a different approach. If a model is uncalibrated, as indicated by a curved plot of Y against $\hat{Y}$, then the researcher may fit a polynomial to Y ($Y = \hat{Y} + \hat{Y}^2 + \hat{Y}^3 + \ldots$) or use some other smoothing function, such as a spline. This procedure does not add anything to the substantive understanding of the relation between the various predictors and the dependent variable, because the researcher has not discovered why the curve is present. Nevertheless, this procedure does enhance the accuracy of prediction of Y and improves the fit of the model.

Table 3.3 provides an illustration of the effects of calibration on explained variance, using an OLS regression model predicting the log of earnings, where the predictors are

TABLE 3.3 The Effect of Calibration on
Model Fit

	R^2	RMSE
Basic OLS regression model	.5237	2.28
Above + quadratic term: $\hat{Y}^2$	.5929	2.11
Above + cubic term: $\hat{Y}^3$	.5939	2.11
Above + quartic term: $\hat{Y}^4$	.5949	2.11

age, age squared, educational attainment (as a set of dummy variables), region, race, hours worked, and weeks worked. Again, the data are from the 2010 American Community Survey.

The addition of $\hat{Y}^2$, $\hat{Y}^3$, and $\hat{Y}^4$ terms in the regression equation increases the explained variance from 0.52 to 0.59, showing that calibration can produce an improvement in predictive accuracy.

Boosting and calibrating are common strategies in DM. Both illustrate the strong emphasis that DM places on improving prediction, and the way that this results in novel analytical strategies.

MEASURING FIT: THE CONFUSION MATRIX AND ROC CURVES

Data miners use the term *fit* to refer to the accuracy of a predictive model, and specifically the extent to which predicted values of a target or dependent variable are close to the observed values of that variable. The simplest measure of fit for a predictive model with a continuous dependent variable is the model's R^2 or adjusted R^2: the percentage of variance explained by the model. But when a predictive model has a dichotomous dependent variable, such as yes/no or zero/one, we need a different way of assessing fit. The most common format provided for assessing fit is called a *confusion matrix,* which is just a two-by-two table. The confusion matrix informs us how accurately the predictive model we have constructed performs in classifying cases. It compares the predicted outcome (yes/no) with the observed or actual outcome (yes/no).

In a real confusion matrix, there would be numbers in the four cells. In the example shown in table 3.4, we have represented the numbers as n_{11}, n_{12}, n_{21}, and n_{22}, just so we can point to specific cells. Note the following with regard to this table.

- Correctly predicted or correctly classified observations appear on the diagonal of the matrix: those cases that were predicted as negative and were actually observed as negative plus those that were predicted as positive and were observed as positive. For an accurate model, most of its cases should ideally appear on the diagonal.
- The percentage of observations correctly classified by the model is $(n_{11} + n_{22})/(n_{11} + n_{12} + n_{21} + n_{22})$.

TABLE 3.4   A Confusion Matrix

		Predicted outcome	
		Negative (0)	Positive (1)
Actual outcome	Negative (0)	n_{11}	n_{12}
	Positive (1)	n_{21}	n_{22}

- However, publications commonly report an overall classification *error rate* instead: $(n_{21} + n_{12})/(n_{11} + n_{12} + n_{21} + n_{22})$.
- Some articles report a measure called *sensitivity*, defined as $n_{22}/(n_{21} + n_{22})$.
- Some also report a measure known as *specificity*, defined as $n_{11}/(n_{11} + n_{12})$.
- The *false-positive rate* is defined as the proportion of predicted positives that were in reality negative: $n_{12}/(n_{12} + n_{22})$.
- The *false-negative rate* is defined as the proportion of predicted negatives that were in reality positive: $n_{21}/(n_{11} + n_{21})$.

In all predictive situations, there is an unavoidable trade-off in prediction between false-positive rate and false-negative rate, or between sensitivity and specificity. Minimizing the false-negative rate will necessarily increase the number of false positives. Conversely, avoiding false positives means that the rate of false negatives will increase.

USING A CONFUSION MATRIX FOR CLASSIFICATION DECISIONS

A logistic regression model with a zero/one dependent variable can report for each observation or case in the dataset the predicted probability that $Y = 1$. Those predicted probabilities will take a continuous range of values from zero to one. But where should a researcher set the "bar" or threshold probability above which an observation should be assumed to have a value of $Y = 1$ and, below that threshold, predicted to be $Y = 0$?

In statistical software, the bar is usually set at $p = .5$. So a logistic regression program treats all the observations with a predicted probability of .5 or greater as predictions that $Y = 1$, and all with probabilities less than .5 as predictions that $Y = 0$.

However, for most real-world decisions, one *would not* assume that the .5 cutoff is the best one for predicting, because there is often an asymmetry in the "costs" of false-positive predictions versus the costs of false-negative predictions. A false positive may cost you far more than a false negative, or vice versa, and this should inform your decision-point.

So how would you determine the decision-point, the predicted probability from your model at which to classify a case as $Y = 1$? Here is one example of the logic to use. Consider a banking situation where a decision has to be made as to whether to offer a $5,000 loan (table 3.5). The model is constructed to predict whether someone will default (not

TABLE 3.5   Adding Cost/Benefit Consideration to a Confusion Matrix

		Decision (prediction from model)	
		Withhold loan, fearing default	*Offer loan*
P_D	Defaults	$0	−$5,000
$1 − P_D$	Does not default	−$200	+$200

pay back the loan). Call P_D the probability that the applicant will default; then $1 − P_D$ is the probability that they will not.

In each cell is the *cost* of the decision regarding each outcome. This information has to be derived from outside the prediction model, from someone who understands the real-world context the model is operating in. If your predictive model indicates that the loan applicant will default and therefore you withhold the loan, you have lost nothing; hence $0 is written in the top-left cell in the table. If your model predicts that the person will not default, so you give them a loan, but in fact they do default, you will have lost the $5,000 you loaned out; hence $5,000 in the top-right cell. If your model predicts that the person will default, so you refuse them the loan, but in fact they would have paid it off, then you will have missed out on $200 in profit from interest (−$200, lower-left cell). And finally, if the model correctly predicts that the person will not default, and you there-fore grant them the loan, you will make $200 in profit from interest (lower-right cell).

The expected value is $0(P_D) − 200(1 − P_D) − 5000(P_D) + 200(1 − P_D)$.

Thus, the decision point is where $−200(1 − P_D) = −5000(P_D) + 200(1 − P_D)$.

Rearranging and solving this equation gives $P_D = .074$. The profitable decision-point is to refuse the loan (expecting default) for any predicted P_D of .074 or greater. Note how different this is from assuming that any probability over .5 should be classified as a default, as the confusion matrix for most logistic regression software reports.

For further reading about including cost considerations in classification models, con-sult Witten, Eibe, and Hall (2001, 163). Adding cost considerations to a confusion matrix in order to decide on the optimum cut point is usually straightforward when costs and benefits have straight monetary value. Unfortunately, the tradeoff between false positives and false negatives, or between sensitivity and specificity, is sometimes difficult to express that way. Deciding where to set the cutoff for a new diagnostic health test is fraught with difficulty, since one has to balance the turmoil produced when a patient is falsely told they have some serious medical problem against the consequences of failing to identify that problem when it really is present.

ROC CURVES AS MEASURES OF FIT

A receiver operating characteristic (ROC) curve is a visual way of deciding which of sev-eral models best classifies cases. It is used in contexts where an outcome is zero/one or

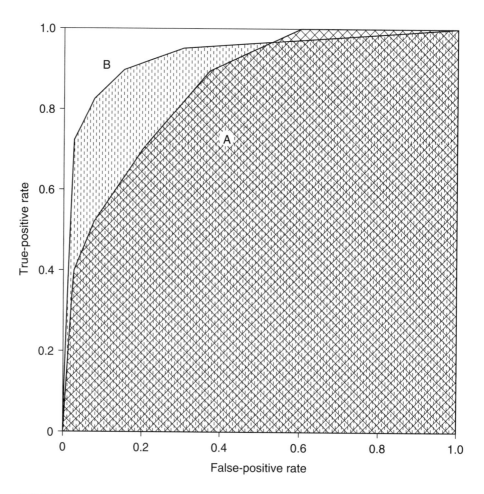

FIGURE 3.3

Examples of receiver operating characteristic curves (from Fawcett 2006).

yes/no and where a model provides a predicted probability of yes or $Y = 1$ for each case. (In DM terms this is a *binary classifier*. Many medical tests are binary classifiers, for example.) The ROC curve plots the rate of true positives (specificity) on the Y axis against false positives ($1 - $ specificity) on the X axis. It therefore depicts the trade-off between true positives (benefit) and false positives (cost)—see figure 3.3.

In the figure, the model represented by line B is generally superior at classification to that represented by line A. But we can also see that where the false-positive rate is very high (greater than 0.6), model A has a better predictive performance (Fawcett 2006).

ROC curves are often used to understand the accuracy of diagnostic tests of some disease, such as a blood test. In addition to the predicted probability of having the disease, obtained from the blood test, one needs some separate objective information as to whether the person actually has the disease. The latter is called the "gold standard" in the medical literature.

An ideal model closely follows the Y axis on the left and then sharply turns parallel to the X axis. It gets as close to the top-left corner of the ROC diagram as possible. The area under such a curve is nearly 1. A very bad model would follow the 45-degree line: this is no better than chance, and the area under this line is 0.5. That diagnostic test would tell you nothing useful.

To summarize this section, DM often constructs predictive models, and the data miner wants some method for assessing the accuracy of a given model. First, the data miner applies a predictive model, which was derived from training data, to other data (other cases or observations) that were set aside as test data. Next, the data miner uses a confusion matrix or an ROC curve to understand the accuracy of the model in predicting a target. One important measure of fit or classification accuracy is the percentage of observations correctly classified (or conversely, the overall error rate). But the researcher often wishes to determine both the false-positive and false-negative rates, and sometimes uses this information, along with cost data, to decide the most suitable cutoff value to use with the predicted probability when classifying cases.

IDENTIFYING STATISTICAL INTERACTIONS AND EFFECT HETEROGENEITY IN DATA MINING

One desideratum underlying a conventional regression model is that the same pattern of association or correlation between variables holds for all the observations in a dataset. When the opposite situation occurs—when a dataset contains groups of observations for which there are very different relations between variables—then regression models can produce highly misleading coefficients. This is known colloquially as the "apples and oranges" problem or more technically as *heterogeneous effects*. For example, if the factors predicting graduation among students in community colleges are quite different from the factors associated with graduation at highly selective four-year colleges, then estimating a single statistical model for a dataset containing both types of students will yield misleading results.

The problem is not that there are different groups within a dataset. That will always be the case. The problem arises when certain subgroups or clusters of cases within a dataset have very different patterns of association between variables than other groups do. One dramatic example is known as Simpson's paradox (sometimes the Yule-Simpson paradox), the amalgamation paradox, or the reversal paradox (Blyth 1972). Two groups of observations in a dataset might both exhibit a *positive* relation between two variables, say X and Y. But when both groups are analyzed together, in the same model, the direction of the relation between X and Y reverses direction: X might appear to be *negatively* associated with Y.

An example is provided in table 3.6, in which outcomes are given for a hypothetical medical trial. The trial was carried out at two locations (sites A and B) and involved giving

TABLE 3.6   Blyth's Formulation of Simpson's Paradox

	Overall		Site A		Site B	
	Standard treatment	*Experimental treatment*	*Standard treatment*	*Experimental treatment*	*Standard treatment*	*Experimental treatment*
Total number	11,000	10,100	1,000	10,000	10,000	100
Number dead	5,950	9,005	950	9,000	5,000	5
Number alive	5,050	1,095	50	1,000	5,000	95
Survival rate	46%	11%	5%	10%	50%	95%

SOURCE: Blyth (1972).

some patients a new, experimental treatment and others the standard treatment. The first two columns compare the outcomes for the experimental treatment and the standard treatment for the trial as a whole, across the two sites. The clearly demonstrate that the survival rate was substantially lower for those receiving the experimental treatment. If we inspected only these two columns we would conclude that the experimental treatment is much worse than the standard treatment and that it therefore ought to be abandoned.

But when we move to the four columns to the right, we find that at *each of the two individual sites* the survival rate was substantially *higher* for those receiving the experimental treatment. This suggests that the experimental treatment is much more effective than the standard treatment. How can we reconcile this with what we see in the aggregated data? The answer is that the experimental technique was administered most frequently at a site with low survival rates for both groups, and the standard technique was administered disproportionately at a site with a much higher survival rates. When the data are combined, then, the higher survival rates achieved in the experimental groups disappear. Or, put another way, the observed negative bivariate relation between exposure to the experimental treatment and the odds of survival reverses when we condition on the site where one received treatment.

A less extreme but more common situation occurs when an observed regression coefficient for a predictor X appears to be small or even not statistically significant. This sometimes occurs because X is strongly positively associated with Y for one group or cluster of cases within the sample, while for another group the same predictor X may have no relation or even a negative relation with Y. Averaging these two effects, as regression does when analyzing the whole sample, results in a misleadingly small coefficient.

Datasets are often heterogeneous in this fashion, but the researcher does not normally know what the subgroups or clusters of cases are in advance, so the "apples and oranges" problem is endemic. Therefore, as a preliminary step in DM analysis, identifying groups or clusters of cases within the dataset is desirable, so that a researcher can subsequently either run separate analyses for each distinctive group or add interaction terms that model different slopes for each group or cluster (Melamed, Breiger, and Schoon 2013).

Several DM clustering techniques can identify clusters of observations with heterogeneous relations between one or more X variables and an outcome, Y. Robert Haralick and colleagues have developed a method using linear and nonlinear manifold clustering (Haralick and Harpaz 2007). Melamed, Breiger, and Schoon offer another solution using singular value decomposition. Unfortunately, these techniques are not yet available in any of the main DM software packages.

A third, more readily available solution uses a technique known as *latent class regression* or *latent class cluster models*. The term *latent class* is used because the heterogeneous groups within a dataset may not be defined by a single measured variable. (If men differ from women in some regression model, or if older and younger respondents show a different pattern of association between variables, that can be relatively easy to identify, since those are single observed variables.) When the subgroups in the data are defined in more complex ways, however, we conceptualize the subgroups as having different values on some unobserved (hence "latent") variable. So how does one identify such subgroups?

Statistical Innovations provides a software package called Latent GOLD that accomplishes this kind of analysis in a clear and user-friendly fashion. The software is described on their website (http://statisticalinnovations.com/products/latentgold.html). Among statisticians, this topic is often called *finite mixture modeling*, and in the last decade considerable advances have been made in developing this technique. Collins and Lanza (2009) have written a useful book about the statistical ideas behind the method.

After identifying distinctive clusters or groups of observations within a dataset, a researcher may decide to analyze all the clusters in separate models. Alternatively, clusters can be represented by a nominal variable and new terms added to the model representing interactions between each cluster and particular predictors. A single model that includes these interaction terms can then be calculated to allow for the groups' heterogeneous effects.

BAGGING AND RANDOM FORESTS

The end product in the conventional statistical paradigm is usually a single regression or similar model that summarizes the relations in a dataset. That model may have gone through several cycles of improvement and modification, but at the end of the day a single model represents the best that a researcher is able to come up with.

By contrast, a DM analysis often follows a different logic, generating several *different* predictive models and combining their results to provide the best possible prediction, a process known in DM as *ensemble learning* (Berk 2006). There are alternative strategies within DM for creating these multiple models and for combining them. One of these— *bagging* (not to be confused with *binning*)—treats a dataset as if it were a population rather than a sample. It draws multiple random samples with replacement from the dataset. For each of those random samples, the DM application fits a model, and from that model calculates a predicted value of the outcome variable for each case or observation. Predictions from those different models can then be averaged to yield a best possible prediction, either for the original dataset or for new out-of-sample observations.

A related approach known as *random forests* is used to aggregate the results of several decision trees. The basic idea is to generate several tree models and average their results to obtain a best prediction. The novel aspect of random forests is that the researcher forces a different subset of predictors to be included in each model, so that each model cannot have an identical structure or content to the previous one. The varied predictions obtained from those multiple models are then combined to yield a best estimate.

Bagging and random forests are optional procedures within JMP and several of the other DM suites discussed above. Examples will be provided in a later chapter.

One rationale for this DM practice of estimating several models and averaging their findings is that in some cases model-building may be *path dependent*. In several kinds of DM models, an algorithm checks each feature to discover which one is the single most powerful predictor of a target. It keeps the most powerful one and then cycles back through the remaining predictors, to select the second-most powerful predictor, and so on for several iterations until it has selected a set of features or variables that collectively maximize the overall predictive power of the model.

This is a widely used and appropriate method for variable or feature selection. However, it has one potential pitfall. Once such an algorithm has chosen a first predictor to be entered into the model, this makes it more likely that some variables will be chosen as the second predictor, compared with some others. For example, the algorithm is unlikely to choose as the second predictor a variable that is very highly correlated with the first variable it chose, since the addition of a second highly related predictor will not enhance the predictive power very much. In other words, the choice of the first variable to some degree sets a path for the remaining iterations of the program, hence the term *path dependence*.

Path dependence implies that certain valuable predictors might be overlooked or omitted in any single model. Hence it makes sense to estimate several models, which are constrained to pick different predictors in each case, thereby avoiding the possibility that certain predictors are overlooked. That is what random forests accomplish.

A related logic informs DM procedures that involve iterative approximations that converge on an optimal solution. One weakness of such algorithms is that, depending upon where the first "guess" is located, the program may sometimes converge upon a local optimum solution that is not the best solution overall.

This is best understood graphically. In figure 3.4, the Y axis represents some measure of error, so the program seeks a solution with the lowest possible value on the Y axis. The X axis represents the value of some parameter being estimated, and the curve represents the path that a program might follow in seeking a solution, a best estimate of X. If the program's initial guess or estimate is on the left of the diagram, at a low value of X, an iterative process that chooses each subsequent solution to be slightly lower on Y will

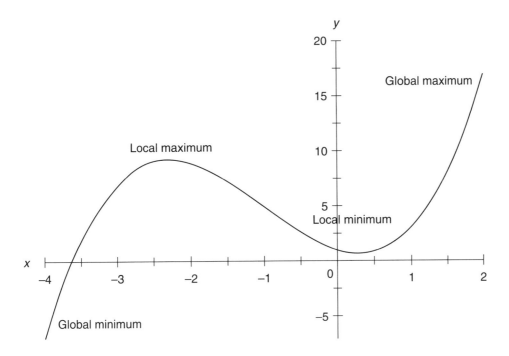

FIGURE 3.4
Global and local minima.

follow the line downwards until it reaches the global minimum—the best possible answer. It will not move up the line when the line turns upward because it is programmed to keep looking for lower values of Y and to stop when it cannot find a lower value. The algorithm will stop at the lowest Y, the global minimum, where the estimate of X is about −4.

But if the program's first guess or estimate of X happens to be on the right side of the diagram, at a higher value of X (say 1.5), the iterative process will lead down-slope to a *local minimum*. Because the algorithm always tries to decrease Y, it will not move back up the line after it reaches the first low point around X = 0.3, and so it will miss the next "valley" where the global minimum resides. It will settle therefore on the local minimum (around X = 0.3), "believing" erroneously that this is the best solution, the estimate of X that minimizes Y.

One antidote to this problem with iterative methods is to estimate several different models, each of which begins at a very different starting point (an initial guess or estimate), and to aggregate the predictions from all these different models to determine one's final prediction. This procedure will not prevent some solutions from being sub-optimal (because they have settled on a local minimum), but it does ensure that there are many other chances to reach the true or optimal solution (the global minimum) and that those will predominate.

JMP Pro and other DM software packages ask the user how many starting points to use. They then run separate models starting at very different starting points, to ensure that they do not get fooled by local minima. The cost, of course, is that they have to run many models instead of one, which may take a lot of processing time with big datasets.

·   ·   ·

To summarize this section on bagging and random forests, researchers working within the DM paradigm have discovered the value of analyzing data several times over, using slightly different samples, or different sets of predictors, or different beginning points. Each individual analysis yields an estimate, and the most robust and accurate prediction is found to be some combination of those estimates. To use an analogy, this is decision by committee, and the claim is made that "voting," averaging, or in some other fashion combining multiple models (also known as *ensemble learning*) provides a more accurate prediction than depending upon a single model or analysis. However, repeating analyses in this fashion and then combining their results is predicated on having fast, capacious computers that can calculate models many times over, a requirement for many DM methods.

THE LIMITS OF PREDICTION

Two eminent DM practitioners have published best-selling books about the limitations of data mining and prediction. Nassim Nicholas Taleb, a financial analyst and statistical modeler, is the author of *The Black Swan* (2005) and *Fooled by Randomness* (2007). Nate Silver, a developer of predictive software in baseball who is also a leading election poll analyst (see the *FiveThirtyEight* blog of the *New York Times*), authored *The Signal and the Noise* (2012).

Both authors provide cautionary points, such as the following:

· Not all natural or social phenomena have an underlying structure that can be discovered. In general, the greater the ratio of noise to signal, the greater the risk that data miners may be misled by overfitting. They may be "fooled by randomness" into seeing a mirage or finding nonexistent structure. (That's why cross-validation and replication are so important.)

· Very dynamic interconnected systems are affected by multiple causes, some of which can trigger positive feedback loops that result in rapid, large-scale, unanticipated change. "Does the Flap of a Butterfly's Wings in Brazil Set Off a Tornado in Texas?" was the title of a famous presentation about *chaos theory*, a theory about nonlinear systems credited to Edward Lorenz. As the imagery suggests, a very small-scale change in one place can trigger very large-scale consequences elsewhere. This imagery might be taken to imply that nonlinear systems cannot be successfully modeled at all. On the contrary, nonlinear systems such as the weather can be predicted, within certain limits (argues Silver), but only within a time frame shortly before the predicted event. Predictions made earlier than this will be completely inaccurate. In other words, one cannot trace any actual tornado back to the flap of a butterfly's wings. One can *imagine* the link, but one cannot *model* that far back. One can, however, fairly accurately predict a hurricane from evidence collected a few days before it happens.

- Other natural systems manifest regularities but are beyond our current predictive understanding. The timing and severity of earthquakes is one example that Silver describes. We can identify certain patterns about the magnitudes of earthquakes, but we cannot accurately predict *when* large earthquakes will happen. The pattern, if there is one, eludes us.

- Certain social phenomena are unsuited to prediction because the actors involved are scanning their environment and responding to any hints of change from the status quo. Under that circumstance, once a hint of movement is perceived—for example, a few stock prices start to rise or fall—many people will anticipate that the market is changing its direction and will jump on the bandwagon. The movement may then become a self-fulfilling prophecy as more people buy or sell off stocks. In such volatile contexts, yesterday's behavior is a poor predictor of tomorrow's action, since participants may gain monetarily from anticipating a change in direction. In this context, a herd mentality can undermine prediction.

- In other contexts, however, the opinions of a collectivity can rival the predictions of individual experts. The average of people's predictions on many issues is frequently superior to most individuals' estimates. That is why information "markets" where numerous individuals bet on outcomes often perform as well as expert decision-makers.

- Experts are often overconfident of their predictions. Equally, individuals with a stake in the continuation of a status quo tend to understate or overlook the risk of change.

These authors' two most crucial points, in our opinion, are these:

- Any prediction should always be accompanied by a probability or confidence interval that represents the uncertainty of the prediction.

- Statistically highly unlikely outcomes, though infrequent, do occur and should therefore be expected and planned for. A one-in-a-million occurrence will happen at some point. Taleb refers to such events as *black swans* and notes their destructive impact on people who make decisions assuming that statistically rare outcomes won't ever happen. One of the causes behind market crashes and bankruptcies is the tendency among quantitatively skilled decision-makers to act as if only the most statistically probable events will occur. Their plans (and fortunes) are devastated when a black swan—an unlikely event—comes to pass.

The portrait we have drawn of DM suggests that the combination of brute computing power and very large datasets enables data miners to discover structures in data that would not have been revealed by applying conventional statistical approaches to datasets containing smaller numbers of cases. We stand by that claim, but it is also important to acknowledge a paradox that data miners continually face and which molds their entire enterprise, namely that even the largest social science datasets—for example the five-million-person, multi-year census files available from the American Community Survey—are not large enough to allow a comprehensive or exhaustive search for structure, and even the biggest, fastest computers find certain empirical tasks intractable.

One consequence of this paradox is that data mining frequently has to make simplifying assumptions to keep problems tractable, or select subsets of variables, because even DM cannot handle all the available measures in one model. Why, given the huge computation and data resources available, does DM still have to make compromises or cut corners or find ingenious ways to estimate or approximate, rather than measuring things directly and exhaustively?

A thought experiment can demonstrate what is at stake. Imagine a situation where we have a dichotomous (yes/no) target or dependent variable and we have determined through some process of exploratory research that, taken together, 10 variables or features provide a good prediction of this yes/no target. Now, for argument's sake, imagine that each of these 10 predictors takes values from 0 through 9. (Say we took continuous predictors such as age or income and split each of them into 10 bins, turning each into an ordinal variable with 10 possible values.)

Hypothetically, one could construct a table, with one row for every possible combination of these 10 ten-valued predictor variables or features. Each of the cases or observations in a training dataset could be sorted, ending up in the single row that represented that case's values on all 10 predictors. After the training data were all sorted in this fashion, the proportion of yes responses for that row could be counted.

This table of training data could then serve as a predictive model. To predict the target (yes or no) for each new case in a test sample, one would just look up in the table the particular row that corresponded to the individual pattern of independent variables for that new case or observation. (For example, look up the row for men, age 65–70, income between \$75K and \$80K, living in New England, etc., for all 10 of a person's variables.) The proportion of yes cases in that row would then provide the predicted probability of yes for a particular new case in the test data. This look-up process could be repeated for each case in the new data file.

Why isn't this kind of exhaustive empirical prediction strategy feasible with big data? Consider what data miners would call the *measurement space*: the size of the table needed to represent all combinations of 10 variables, each with 10 values. It would have to be 10^{10} in size: ten billion rows in total. Also, consider what amount of training data would be needed such that (say) a hundred cases or observations would be available for each row within the table from which to count the proportion of yes answers for prediction to new data. One would need a training data set of a hundred times ten billion cases—a trillion cases—to fill up the table sufficiently to allow for a purely empirical look-up strategy.

Even big data is not big enough for an *exhaustive* prediction strategy; short of astronomy, we are unlikely to find datasets with a trillion cases. So data mining is unable to handle an exhaustive direct measurement strategy for an imagined problem of 10 variables, each with 10 values.

What this thought experiment is intended to communicate is that DM faces important limitations stemming from the size of training data and also from computational load. On the other hand, DM has several strategies that successfully avoid these problems and enable DM methods to successfully analyze data with hundreds of variables.

- First, DM places a high premium on reducing the number of variables that will go into any model. One approach involves *feature selection*: scanning through large numbers of variables to discover which small subset is the most powerful for predicting a given target, and dropping the rest.

- A second approach involves combining some predictor variables into indices, scales, or factors, a process called *feature extraction*.

- A third approach avoids a huge measurement space by realizing that many of the possible combinations of values of variables will not be important in practice, either because there aren't many cases with those particular combinations, or because one can obtain good estimates of the effects of individual variables without considering all their possible interactions or combinations of values.

- *Data partitioning* (or *decision trees*) is one example. These methods search for statistical interactions between variables, but they do not exhaustively consider the entire measurement space with its millions of possible interactions or cells. Instead, they work one variable at a time, initially picking the single variable that best partitions the data on *Y*, then recursively finding additional variables to partition the data further. These techniques do find interactions that matter in terms of predicting *Y*, but by proceeding one variable at a time they identify maybe a hundred important combinations of values of variables (or interactions), rather than billions. Tree or recursive partitioning methods select a subset of predictors and interactions from a larger number of possible predictors and interactions.

- *Neural network* models play a similar role. They can incorporate complex interactions between predictors into their predictive models in an automated fashion, without the data analyst having to specify those ahead of time.

- Finally, some methods take advantage of the fact that a huge measurement space can be drastically reduced if we make a simplifying assumption, namely that each variable affects a dependent variable independently of each other variable, or more precisely that predictors are *conditionally independent*. This is equivalent to saying that interactions between predictors do not matter. Methods that follow this simplifying assumption, including the naive Bayesian classifier (discussed in a later chapter), are fairly accurate in some contexts.

Let's summarize our argument with respect to "big data is never big enough." We began by noting that, in principle, DM methods could take an "exhaustive" approach to discovering structure and prediction, for example by considering every possible interaction between predictors, or by using every available predictor. We used a thought experiment to show that an exhaustive strategy often isn't possible as a practical matter, because the number of combinations or interactions between predictors becomes astronomically large, so large that no dataset is going to have enough cases to cover all the combinations. Faced with that, DM methods adopt search strategies that are not exhaustive. Although they still try out many possible models, they usually don't try out *all* possibilities. In practice, DM reduces the measurement space or the number of possibilities considered. This is accomplished in several ways: (1) by initially selecting a subset of important predictors from a larger list—*feature selection*; (2) by combining variables into scales or other composites—*feature extraction*; (3) by sometimes ignoring interactions among predictors to obtain an simpler but perhaps still accurate prediction; and (4) by looking for clusters of similar cases in the data, and analyzing each cluster or group separately.

4

IMPORTANT STAGES IN
A DATA MINING PROJECT

Having introduced the paradox of too little big data and noted the challenges caused by high-dimensional data, we can now discuss how a DM analysis typically proceeds. There are six conceptually separate steps: (1) deciding whether and how to sample data before analyzing it; (2) building a rich array of features or variables; (3) feature selection and feature extraction; (4) constructing or fitting a model using that smaller list of features on the training data; (5) verifying or validating that model on test data; and (6) trying out alternative DM methods and perhaps combining several (ensemble methods) in order to discover whether they offer a better solution. In this chapter we provide more detail for the first four of these.

WHEN TO SAMPLE BIG DATA

Data miners sometimes avoid analyzing a whole large dataset; they draw a smaller random sample of cases from it and analyze that instead. One reason for doing this is that even a fast computer may run for hours analyzing millions of cases, while the identical analysis performed on a random and therefore representative sample of (say) 20,000 cases might well reveal just the same patterns and run much faster. In this instance, sampling big data is just a way to speed up analyses and avoid the possibility of a computer crashing due to insufficient memory. (An alternative strategy is to carry out initial analyses using a smaller random sample and only analyze the whole dataset at the end, after one has decided on variables and models based on the smaller sample data.)

A second and quite different reason for sampling from large datasets occurs when a researcher is interested in predicting relatively rare events or cases. So, for example, an analyst may want to detect fraudulent transactions by identifying some distinctive pattern of characteristics that those transactions have in common. This researcher's database may contain millions of legitimate transactions (say, coded as 0 for the target variable) but perhaps only a thousand identified fraudulent transactions (coded as 1). In other words, there is a very lopsided ratio of fraudulent to legitimate transactions, but these are very important "needles in a haystack."

Some modeling and classification techniques do not work well with lopsided distributions on the dependent variable. A logistic regression model, for example, faced with nine value-zero outcomes to every value-one outcome, tends to build a model that predicts the zeros quite well but at the expense of missing many ones. The overall model might fit relatively well, perhaps classifying correctly 95% of the time, but it might still misclassify half of the fraudulent transactions.

To avoid that kind of problem, when focusing on relatively rare outcomes it is better to include all of the rare (e.g., fraudulent) cases, and randomly sample from the other kind of plentiful cases, aiming at roughly a 1:1 ratio of the two types in the new dataset. DM techniques will predict or classify much better given this relatively balanced dataset than they would when applied to a very lopsided sample. Sampling before analyzing is indispensible in this kind of context.

BUILDING A RICH ARRAY OF FEATURES

It might seem surprising that data miners routinely begin a project by constructing new variables, even when their dataset already has many variables or features. In fact, some data miners spend more time on constructing a rich set of features than they spend on running models. That's because the success of modeling *depends on having the right features* and the researcher may not be sure in advance which predictor variables will turn out to be strong predictors or classifiers. It is prudent to begin any DM project by constructing new variables, knowing that the list of variables can later be pared down, leaving just the ones that turn out to be powerful predictors of a target or dependent variable, or which work well in cluster analyses or as classifiers.

In practice, data miners:

· Consult so-called *domain experts* about what factors those experts think are important in predicting outcomes, and then construct measures that represent those factors. Data miners are often outsiders brought into an organization to analyze activities that organizational insiders already know a lot about. It is wise to debrief these everyday experts and gain their insights to inform variable construction.

· Create new features that are *ratios,* constructed out of existing variables. In the real estate industry, for example, cost per square foot of property may be a more useful measure than either the total cost or the total size of a property. In health research, body mass index (BMI) is a complex ratio of weight to height that functions as a useful predictor for various kinds of health outcomes. In demography, many critical variables are rates (children per 10,000 women of childbearing age, divorces per 1,000 marriages per year, and so on). So data miners should ensure that they have thought about appropriate ratios and rates when constructing features in a data set.

· Construct new versions of continuous variables that are intended to capture nonlinear effects of the variable on a target dependent variable. This binning can be done using data partitioning or tree software or using optimal binning, as discussed earlier. Examples will also be given in a later chapter.

· Construct new variables to represent interactions between other features or variables but which can subsequently be entered into models as variables in their own right. CHAID and CART will identify interactions, as detailed below.

· Some data mining procedures require that the researcher rescale predictors before models are run. The rationale for rescaling predictors is that some variables are measured in units such as dollars and take values from zero to one million or so, while others may have just a few categories (say one through five), and yet others may be probabilities, with decimal values between zero and one. Some DM applications are biased toward picking variables with a large range of values or a large variance in preference to variables with a smaller range of values. The solution to that difficulty is to rescale all predictors so they have the same range. (Some applications perform this rescaling automatically, so the researcher doesn't have to bother.)

· The two most common types of rescaling are standardization (into z-scores) and normalization. Standardization into a z-score involves an arithmetical transformation: the mean value for that variable is first subtracted from each observed value and the resulting number is then divided by the standard deviation of the variable. Normalizing, on the other hand, transforms each observation by subtracting the minimum value for that variable from its observed value and then dividing by the range of the variable. Both techniques render variables commensurate in scale.

· A cluster analysis may be also carried out to identify groups of similar cases in the dataset, without reference to the dependent or target variable. The researcher can pick the number of clusters in advance (often around four). Those clusters can then be used to define a new nominal variable that can be added to the dataset.

Using these strategies, data miners create new features or variables to be employed in subsequent stages of DM analysis along with pre-existing variables. Some of the new variables may turn out to be important predictors, but many will be discarded. This winnowing is fine; unless one begins with a rich set of features, one is unlikely to end up with a strong model.

All together, the various activities that create rich features, along with the selection of the most powerful predictors (to be discussed in the next section), plus dealing with missing data, are referred to as *preprocessing* data.

FEATURE SELECTION

Feature-selection methods allow a researcher to identify which among many potential predictors are strongly associated with an outcome variable of interest. They also help avoid problems with multicollinearity among predictors.

DM offers several alternatives for selecting a subset of independent variables that are the most effective predictors of a dependent variable. One method is already well known to quantitative social scientists: *stepwise regression* follows a DM-like logic. After a dependent variable is specified, a forward stepwise program works its way through all the independent variables, estimating for each the predictive power of a regression model containing just that independent variable. It chooses the best predictor among these. In a second step, it cycles back through the list of remaining predictors and assesses which of those best improves the fit if it is added to the first in the regression model. It adds that best predictor to the former one, and repeats the process many times until it has identified a subset of predictors that in combination best predict the dependent variable. Tree or recursive partitioning methods are analogous to stepwise regression insofar as they test each potential predictor and select the most powerful predictors, while also identifying interactions between predictors.

Other DM algorithms for feature selection are claimed to be superior to stepwise regression, either in their speed of computation and/or because they are less biased. One approach is known as LARS (least angle regression) or LASSO (least absolute shrinkage in selection optimization) (Hastie, Tibshirani, and Friedman 2009; Miller 2002). LASSO feature selection is implemented in the Professional edition of SPSS's Statistics software (choose Regression → Optimal Scaling CATREG, and pick the regularization option).

Another feature-selection algorithm, which is claimed to be more accurate than LASSO and also has the advantage of being very fast, is called *VIF regression* (because it uses *variance inflation factors* to select potential predictors). It is freely available as a program in R (Lin, Foster, and Ungar 2011).

Within R, type `install.packages("VIF")`. Additional information is online at http://cran.r-project.org/web/packages/VIF/VIF.pdf. We provide an example in a later chapter.

FEATURE EXTRACTION

Three procedures, *principal component analysis* (PCA), *independent component analysis* (ICA), and a combination of *random projection* and *singular value decomposition*, provide alternative tools for constructing new variables that are weighted sums of existing variables.

PCA is the most established technique and is available in many software packages, so we recommend using it. PCA finds a set of components (or *factors*, or *scales*) that taken together best explain the total variance within a dataset (Dunteman 1989). Each component is constructed by adding together a number of previously measured variables, each with its own weight. These variables are selected and their weights are calculated in such a way that the resulting components or scales explain as much of the overall variance in the data matrix as possible.

In a second step, each of these components is "rotated" so that it is now uncorrelated with any other dimension. What this yields is a small number of new variables or features which summarize most of the variance contained in the larger number of original variables. So PCA achieves dimension reduction by reducing the number of variables.

It is not a given that components that together explain much of the variance in a dataset will also turn out to be good predictors for one particular dependent variable or target or label. That will have to be determined at a subsequent stage during modeling. However, PCA creates new variables. Analytical software can subsequently decide what the best predictors for modeling are.

The downside of PCA is that the components or factors it creates may not be meaningful or interpretable. The PCA procedure "loads" original variables onto components by weighting the former in such a way that the component accounts for a lot of the variance, but not infrequently this combines conceptually very different variables into a single component. What does it mean if a component combines questions or measures about totally different subjects, for example loading attitudes toward abortion with measures of family income, age, and length of daily commute? If a thematically incoherent component then turns out to be a significant predictor in a model, how does one interpret that fact?

This brings us back to the tension between data analysis focused on understanding mechanisms and causal processes versus analyses emphasizing predictive accuracy. If the purpose of building a model is to predict accurately and then to base decisions upon that prediction, the conceptual incoherence of PCA scales doesn't much matter so long as they "work." If the purpose is to understand a causal process, then PCA's production of incoherent or uninterpretable predictors is a problem.

PCA software works well with a hundred variables and a few thousand cases, but it slows down and may collapse when confronted with very large datasets, because manipulating huge matrices becomes computationally very time-consuming. Luckily, data miners have been able to extend the logic of PCA to analyze big data in reasonable amounts of processing time, by combining two techniques called *random projection* and *singular value decomposition*.

Random projection first multiplies a data matrix by a random matrix, in effect making many new variables, each consisting of an old variable weighted by a random number. It then adds all those newly weighted variables together to create a new variable. At first impression this seems a very odd idea: creating new variables, similar to scales, that that are literally random mixes of pre-existing variables. Singular value decomposition then analyzes these newly created variables to create a smaller number of dimensions or attributes that can then be used in a DM model (Vempala 2004; Halko, Martinsson, and Tropp 2011.) Singular value decomposition is analogous to PCA in that it reduces a large number of variables to fewer new ones.

Mathematicians have shown that the smaller number of features or variables produced by adding randomly weighted versions of the original variables can preserve structure that was present in the larger numbers of original variables (Halko, Martinsson, and Tropp 2011; Martinsson, Rokhlin, and Tygert 2011).

ICA is another recently developed approach to feature extraction that is analogous to PCA. Its authors claim that it is far superior to PCA in its ability to find components that predict a target (Hyvarinen, Karhunen, and Oja 2001). A program called FastICA is available as a free download from http://research.ics.aalto.fi/ica/fastica/.

CONSTRUCTING A MODEL

Once a researcher has constructed a dataset rich in features or variables, modeling can begin. A data miner will choose what kind of model to use, but this first step is only temporary, since typically a researcher will analyze data using several different kinds of models or approaches and compare their prediction accuracy before settling on a final approach.

If the purpose of analyzing the data is to predict a dichotomous (yes/no) variable, data miners have a large palette of classifiers that will accomplish this: nearest-neighbor methods, tree methods, naive Bayesian and Bayesian classifiers, support vector machines, and neural networks, in addition to older, well-established statistical methods such as logistic regression, probit, and discriminant analysis.

When the target or dependent variable is a continuous measure, the list of applicable techniques is still long, including tree methods, neural network models, Bayesian regression, and support vector machine regression, in addition to conventional regression approaches.

Everyone new to DM asks the same question at this point: "But which method works best?" The correct answer pleases no one: "It depends." When researchers have attempted to compare the accuracy of these different techniques using multiple datasets, they have found that no single technique consistently outperforms all the others. If one analyzes a single dataset, it is often the case that one technique will outperform the rest, but when one shifts to analyzing a different dataset then the ranking of methods will completely change. The method that was outstanding before is now near the bottom of the list, while some other method rises to the top.

Perhaps with time, researchers will develop a theory of which DM methods are best suited to which datasets, but that has not occurred up to now. It seems that the peculiarities of a dataset really matter—aspects of its structure that we don't easily grasp. That does not present a practical barrier to analysis; it just means that any sensible data miner tries several modeling techniques for a particular dataset, and notes how well each performs in this unique context.

PART 2

WORKED EXAMPLES

PREPARING TRAINING AND TEST DATASETS

Earlier, we discussed how cross-validation (CV) works as a sort of quality control mechanism in data mining, and pointed out how CV methods contrast in an interesting manner with conventional tests for statistical significance. We will now discuss explicitly the logic of CV, and then provide a guide for how one carries out this technique in practice using a number of statistical packages.

Many data mining texts deal with the logic of CV in a rather cursory fashion. The focus is on its practical application: how CV presents a solution to one or another problem that tends to be encountered when employing computationally intensive methods with big data. In some texts CV is presented as a way to prevent overfitting (Nisbet, Elder, and Miner, 2009; Kuhn and Johnson 2013); in others, as a means for model selection (Murphy 2012); and in others, as a way to evaluate model accuracy (Han, Kamber, and Pei 2012). In fact, CV is all of these, but the reasons why this is the case, and indeed why these problems are interlinked, tend to be left rather obscure. We here attempt to fill in this conceptual gap.

The problems data miners address with CV methods are ones which are central and familiar in scientific practice. In the scientific investigation of any particular problem, the result found in a single study can never be taken too seriously, by itself, as a valid description of how the world generally works. This is because the chance nature of sampling, and the possibility of random occurrence in an experiment, render it all too possible that findings from a single study are the result of the confluence of particular fortuitous circumstances. For results to be believed and accepted, they must obtain support from multiple subsequent investigations. In short, results must be replicated *independently,* ideally by entirely different researchers.

CV procedures permit researchers to employ this logic within a single investigation. In the simplest method of CV, researchers randomly split their data into subsamples prior to building a predictive model. Because the data splitting is *random,* for the limited purposes of the investigation at hand the subsamples generated constitute independent sets of observations. They are not independent in a global sense, since they were drawn from the same population (i.e. the full data set); but within the universe defined for the study at hand, and defined by the data that we are using, the subgroups are rendered independent of each other through randomization. Researchers build a model using one set of observations and then test it on another. This latter step represents an *independent* test of the model's accuracy.

Randomization is typically used to ensure that, on average, the subgroups produced are as similar as possible in terms of relevant characteristics (see e.g. Rubin 1978). However, it has another convenient result, which data mining CV methods exploit: the random variation among subgroups produced through random assignment. The idiosyncratic features of any particular randomly created subgroup are by definition unlikely to recur in the other subgroups. In contrast, empirical regularities across the subgroups are likely to be characteristics of the population as a whole—that is, they will tell us the *signal* to which we want to attend; the random variation across the subsamples can be thought of as the *noise* which we would like to analytically separate out.

This is of particular importance because of the very flexibility and power of data mining methods for creating predictive models. Because models such as neural networks and partition trees are capable of fitting themselves tightly to the data, they are highly susceptible to permitting the noise to play a greater role than one would wish in generating the model built on any particular set of observations. The very plasticity and power of the models becomes, in this sense, a curse. They will produce a model which is highly accurate, attaining near-perfection in predictive accuracy for the particular set of observations upon which it was built. But this apparent result is deceptive, or "overoptimistic" in the words of an early researcher (Larson 1931), for such a model will not perform well at all out of sample. This is what data miners refer to as *overfitting*. Using CV for model selection and evaluation can help reduce the possibility of its occurrence.

Consider why this is ultimately important. Data mining algorithms can be powerful tools for prediction, and can thus improve practical diagnostic ability. That is, if a data mining algorithm is trained on a set of data in which researchers have access to the true value of the outcome variable, and validated on an independent set where values of the outcome are also known, it can later be deployed in data in which the outcome variable, the quantity of interest, is *not* known. For example, data mining tools can potentially improve practitioners' ability to distinguish cancerous from noncancerous cells. Given this practical application, it is all the more important that the models be accurate; and this is ensured through rigorous application of CV for model selection and evaluation.

We have one final comment on the importance of CV methods. It has become abundantly clear to us in the course of our research that the predictive strength of computationally intensive data mining methods comes at a cost, in terms of the ability of the models to be fully comprehended by humans. Kuhn and Johnson (2013) describe this as the "tension between prediction and interpretation." Data mining models often garner their power through increasing complexity, and this renders them rather dizzying if not simply opaque to human analysts. But Kuhn and Johnson argue that, especially in life-and-death situations, this ought not to matter, and that indeed preferring a comprehensible but relatively poor-performing model to one which is a "black box" but is highly predictive would be "unethical." In the context of models whose results cannot be readily understood, but which have the appearance of being highly accurate, CV appears as an essential means of generating trust through rigorous testing.

In sum, CV provides an independent test of the model developed with a data mining technique. It assists with both choosing the "best" model (model selection) in terms of its capacity for out-of-sample prediction, and with evaluating the "true" predictive capacity of a given model (model evaluation). This helps guard against the possibility of selecting a model which is too dependent on the particular data it was built on—that is, it guards against overfitting. All of these functions are connected by a common reference to the logic of the independent test and the trustworthiness of replicable results. Now we present a brief discussion of different methods of CV, and then proceed to show how CV is performed using a number of statistical programs.

CROSS-VALIDATION METHODS: AN OVERVIEW

"Independent" datasets can be generated in a number of ways. The simplest conceptually, but the most complicated in terms of the actual work required, is to work with separately collected data. If we have built a predictive model for mortality using data from one hospital, we can test it on data gathered at a different hospital. However, this situation, though perhaps desirable, is fairly rare. Data collection is expensive, and it is unlikely that researchers and funders would want to double research costs simply so that predictive modelers can have a clean test dataset.

Otherwise, there are three methods for generating independent data from a single dataset: *bootstrapping, random holdback,* and *k-fold.* The first involves randomly sampling, with replacement, from the data that we have. Typically this is done a large number of times, creating many separate datasets of the same size as our original dataset. If we believe that our original data were a relatively random sample drawn from a population, then bootstrapping from it provides an unbiased method of generating a random sample of all possible random samples. Each of the multiple bootstrapped samples can be used to analyze the data, giving a range of results (coefficients or predicted probabilities, for example) which can then be averaged to obtain an overall result.

Bootstrapping presents certain advantages over other methods that will be discussed below. In particular, through bootstrapping we can generate not only an estimate of the error rate but also a standard error of the prediction, as well as a standard error of the error rate (Efron 1979, 1983; Efron and Gong 1983).[1] Moreover, bootstrapping produces a *nonparametric* standard error—which does not depend upon distributional assumptions that may not hold empirically—and indeed has entered into conventional statistical modeling primarily in this capacity. Finally, because bootstrapping generates numerous datasets, rather than just one, on which to test the model, it results in a "smoothed" estimate of the error rate. However, bootstrapping is quite computationally intensive and can be time-consuming to use with large datasets.

The bootstrapping approach is particularly valuable when one has a small sample to begin with, where statistical power is really an issue. In other cases, however, we have data to burn—increasingly true in the era of big data. In this latter situation, we can adopt a much simpler approach than bootstrapping, called *random holdback*: we can simply randomly split our data into training and test sets, build our model using the first, and test it on the second. We can decide to split the data between the training and test parts in whatever proportions we want—50/50, 70/30, and so on.

Alternatively, we can take a third approach, using what is called *k*-fold cross-validation. This involves dividing the data up randomly into *k* parts (or folds) of equal size, where *k* is a number chosen by the researcher. (Typical values for *k*, used in popular software packages, are 5 or 10 folds.) The researcher then builds *k* separate models, each using all but one of the folds and then tested on this remaining one. In essence, then, we have *k* training and *k* test sets, and each of the resulting *k* models is tested on data which were not used in its generation. Results can then be combined by averaging, or we can choose the best-fitting model. This method is also good for relatively small datasets.

We'll now demonstrate how to perform *k*-fold and holdback CV using several different statistical software packages.

STATA

Stata is not really a data mining package, so CV isn't built into it in such a manner as to make it particularly easy to use. Holdback CV needs to be done "by hand," as far as we know.

In order to perform holdback CV, the first thing that needs to be done is to randomly divide the data into two parts. Stata permits random sampling, which will allow the researcher to create separate datasets, but we think it is far easier to simply generate a variable that permits random division. One can do this by generating a random binomial with the code:

$$\text{gen x} = \text{rbinomial(n, p)}$$

TABLE 5.1	Results from Stata's Crossfold Program
Crossfold number	Root mean square error
1	0.3352256
2	0.3308182
3	0.3365854
4	0.3280907
5	0.3264875

This call generates a new variable named x which is distributed as binomial. The parameter n is the number of binomial trials per case, and p is the probability of "successes." For random assignment, $n = 1$, and p depends on the training/test breakdown you want. Setting p to .5 will generate a new variable with a 50%–50% breakdown of ones and zeros; $p = .7$ produces a 70%-30% breakdown, and so on.

Independent testing is another story. As far as we know, this would involve building a model (e.g. a logistic regression) on one part of the data (where x == 1), saving parameter estimates in a vector, and then predicting the outcome in the rest of the data (where x == 0) using a regression equation generated through multiplying a matrix of variables by this vector of coefficients. This process is somewhat arduous, and gets the user into the field of matrix programming in Stata, which is fairly advanced. In short, holdback validation is difficult to do in Stata, principally because its designers haven't built the system with data mining concerns in mind.

K-fold CV can be done straightforwardly with a user-generated program called crossfold (Daniels 2012). Crossfold uses the following Stata syntax:

```
crossfold regress yvar xvars, k(k)
```

"Regress" in this syntax could be replaced with logit or other estimators. We are not sure, and documentation does not tell us, precisely how many estimators are supported by crossfold. In any event, it provides fit statistics from k models (with k chosen by the researcher), and permits the choice of fit statistics—RMSE, mean absolute error, or pseudo-R^2. Typical output is shown in table 5.1. This is not the most informative CV technique, but it does provide k independent tests of a model.

R

We are not aware of a specific R routine which performs holdback CV and which could be combined with any analytical routine. There are some R routines which *incorporate* CV via holdback (presuming one has already created separate test and training sets). For these routines, holdback CV is quite easy; for others, it is as difficult as it is in Stata.

However, numerous *k*-fold CV routines exist in R. One *k*-fold CV routine which is particularly intuitive is cv.glm, which is part of the package called *boot* (Canty and Ripley 2010). It is used to cross-validate previously fit generalized linear models.

One can call this with the following syntax:

```
cv1<-cv.glm(data, glmfit, k)
```

Where `data` is some dataset, `glmfit` is the results of a previously fit generalized linear model fit using `data`, and `k` is the number of folds desired. After running this model, entering

```
cv1$delta
```

returns a vector of two numbers: a cross-validation fit, and an adjusted cross-validation fit (if a value of *k* was entered rather than using the default leave-one-out CV).[2] The latter number is given because some statistical work suggests that *not* using leave-one-out CV can generate biased estimates of validation fit (Davison and Hinkley 1997), so the program performs some operations to compensate for this bias.

JMP PRO

CV is very, very easy in JMP Pro. It is done in one of two ways. For some modeling routines, JMP Pro requires you to supply a validation variable—a nominal variable containing different values indicating the training and test portions. What we want is a variable in which the values are randomly assigned in the proportions we desire. This can be done quite easily. In the main menu of JMP Pro, click Cols New Column. The window which opens is shown in figure 5.1.

We change the column name from the default to "valid" (as in validation). We change Modeling Type from the default Continuous to Nominal, and then under Initialize Data, we select Random. This permits us to choose different distributions to draw from: the normal, the uniform, and the binomial (which is what Random Indicator is drawing from). We select Random Indicator and change the proportions for values 0 and 1 to 0.5 and 0.5 (the value for 2 is set to 0). Simply clicking OK proceeds to generate this validation variable. The variable can simply be entered into Validation fields in later model-building windows, as in the Stepwise Regression launch platform shown in figure 5.2.

Other model platforms have built-in CV settings in JMP. The Partition platform (for partition trees), for example, allows the researcher to indicate a "validation portion" in the main model platform window. They also allow users to choose *k*-fold CV in the model launch window. Neural nets similarly allow users to specify a holdback portion. We will go into this in greater detail in the partition tree and neural network sections below.

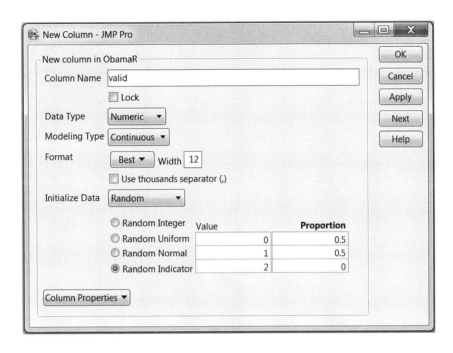

FIGURE 5.1

Creating a validation column in JMP Pro.

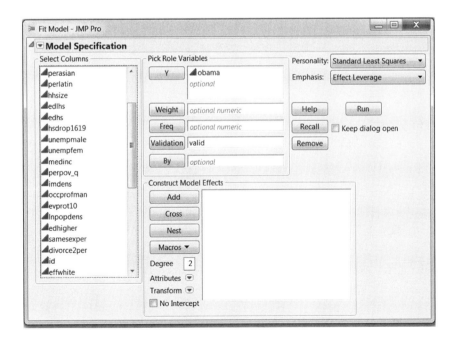

FIGURE 5.2

Adding cross-validation to stepwise regression in JMP Pro.

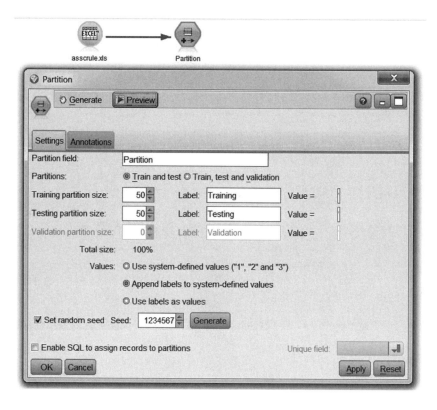

FIGURE 5.3
Cross-validation in SPSS Modeler.

SPSS MODELER

SPSS Modeler, the specialized data analytics package of SPSS, makes CV by holdback particularly easy. The program, which we will describe in more detail later, involves generating "streams" of statistical operations through point-and-click; each stream consists of "nodes" which can perform operations. Each node has an associated window in which numerous parameters can be adjusted. The nodes are selected from "palettes" which contain similar-type nodes.

In the Fields palette, choose the Partition node and double-click. This opens the screen shown in figure 5.3. Within this node, as can be seen, one can set the breakdown of training and test (and validation) samples. This generates a variable called Partition (or some other name if the researcher changes it) which can be selected as a validation variable in modeling nodes.

K-fold CV can be also performed for some other applications in Modeler (*K*-nearest neighbors, 5.0 partition tree, neural net), but within the nodes for these specific modeling operations, not as a separate node.

IBM has been enhancing SPSS Statistics—the regular statistics program that is used in hundreds of undergraduate classrooms—with several data mining applications. Some of those have internal options for CV. However, it is easy enough to divide any SPSS dataset into two random parts—for training and testing—using ordinary SPSS syntax. In the example below we divide our data randomly such that 80% of cases are identified as training and the remaining 20% as test; users can choose their own proportions. The syntax reads:

```
USE ALL.
COMPUTE filter_$ = (uniform(1)< = .80).
VARIABLE LABELS filter_$ 'Approximately 80% of the cases
   (SAMPLE)'.
FORMATS filter_$ (f1.0).
FILTER BY filter_$.
EXECUTE.
Filter OFF.
recode filter_$ (0 = 0)(1 = 1) into datagroup.
var label datagroup 'training or test'.
value labels datagroup 0 'test dataset' 1 'training data-
   set'.
execute.
```

The variable "datagroup" takes values of 1 for observations randomly assigned to the 80% training subset and 0 for those to be used for the test dataset.

6

VARIABLE SELECTION TOOLS

When analyzing big data, we are faced with an overwhelming welter of information. We have too many cases, or too much information about each case, for effective use of standard statistical methodologies. We have already seen how having too many cases can cause programs to crash or run unduly slowly, and how this can sometimes be addressed simply by sampling our data. A more complicated situation emerges when we have too much information gathered about each case—in other words, when we have more variables than we know what to do with.

Data miners use the letter N to refer to the number of observations or cases, and the letter P to refer to the number of variables, predictors or features. In the situation where P is very large, what we seek is a technique that reduces the amount of information we need to process by selecting those variables which are most important and discarding the others.

One solution is to turn to a class of techniques called *subset selection* or *regularization* methods. This family of methods were developed precisely in order to automate the process of variable selection (and for this same reason it is often criticized by conventional data analysts for being atheoretical and data-driven). The methods in question operate by discovering, from among a long list of predictors, those which perform best in terms of explaining variance on the dependent variable.

STEPWISE REGRESSION

Stepwise regression was the first "automated" routine that was developed for choosing variables, and it is certainly the one most frequently and vehemently denounced by detractors of such algorithms. It was developed for situations in which a researcher is blessed with an abundance of independent variables in a dataset (i.e., large P) but has little or no theoretical framework for choosing which of them to include in a model. This is probably still the situation in which it is most often employed, but there are other situations in which it can be profitably used and for which it is probably more justifiable.

In our experience, stepwise regression may be used not only to weed through large numbers of potential predictors representing main effects but also to sift through higher-order interaction terms between predictors. Let's imagine we have 12 predictor variables which we want to include in a model. But we want to be realistic about the fact that the world does not consist only of main effects but also of interactions between predictors, and we want to allow for the possibility that some of the interactions might explain substantial variance in the outcome variable. If we wish to include only two-way interactions, the number of features or predictors in the model rises from 12 to 88. That number increases to 100 if we also include quadratic terms—interactions of a variable with itself—to allow for curvilinear relations between a predictor X and an outcome Y. If we also decide to allow for three-way interactions, (say of age by gender by income) the number of predictors in the model reaches 320 terms. However, not all of those 320 variables are likely to be statistically significant or important predictors. So we begin to see the appeal of a feature selection algorithm which can tell us which among these 320 variables are important.

Stepwise regression routines work in one of three ways. The first, *forward selection,* begins with a model that contains only an intercept term. It then examines each independent variable individually and chooses the one that is "best" (we will get to how "best" is determined in a minute). After entering this variable into the predictive model, the program repeats this process, considering the remaining candidate predictors over and over—adding one superior predictor at a time—until it chooses the "best" model (once again, we'll define that a little later).

The second method, *backward elimination,* begins by including all available variables in an initial regression, and then tests each one to see which can be most profitably dropped from the model. It ends with a more pared-down model in which only the variables that "count" remain. Finally, there is a method known as *forward-backward stepwise regression,* which as the name suggests is a combination of forward selection and backward elimination. Like forward selection it starts with a null model and enters variables iteratively when they meet a criterion, but it also eliminates them if and when they subsequently fall below some threshold of relevance.

Variables are selected for inclusion or exclusion in one of two ways. The first involves the use of p-values for the individual predictor variables. For example, the researcher might instruct the program to include variables only if they have p-values of .05 or lower and to eliminate them if their p-value rises above .10. This variable inclusion criterion, which is oriented entirely toward the individual predictors, is what is used exclusively in the stepwise algorithms of some commercial packages—Stata's, for instance.

An alternative approach is to employ some measure of overall or global model fit, usually one that penalizes a model for adding more predictors. Fit measures include adjusted R^2, Akaike's information criterion (AIC), the Bayesian information criterion (BIC), and Mallows's C_p. Variables are included or excluded on the basis of the improvement each makes to the regression model as a whole as evaluated by the change in the fit statistic designated by the researcher.

The "final model" is chosen in a manner similar to how the individual variables are chosen. If p-values are utilized in variable selection, then the algorithm will stop building a stepwise regression model once all of the variables that meet the researcher-specified criteria are in the model (for instance, all variables in the model have p-values of .05 or lower, and no other variable could be entered into the model which would have such a p-value). If, on the other hand, a global fit statistic is utilized, the algorithm will choose the model which optimizes that fit statistic—that is, the model with the highest adjusted R^2 or the lowest BIC, for example.

Both methods are quite susceptible to type I error, because by chance alone, we are quite likely to find, in a large set of predictors, one that is significantly related to the outcome. While this may be rather obvious in the case of p-value-based methods of selection, it is also true of selection methods that use global measures of model fit. Given enough predictors, one is bound, by chance, to be able to raise predictive capacity sufficiently to surmount the threshold for inclusion. The best ways to avoid type I error appear to be those which use a measure of model fit as a "stopping rule" and which select variables on the basis of p-values—but p-values which take the multiple-comparisons issue into account. We could, for instance, apply the Bonferroni rule, setting the p-value at α/p, where p is the total number of candidate predictors and α is 0.05. Such Bonferroni p-values are very stringent, though. Another approach, suggested by Foster and Stine (2004), is to test variables in ascending order according to their t statistics, beginning conservative threshold and gradually raising that threshold while working towards the less predictive variables.

Like any other data-driven approach, stepwise regression is highly likely to overfit the model in question (though using a tougher threshold for inclusion will remedy this to some extent). Validating the model on a separate test set of data is therefore important. When possible, the cross-validation fit should be reported.

AN EXAMPLE IN JMP

We will demonstrate the utility of stepwise regression using JMP's Stepwise algorithm, which we like because of the numerous options for stopping rules that it provides and because of the ease with which interactions and polynomial terms can be added to the

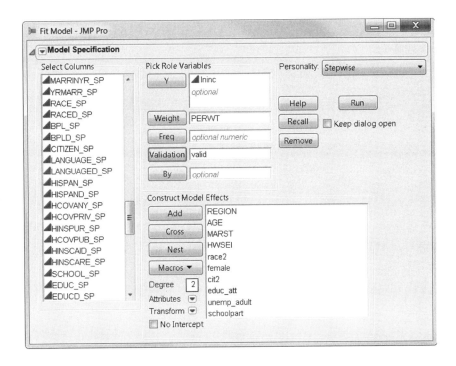

FIGURE 6.1
Stepwise regression in JMP Pro.

model. (However, stepwise regression is available in many other statistical packages, including SPSS and SAS.)

For this demonstration, we will use data from the U.S. Census Bureau's 2010 American Community Survey, from which we have randomly drawn a dataset of 15,000 cases. We will be predicting the (logged) personal income of adults in the United States using a fairly small number of main effect variables—region, age, marital status, occupational prestige, race, gender, citizenship, educational attainment, employment status, and educational enrollment.

To run a stepwise regression using JMP, we go to Analyze and choose Fit Model (figure 6.1). In the top-right corner of the Fit Model dialog box, we click the Personality menu and choose Stepwise. We can add a probability weight (a variable called PERWT provided by the survey to correct for nonresponse). We also tell the program the name of a Validation variable, which we called "valid" and had previously created in JMP, and which randomly divides the dataset into a training dataset and a test set (in a 2:1 ratio). Next, we click Run. This opens the Stepwise launch platform (figure 6.2), which lists all the terms or variables we are including in our model.

We should explain that JMP does something clever with non-dichotomous categorical variables in stepwise regression. Rather than representing the categorical variable as a

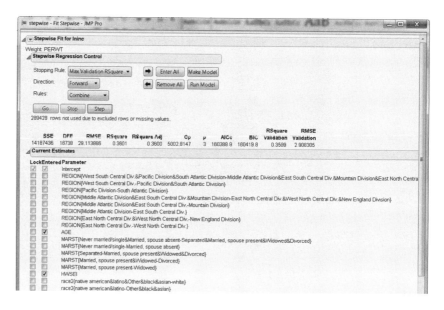

FIGURE 6.2

Output from stepwise regression in JMP Pro.

set of zero-or-one dummy variables, with one baseline category omitted, JMP codes categories hierarchically. It first splits the categories into the two groups which have the most disparate means for the response variable, and adds a dummy variable for this contrast. Within these two groups, it then splits them again into two more groups in the same manner, and so on. For example, consider what JMP does with the "educational attainment" variable. It splits first into two groups: *less than high school* versus all other categories. Next, it splits the latter group into *high school + some college + no degree* versus *associate's + bachelor's + higher than bachelor's*. The former group it can only split once, but the latter group again splits into *associate's + bachelor's* versus *higher than bachelor's*. The point is that these groups are clustered hierarchically in terms of the outcome, such that groups with more similar means on the outcome variable will remain together in one group. This hierarchical differentiation has the benefit of permitting the program to choose a more parsimonious regression model than one that includes all the separate values of a categorical variable as dummies, if that parsimony is beneficial to model fit.

As shown in the screenshot (figure 6.2), we have specified a validation variable, and so we will use maximum validation R^2 as the stopping rule. Other options are k-fold cross-validation R^2 (available only if a validation variable is not specified), p-value thresholds (to enter and to leave the model), minimum AIC, and minimum BIC. Next, we specify what direction the stepwise algorithm should proceed in. We choose forward stepwise regression. Other options are backwards and mixed, the latter available only when p-value stopping rules are utilized.

The Rules menu relates to our hierarchically ordered categorical variables. In the default setting, Combine, as well as with the "Restricted" option, the selection of a more fine-grained differentiation will trigger the automatic inclusion of higher-level groupings. If you don't want this, change the setting to No Rules (which we strongly advise against). Incidentally, models with interaction terms operate in a similar fashion in JMP's stepwise algorithm. That is, the selection of an interaction will automatically lead to the inclusion of all constituent terms, unless No Rules is selected.

JMP permits you to run the program one step at a time, to watch the progress of the model as it evolves. The first step in the main-effects-only model includes occupational prestige, which achieves an R^2 of .21. The next step includes age, which raises the R^2 to .36, followed by an indicator for unemployed working-aged adults (R^2 = .44). When we permit the stepwise regression to run to the end and to choose the best model for predicting log income, the algorithm proceeds to select 24 parameters, and achieves a validation R^2 of .495, as shown in table 6.1. The progress of model fit can be seen by choosing, in the top corner of the output window, the "red triangle" menu, Criterion History, and then RSquare History. (Many of JMP's windows contain menus, styled as red triangles pointing down. Though this book is printed in black and white, we will still refer to these menus as red triangles.) As shown in figure 6.3, most of the improvement in model fit was achieved in the first 10 steps, and only very modest improvements were made after 20 steps or predictors. Nonetheless, the fit did continue to improve incrementally afterwards.

We can certainly do better than this in terms of fit if we include interaction terms. This is done by choosing Relaunch Model, which returns us to the Fit Model box. We now set Degree to 2 (for two-way interaction terms). In the Select Columns box, we highlight all of our variables, and then from the Macros menu we choose Factorial to Degree. This automatically enters all possible two-way interactions as candidate variables. For good measure, we also include quadratic terms for age and occupational prestige. This time, the program takes 54 steps to build the optimal model in terms of validation fit. The selected model now has an R^2 of .6123 in the training set and .6064 in the test set, and has entered a total of 68 parameters in the model, including the interaction terms.

Many of the terms selected were interactions, which trigger the inclusion of constituent terms. Thus, all main-effect variables were used to some degree in the model, but not all separate categories of nominal or categorical variables were utilized. For example, only three region contrasts were included, and the educational attainment variable was not thoroughly disaggregated.

With a model this complex, in which many interactions were utilized, along with groupings of categorical variables, interpretation of the parameters is difficult. Consider the age parameter. The model has selected the age main effect, the quadratic term, and eight interaction terms involving age. Here there is a strong trade-off between predictive accuracy and interpretability. With this level of complexity, it is difficult, though certainly

AU: Please
provide a
column head for
the leftmost
column, if
possible.

TABLE 6.1   Main Effects Regression Model

	β	p
Region: West South Central, South Atlantic and Pacific vs. else	−0.030	.001
Region: West South Central vs. South Atlantic and Pacific	−0.097	.001
Region: South Atlantic vs. Pacific	0.075	.028
Region: Mid Atlantic, East South Central, and Mountain vs. East North Central, West North Central, and New England	−0.023	.049
Region: East North Central and West North Central vs. New England	0.038	.104
Region: East North Central vs. West North Central	0.085	.071
Age	0.040	<.001
Marital status: never married and married, spouse absent vs. separated, married, spouse present, widowed and divorced	−0.229	<.001
Marital Status: separated vs. married, spouse present, widowed and divorced	0.062	<.001
Marital Status: married, spouse present and widowed vs. divorced	−0.133	<.001
Marital Status: married, spouse present vs. widowed	−0.189	<.001
Occupational prestige	0.061	<.001
Race: else vs. white	0.046	<.001
Race: Native American and Latino vs. black, Asian, and other	0.193	<.001
Race: other and black vs. Asian	0.261	<.001
Female	−0.281	<.001
Noncitizen	−0.110	.007
Education: less than high school vs. rest	−0.639	<.001
Education: high school and some college vs. AA, BA, and higher	0.141	<.001
Education: high school vs. some college	−0.146	<.001
Education: AA and BA vs. higher	0.193	<.001
Unemployed	−1.435	<.001
In school	−1.039	<.001
Constant	3.204	<.001
R^2	0.508	
Validation R^2	0.495	

not impossible, to interpret just what the "effect of a one-unit change in age on income" would be. However, including these interaction terms did increase out-of-sample predictive accuracy.

SUMMARY

Stepwise regression can be used to select, from a large set of independent variables, those that are most predictive. It is typically used in contexts where a researcher has many

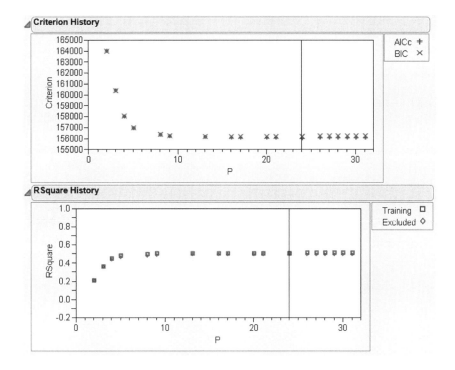

FIGURE 6.3
The progress of stepwise model fit in JMP Pro.

features in the dataset. The technique can also be used to identify those interaction terms between predictors that enhance the predictive power of a model. There are usually many possible interaction terms, and stepwise regression can be used to discover the useful ones.

It is best to use stepwise regression with some form of cross-validation, because this technique will overfit data. The R^2 or fit statistic for the training data will therefore be artificially high. However, if one attends to the predictive power of a model for the test sample, then overfitting ceases to be a problem. The R^2 for the test dataset is a valid measure of the predictive strength of the regression model.

THE LASSO

As mentioned, stepwise regression, like many data mining approaches, is disparaged by some data analysts who view the method as atheoretical "data fishing" or "data dredging." Such researchers feel that statistical modeling should always be driven by theory about causal processes and the variables that represent them. But stepwise regression has also been criticized from within the friendly terrain of data mining research itself. These critics note that the all-or-nothing nature of its variable selection process—variables are either included or left out—makes stepwise regression unstable and therefore somewhat unreliable. Small changes in the data, such as different random samplings from a larger set of cases, can lead to different subsets of variables being chosen by the stepwise algorithm. Therefore, a method that, rather than keeping or discarding variables wholesale, instead enacts selection more gradually and continuously seems preferable.

The LASSO (which stands for the least absolute shrinkage and selection operator) is just such a method. It imposes a penalty on the model's regression coefficients in such a way that those of the less predictive variables are shrunk toward zero. At the point where the regression coefficients reach zero, they effectively leave the model. This makes the LASSO similar in form to the backwards elimination form of stepwise regression. But unlike backwards elimination, model simplification in the LASSO does not occur through the establishment of an arbitrary threshold. The gradual nature of the LASSO's shrinkage process means that the inclusion or exclusion of one variable does not immediately and profoundly affect the coefficients of those that remain. The LASSO is thus more stable and produces less bias than stepwise regression, but still results in similar model simplification.

Mathematically, the LASSO's penalty relates to the sum of the absolute values of the regression coefficients (this is the *Manhattan* or *city-block distance* of the vector of coefficients, also called their L_1 *norm*), usually after all predictors have been standardized as z-scores. In its initial formulation (Tibshirani 1996), the sum of these absolute values was constrained to be less than a tuning parameter, t. If t is set to be greater than or equal to the observed sum of the absolute values of coefficients from the baseline OLS model, no shrinkage would occur and the LASSO fit would equal the least-squares fit. Shrinking this tuning parameter below that sum, then, has the effect of constraining these coefficients. Other variants, like the method we use, use a transformation of this parameter which increases constraints more at higher values.

To demonstrate, we begin by presenting a full OLS regression model predicting vote percentage for Obama in 2012 in U.S. counties. This "ordinary" regression is going to be used as a benchmark against which to compare the LASSO. We have picked a fairly large set of independent variables here—22 total—which describe several demographic dimensions of these counties (population density, racial mix, age structure, economic characteristics, etc.). Table 6.2 shows the results of this regression. To be sure, this model is of some interest in its own right, and it explains a good percentage of the variance in voting: 58%. But clearly we have some predictors which are related, and we may be interested in a more stripped-down, parsimonious model. This is an excellent opportunity to make use of the LASSO.

There is a user-generated Stata program which implements the LASSO ("lars," specifying the "lasso" function), but it appears to be in the early stages of development. The capacity for the LASSO also exists in JMP Pro 12 and in SPSS Statistics, as long as one has purchased the SPSS Categories package. R has at least two routines which perform the LASSO. They are called "penalized" and "lars," and both are freely available through

TABLE 6.2 Results from an OLS Regression Predicting Obama's Vote Share in County-Level Data

Variable	Coeff. (SE)	Standardized (Beta) Coeff.
Population density (log)	2.398 (0.157)***	0.278
% under 18 years	−0.775 (0.101)***	−0.177
% 18–34 years	−0.534 (0.0710)***	−0.177
% 65 and older	−0.636 (0.100)***	−0.179
% non-Hispanic white	−0.476 (0.0311)***	−0.625
% Asian	0.165 (0.116)	0.0260
% non-Hispanic black	0.0147 (0.0309)	0.0145
% Latino/a	−0.0748 (0.0360)**	−0.0651
% college graduate	0.563 (0.0613)***	0.329
% high school graduate only	0.314 (0.0477)***	0.147
% less than high school education	−0.214 (0.0514)***	−0.106
Male unemployment rate	0.920 (0.0729)***	0.232
Female unemployment rate	−0.0808 (0.0795)	−0.0184
Poverty rate	0.249 (0.0642)***	0.101
% foreign-born	−0.174 (0.0643)***	−0.0637
% divorced	−0.104 (0.0424)**	−0.0438
% same-sex-couple households	1.718 (0.582)***	0.0374
% evangelical Protestant	−0.277 (0.0133)***	−0.304
Average household size	−8.242 (1.341)***	−0.135
% professional/managerial	−0.369 (0.0487)***	−0.163
Median income	−7.34e-05 (4.16e-05)*	−0.0567
High school dropout rate	−0.0173 (0.0337)	−0.00655
Constant	130.0 (7.903)***	
Observations	3,114	
R^2	0.586	

I J OE: Standard errors in parentheses.

***p < .001; **p < .01; *p < .05.

cran.r-project.org. We will assume a baseline familiarity with R and focus here on the "penalized" package (Goeman, 2010; Goeman, Meijier & Chaturvedi 2012).

We begin with a simple call of the R function, involving mostly default settings of the program:

```
lasso1<-penalized(obama, ~lnpopdens+agelt18+age1834+age65o
   ver+imdens+perwhite+perasian+perblack+perlatin+edhigher+
   edhs+edlhs+unempmale+unempfem+perpov_q+divorce2per+sames
   exper+evprot10+hhsize+occprofman+medinc+hsdrop1619,
   lambda1 = 500, standardize = TRUE)
```

This runs the model. The `lambda1` option sets the penalty relating to the sum of absolute values of coefficients; larger values will result in more shrinkage toward zero of regression coefficients. It is also possible to utilize a separate option called `lambda2` which relates to the square root of the sum of squares of regression coefficients (their Euclidean distance or L_2 norm). Including lambda 2 instead of lambda 1 thus leads penalized to perform *ridge regression*. It is possible in penalized to set both lambda1 and lambda2 in order to penalize the model in a more complex fashion. One may also exclude certain covariates from penalization, and may penalize the various coefficients differently. But we will focus here on a straightforward case of the LASSO. We have also standardized our variables as *z*-scores in advance (with `standardize = TRUE`).

To see the regression coefficients, we enter:

```
coefficients(lasso1, 'all')
```

Table 6.3 shows our results. We initially set a low penalty parameter here (a value of 2 for `lambda1`): see the column labeled 2. Therefore, the variables all have non-zero coefficients and are nearly identical to the OLS estimates. In fact we have to make the penalty much higher to see substantial model alteration. Nothing at all drops out until the penalty reaches 500. In the 500 column, some of the coefficients for predictors have dropped to zero. Even after doubling the penalty again (to 1,000), we retain 15 covariates. This is undoubtedly because many of our covariates actually contribute to explaining variance in the outcome, and because of our relatively large ($N = 3{,}114$) sample size.

Once the variables start being shrunk to zero, however, some interesting things happen. While most coefficients shrink monotonically as the penalty increases, the coefficient on percentage black actually rises until `lambda1 = 1,000`, after which it drops off only slightly. The small coefficient on black population share in the initial model had been surprising; this suggests that in a multivariate model the effects of this variable are largely masked by related covariates, but that it is an important predictor in and of itself. Another variable, divorced people as a percentage of ever-married adults, drops to zero at `lambda1 = 500`, re-emerges at 1000, and then again shrinks to zero. In the final column of the printout, with a penalty of 5,000, we have a much smaller set of covariates to examine, each of which explains a fair amount of the variance in the data.

Penalized can also produce a graph showing how the regression coefficients shrink as the penalty increases. To see this graph, we first tell the program to calculate the coefficients as it increases the penalty in regular intervals (`steps = 100`). While it is entirely possible to draw the graph using a large number of variables as in the above model, the resulting graph will be a touch overcrowded. For clarity of presentation, we estimate a simpler model:

```
lasso1<-penalized(obama, ~lnpopdens+imdens+perblack+perwhi
    te+edhigher+evprot10, lambda1 = 2, steps = 100, trace =
    FALSE, standardize = TRUE)
```

TABLE 6.3   Regression Coefficients from LASSO Predicting 2012 Obama Vote
Share, with Varying Penalties

	Value of lambda1 penalty				
	2	100	500	1000	5000
Population/sq. mile (log)	2.396	2.313	2.139	2.063	1.631
% age < 18	−0.7730	−0.689	−0.474	−0.375	−0.131
% non-Hispanic white	−0.4756	−0.452	−0.372	−0.300	−0.172
% black	0.01499	0.027	0.079	0.125	0.116
% BA or higher degree	0.5619	0.527	0.402	0.246	0.166
Male unemployment rate	0.9195	0.916	0.973	1.025	0.699
% evangelical Protestant	−0.2767	−0.274	−0.263	−0.249	−0.163
% Asian	0.1646	0.150	0.101	0.0301	0.000
% HS diploma	0.3139	0.301	0.233	0.126	0.000
% less than HS	−0.2140	−0.200	−0.171	−0.158	0.000
Poverty rate	0.2489	0.238	0.153	0.070	0.000
% same-sex households	1.716	1.644	1.504	1.355	0.000
Avg. household size	−8.242	−8.263	−7.425	−5.926	0.000
% prof./managerial	−0.3682	−0.333	−0.201	−0.053	0.000
Divorce rate	−0.1036	−0.062	0.000	0.012	0.000
% age 18–34	−0.5319	−0.439	−0.161	0.000	0.000
% age 65+	−0.6331	−0.509	−0.177	0.000	0.000
% foreign-born	−0.1735	−0.159	−0.087	0.000	0.000
% Latino	−0.07460	−0.063	−0.026	0.000	0.000
Female unemployment rate	−0.07988	−0.036	0.000	0.000	0.000
Median income ($1000s)	−0.073	−0.030	0.000	0.000	0.000
HS noncompletion rate	−0.01715	−0.010	0.000	0.000	0.000

—and we tell it to create a plot of this relation. It helps to standardize the coefficients here so that their different scales do not lead to some being overwhelmed by others:

```
plotpath(lasso1, log = "x", standardize = TRUE)
```

The resulting graph (figure 6.4), along with standardization, lets us visualize which variables remain important to the model. We can see that the variables that remain in the model longest are those which, at the beginning, were most highly correlated (positively or negatively) with Obama's share of the vote: the percentage of county population that is non-Hispanic white, population density, male unemployment rate, the percentage of the population that is evangelical Protestant, and the percentage of the adult population with a bachelor's degree or higher. A regression model with only these five variables has an adjusted R^2 of .49, compared to .58 in the full model. Clearly these five variables can tell us quite a bit about aggregate electoral patterns.

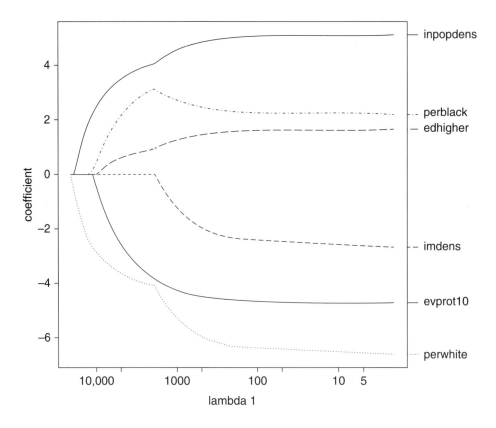

FIGURE 6.4
Shrinkage of coefficients at different settings of the penalty parameter in LASSO (from R).

However, dropping variables from the model, though making the model substantially more interpretable, does reduce the total predictive value. Typically, we want to balance parsimoniousness with predictive accuracy.

The penalized package also allows us to use *k*-fold cross-validation to determine how well a model fits. We can perform cross-validation of a model with the following code:

```
cross<-cvl(obama, ~lnpopdens+agelt18+age1834+age65over+imd
   ens+perwhite+perasian+perblack+perlatin+edhigher+edhs+ed
   lhs+unempmale+unempfem+perpov_q+divorce2per+samesexper+e
   vprot10+hhsize+occprofman+medinc+hsdrop1619, lambda1 =
   500, fold = 10, standardize = TRUE)
```

Here we create an object called "**cross**" in which is stored cross-validation results from a model predicting Obama's vote share using 22 independent variables. After the model, we must set the penalty parameter (**lambda1 = 500**) and the number of folds to be used in cross-validation (**fold = 10**). After running the model, we call elements

TABLE 6.4   Fit Statistics at Different Values of the Penalty Parameter in the LASSO

	Value of lambda1 penalty				
	2	*100*	*500*	*1,000*	*5,000*
Cross-validation log-likelihood	−11,483.17	−11,496.82	−11,516.6	−11,568.63	−11,888.41
Full data log-likelihood	−11,443.92	−11,445.92	−11,475.19	−11,533.25	−11,827.07
Nonzero coefficients	23	23	19	16	8

of the object. The first element, `$cvl`, returns the log-likelihood of the model on the cross-validation data. With the element `$fullfit`, we can call the fit on the full data.

```
cross$cvl
cross$fullfit
```

We can repeat this a number of times at different settings of lambda1, and examine the relative fit of the model with different penalty parameters. In table 6.4 we show cross-validation log-likelihoods for the above model, with the values of lambda1 we used above to demonstrate model shrinkage. We see that the lowest log-likelihood statistics listed are at `lambda1 = 2`. This would seem to suggest that less, not more, shrinkage yields a better fit in this model. But these few results alone do not allow us to conclude that 2 is the best value for lambda for maximizing out-of-sample accuracy. To do this, we would have to proceed like a maximum-likelihood algorithm, trying different values and moving closer and closer to the minimum cross-validation log-likelihood.

This sounds like a lot of work which ought to be automated. And luckily, it has been. Penalized will permit us to find the best value for lambda1 with the 'optL1' function. This function allows us to set minimum and maximum values of lambda1, and it will find the value that minimizes the cross-validation log-likelihood. We set the minimum to zero, and allow lambda1 to range up to 1,000:

```
bestfit<-optL1(obama, ~lnpopdens+agelt18+age1834+age65over
    +imdens+perwhite+perasian+perblack+perlatin+edhigher+
    edhs+edlhs+unempmale+unempfem+perpov_q+divorce2per+
    samesexper+evprot10+hhsize+occprofman+medinc+hsdrop1619,
    minlambda1 = 2, maxlambda1 = 1000, fold = 10, standard-
    ize = TRUE)
bestfit$lambda
```

Here, after performing 21 iterations, the program settles on an optimal value for lambda1: 27.14285. As stated before, at this low value the penalty parameter will only marginally affect our regression coefficients, though it does increase predictive accuracy slightly.

SUMMARY

The LASSO is a powerful variable selection tool, used to find a subset of available predictors that together have strong predictive power. Data miners use it to optimize both model simplicity (parsimony) and predictive power. Unfortunately, the LASSO is not yet available in some of the more user-friendly data mining packages, so we demonstrated the technique using the free R language.

In the example, we used the LASSO to predict the percentage of the vote in U.S. counties that went to President Obama in the 2012 election. The program identified higher population density, lower percentage of the population under 18, lower percentage white, higher percentage of blacks and percentage with college degrees, and higher male unemployment rate as core predictors of Obama's vote share at the county level.

VIF REGRESSION

VIF regression is another very recently developed data mining tool for simplifying a model by selecting variables (feature selection). Developed in 2011 by Lin, Foster, and Ungar, VIF regression was designed specifically for use with *very* large datasets, and especially those which are very wide (large numbers of variables). It was developed as an alternative to stepwise regression and best-subset regression, both of which are computationally intensive and therefore tend to run very slowly. Other feature selection methods, like generalized path seeker (GPS), run much more quickly but pay a price in reduced predictive accuracy (Lin, Foster, and Ungar 2011). VIF regression is designed to speed up stepwise regression without a substantial trade-off in terms of accuracy.

VIF is a complicated, multistage algorithm, which blends together a number of preexisting techniques (like forward stagewise regression and alpha-investing rules) and adds its own unique element. It is a variation on forward stepwise regression (because with a large number of candidate features, backwards elimination is highly inefficient). We will run through what exactly this algorithm does, and then show how it can be implemented using R.

The main benefit of VIF regression is in reducing the amount of computation that occurs when we run a stepwise regression. But why does stepwise regression require so much mathematical calculation? There are two reasons. First, at each iteration or step in model building, it considers *each candidate variable* for inclusion. This means that at every step, stepwise considers many variables, and since it performs a large number of steps, it does this many times. By contrast, VIF regression runs through the candidate variables only once. Secondly, at each step, stepwise generates estimates for *each* parameter. And it runs not just one regression, but as many regressions as there are candidate variables at each stage. VIF regression gets around this second problem by employing what is called *forward stagewise* regression.

VIF regression starts with a null model—that is, a model containing only an intercept—and calculates residuals from this model. It then selects the first variable in the prespecified list of predictors (the order of which is somewhat important here), and regresses these residuals on this variable. If the variable meets certain criteria for inclusion, it is entered into the model, and new residuals are calculated. If not, the algorithm moves on to the next variable.

At each step, then, only the residuals from the previous stage are regressed on the new candidate variable. This forward stagewise regression permits a substantial reduction in computation. Rather than running a full regression and calculating all the parameter estimates, VIF regression in essence calculates only a series of bivariate correlations.

However, there is a difficulty with this procedure. The *t*-ratios evaluating these bivariate correlations are likely to be biased against variables for which multicollinearity with the variables already selected for the model is substantial. As a result, a "naive" forward stagewise regression algorithm is biased toward selecting variables which are uncorrelated with the variables already in the model rather than selecting what might be the most predictive variable. Some correction must be made to remove this bias.

The correction is what gives VIF regression its name. VIF regression adjusts the *t*-ratios to account for multicollinearity by making use of the "variance inflation factor" of each variable as it comes under consideration. But since the VIF is calculated by regressing a new variable on all the variables already in the model, this presents a conundrum. Performing these regressions would eliminate the savings in computation that was the purpose of using forward stagewise regression in the first place. The solution is to avoid calculating the VIFs using the full dataset. Instead, a small subset of cases is randomly sampled, and VIFs are estimated from this smaller amount of data.

Finally, an allowance is made for an inflation of the probability of type I error over multiple hypothesis tests. Simply put, when we conduct a test for statistical significance, we allow for the possibility of erroneously rejecting a true null hypothesis (type I error), and we choose the probability that this will happen by setting our alpha. But as we conduct multiple hypothesis tests, the likelihood of a rare event increases, so simply applying the same alpha level to each test is not appropriate.

Bonferroni corrections for multiple hypothesis tests simply divide alpha (usually $p < .05$) by n, the number of tests to be performed (i.e. the number of candidate variables). But this correction is problematic if the number of tests is very large, and it elevates the probability of type II error by setting the effective alpha for entry very, very low indeed.

Instead, VIF regression employs a procedure, called an *alpha-investing rule*, which strikes a middle ground between unconstrained multiple-hypothesis testing (which produces a lot of type I error) and the application of a Bonferroni rule (which tends to knock out potentially significant predictors; see Foster and Stine 2008). The idea is that we begin with a certain "wealth," or allowance for type I error (say 0.05 or 0.10). We then perform a hypothesis test. If the null hypothesis is rejected, we *add* to our wealth. And if we fail to reject it, we subtract from our wealth. After all the wealth is exhausted, no more hypothesis tests are permitted. The critical level for inclusion, meanwhile, changes as a function of the current wealth and the number of iterations since the last null-hypothesis rejection. This procedure has been shown to effectively control the likelihood of false rejections of the null hypothesis (Foster and Stine 2008).

So, VIF regression runs through each candidate predictor only once, and admits it only if it passes a fairly high bar for inclusion. But doesn't this mean that the algorithm could "miss" important predictors? The algorithm's creators assure us that this is not the case. If highly predictive variables are uncorrelated with residuals, they will certainly be selected. If a new variable is highly correlated with residuals, then the alpha-investment rule guarantees that the model as a whole will be predictive, though it doesn't guarantee that any one variable will enter the model per se. Users of this technique are advised to prioritize the most important variables by listing them first. The program's authors claim that, for prediction purposes, it doesn't matter whether one or another highly correlated variable enters the model. "If this importance can be washed out or masked by other variables," they write, "then for prediction purposes, there is no difference between the variable and its surrogates, thus neither of them can be claimed 'true'" (Lin, Foster, and Ungar 2011, 239). "Globally important variables" will not be missed, and high-signal predictors will not be missed as long as there aren't other variables which are substantially correlated with them.

The VIF regression algorithm has been shown to be substantially faster than competing algorithms (GPS comes closest), and good at controlling the marginal false-discovery rate (though not as good as stepwise, the forward-backward greedy algorithm [FoBa] or GPS). It has better out-of-sample performance (more predictive accuracy) than GPS and the LASSO, and as good as FoBa and stepwise.

RUNNING VIF REGRESSION: AN EXAMPLE USING R

To our knowledge, the only way to implement VIF regression is through the R package VIF, written and maintained by Dongyu Lin (2011), one of the developers of the method. We perform an example of VIF regression using our county-level 2012 election dataset. As with our example demonstrating LASSO, we will be modeling Obama's share of the vote at the county level.

We first download the package from http://cran.r-project.org, and install it in working memory:

```
install.packages("VIF")
library(VIF)
```

Next, we turn a set of predictors into a matrix, because VIF works better if it deals with the X's as a single object. R's `cbind` command will suffice for this purpose. Note here that all of the variables have the letter z as a prefix. We do this to signify the fact that we have z-score standardized all of the predictors we are using. This must be done to put all variables on the same scale so that their relative contribution to explaining variance can be properly assessed. This is generally necessary in any feature selector in order to not bias the algorithm in its selection. However, while a package like "penalized" standardizes the variables for you as an option, with VIF you must have already done it yourself, ahead of time.

```
X<-cbind(zlnpop, zlnpopdens, zagelt18, zage1834, zage3564,
    zagegt65, zperwhite, zperblack, zperamind, zperasian,
    zperpacisl, zperother, zpermultirace, zperlatin, zhh-
    size, zlthsed, zhsed, zsomecol, zbached, mastersed,
    zprofed, zdoced, zmalunemp, zmedinc, zperpov, zimdens,
    zprofmanocc, zdivorce2, zsamesex, zhigheredpop)
```

Now that we have gathered all of our candidate predictors into a matrix, we are ready to perform VIF. We run it with the call:

```
mod1<-vif(zobama,X, w0 = 0.05, dw = 0.05, subsize = 200,
    trace = TRUE)
```

This generates an object called "mod1," into which the results of the VIF variable selection process will be stored. The w0 option tells the program the initial wealth we want the model to spend, and dw tells it the change in wealth if another variable is added to the model. For more conservative model that selects fewer variables, we would set these values lower. Conversely, setting initial wealth or change in wealth higher will result in the inclusion of more variables. Subsize tells the program the size of the random subsample on which to calculate the variance inflation factor of each variable under consideration. Finally, trace = TRUE lets us see what goes on as VIF runs through the set of 30 variables we have offered it for evaluation. Doing so generates the output shown in figure 6.5.

We can see that there are 30 rows, one for each of the 30 predictor variables, and five columns. The first number in a column (after the [1] symbol) simply tells us which variable the program is evaluating. The other columns tell us:

1. the current wealth (before the current variable is evaluated)
2. the current test level (which, remember, alters with each new variable, depending on whether prior variables made it into the model or not)
3. the t-statistic for the variable under evaluation
4. the p-value for this t-test

What does all this mean? Well, consider what happens in the first two lines. In line 1, we have the wealth that we chose to begin with: 0.05. To be included in the model, the variable must be significant at $\alpha = .025$ (or the current wealth divided by 2). We see that the result of the t-test is 22.77, which is significant far below $p < .001$ (rounded here to 0). This means that the first variable we offered to VIF, zlnpop (the z-standardization of the natural log of population density), explained sufficient variance to be included in the model. In line 2, we see the result: the model wealth has increased, while

```
> mod1<-vif(zobama,X, w0=0.05, dw=0.05, subsize=200, trace=TRUE)
[1] "1 0.05 0.025 22.771554296814 0"
[1] "2 0.075 0.01875 6.95294747856659 3.57736062994718e-12"
[1] "3 0.10625 0.0177083333333333 5.72354728131594 1.04322517291422e-08"
[1] "4 0.138541666666667 0.0173177083333333 5.59771973911076 2.17189479734259e-08"
[1] "5 0.171223958333333 0.0171223958333333 4.83686222030236 1.31904790978687e-06"
[1] "6 0.2041015625 0.0170084635416667 0.828564198610133 0.40735105353865"
[1] "7 0.187093098958333 0.0133637927827381 27.0053667414444 0"
[1] "8 0.223729306175595 0.0139830816359747 3.80020276492099 0.000144577740259999"
[1] "9 0.25974622453962 0.0144303458077567 13.5027750931116 0"
[1] "10 0.295315878731864 0.0147657939365932 5.57551515371425 2.46798421699168e-08"
[1] "11 0.330550084795271 0.0150250038543305 0.793302156109217 0.42760180093179"
[1] "12 0.31552508094094 0.0131468783725392 0.759470464593518 0.44757117560337"
[1] "13 0.302378202568401 0.0116299308680154 5.24342826272885 1.57620108520717e-07"
[1] "14 0.340748271700385 0.0121695811321566 1.4465381095496 0.148026331031677"
[1] "15 0.328578690568229 0.010952623018941 10.5970808072016 0"
[1] "16 0.367626067549288 0.0114883146109152 11.6686643604467 0"
[1] "17 0.406137752938373 0.0119452280275992 5.68462572632097 1.31099446853966e-08"
[1] "18 0.444192524910773 0.0123386812475215 4.976982834295 6.45832303414196e-07"
[1] "19 0.481853843663252 0.0126803643069277 6.14694924012578 7.89873944029296e-10"
[1] "20 0.519173479356324 0.0129793369839081 2.26986290639511 0.0232159023444118"
[1] "21 0.506194142372416 0.0120522414850575 0.498836920414769 0.617894275430784"
[1] "22 0.494141900887359 0.01123049774744 1.41894577497042 0.155914825535024"
[1] "23 0.482911403139919 0.0104980739813026 18.4175936639235 0"
[1] "24 0.522413329158616 0.0108836110241378 3.98169787457411 6.84247222204615e-05"
[1] "25 0.561529718134478 0.0112305943626896 0.531800210693972 0.594864376832877"
[1] "26 0.550299123771789 0.0105826754571498 0.570307523144667 0.568469139224964"
[1] "27 0.539716448314639 0.00999474904286369 6.86589616654364 6.60760335335908e-12"
[1] "28 0.579721699271776 0.0103521732012817 2.75214879766392 0.00592056128820428"
[1] "29 0.619369526070494 0.0106787849322499 2.24618282745469 0.0246922997211378"
[1] "30 0.608690741138244 0.0101448456856374 1.159582223814 0.246218941876399"
> |
```

FIGURE 6.5

Output displaying variable selection from VIF regression in R.

critical value for inclusion of the *next* variable is set lower (at α = .018). Once again, the *t*-statistic for this second variable is quite high (6.953), and the variable is admitted into the model.

We can see what happens, conversely, when a variable fails to make it into the model by looking at what happens before and after variable 6. Note that the model wealth rises for each variable from 1 through 6. This is, remember, the wealth of the model *before* the new variable is auditioned. Variable 6 does not make it into the model (which we can tell by looking at the *t*-value, 0.829, and the *p*-value, 0.407). Note that for variable 7 the wealth dips slightly (from 0.204 to 0.187).

After we have run through our variables, what do we get in terms of model fit? Actually, the VIF routine does not fit the model for you. Instead, it tells you which variables you ought to include and which you should reject. It is, then, a pure *feature selector*.

To see the selected variables, call:

`mod1$select`

R returns:

```
[1]  1  2  3  4  5  7  8  9  10  13  15  16  17  18  19  23  24  27  28
```

This tells us the ID numbers of the variables—19 in total—which were selected by the model. We see, by examining the list, that many variables are missing: variables 6, 11, 12,

```
call:
lm(formula = zobama ~ X2)

coefficients:
    (Intercept)         X2zlnpop     X2zlnpopdens       X2zagelt18       X2zage1834       X2zage3564
     -2.199e-09        -3.971e-02        2.688e-01       -2.985e-02        3.584e-02        1.275e-01
    X2zperwhite      X2zperblack      X2zperamind      X2zperasian  X2zpermultirace      X2zperlatin
     -2.354e+00        -1.306e+00       -4.710e-01       -1.571e-01       -2.679e-01       -1.171e+00
      X2zhhsize        X2zlthsed          X2zhsed       X2zsomecol        X2zbached      X2zmalunemp
     -1.752e-01        -7.381e-01       -3.069e-01       -3.513e-01       -2.283e-01        2.439e-01
      X2zmedinc    X2zprofmanocc      X2zdivorce2
     -1.008e-01        -1.479e-01       -4.882e-02
```

FIGURE 6.6

Output from VIF regression in R.

14, 20, 21, 22, 25, 26, 29, and 30. It is important to remember that the selection of variables by VIF regression depends, to some degree, on the order in which you list them. VIF only tries each variable once, and is simply attempting to maximize explanatory power without overfitting. So if we are trying to ensure that the algorithm picks the "true" variables, it is a good idea to run it a number of times, switching up the order of the variables each time.

If we reduce the value of the dw parameter, we reduce the number of variables admitted to the model. That is because the critical value for inclusion in the model depends on model wealth. Adding less wealth upon the rejection of a null hypothesis leads to lower critical values for inclusion, and thus for fewer features selected. When we set dw to 0.05, VIF selects 19 variables. But this parameter does not lead quickly to a more parsimonious model. When we drop dw to 0.01, 0.001, and 0.0001, we select 18, 18, and 17 variables, respectively. Another option is to reduce the initial wealth of the model. But once again, one must, with this selection of variables, set w0 quite low before the model becomes substantially smaller.

After settling on the variables for inclusion, we simply run a linear model with only those selected variables. We manually construct a matrix that includes only the subset of selected variables, and then run a linear model on this subset. R regression output appears in figure 6.6.

```
X2<-cbind(zlnpop, zlnpopdens, zagelt18, zage1834, zage3564,
    zperwhite, zperblack, zperamind, zperasian, zpermulti-
    race, zhhsize, zlthsed, zhsed, zsomecol, zbached,
    zmalunemp, zmedinc, zprofmanocc, zdivorce2)
mod2<-lm(zobama~X2)
```

VIF has selected the variables which we have already seen to be important in the prediction of county-level Obama vote share: population density, the percentage of the population that is non-Hispanic white, the percentage of the population that is black, the proportion of young adults in the population, and the male unemployment rate. Thus, this highly efficient algorithm produces results which largely agree with the results of models we have seen before.

As the expansion of the data mining universe proceeds apace, forever churning out new algorithms, researchers have developed yet another technique which allegedly improves upon VIF regression. This latest method, *robust VIF regression*, addresses the tendency of "standard" VIF regression to be sensitive to the presence of outliers in the data (Dupuis and Victoria-Feser 2013). VIF regression is an interesting way of selecting variables in an efficient manner to maximize predictive accuracy.

7

CREATING NEW VARIABLES

Experienced data miners repeatedly tell newcomers that what takes the most time and requires the greatest care in data mining is typically not running the analysis (the modeling stage) but the stage prior to data analysis when the researcher creates the variables or features that are going to be entered into models. This is partly because researchers use their knowledge of the subject matter to ensure that important variables are not left out. Researchers also construct ratios that seem conceptually important (cost per square foot, shootings per 100,000 population, etc.) and which may prove empirically powerful predictors. Beyond this, though, data miners know that the *form* of variables can be important for the analyses that follow, so they have to consider possible transformations of their variables.

The simplest and most common situation concerns standardization. In some but not all DM methods, the algorithm will favor variables that have many categories (or a large range of values), such as age in years or income in dollars, as being more predictive or consequential than a variable with fewer categories or a smaller range of values, for example marital status. By "favor" we mean that the program will deem a predictor with many categories or a large range a more powerful predictor than one with fewer. This bias stems from the way that we represent our data, rather than reflecting real structure in the data. For example, we might choose to represent income in dollars, or in logged dollars. We might represent age in years or age in groups like teens, twenties, thirties, and so on. Depending on which of these choices we make, the variable's relation to the outcome will change, sometimes affecting the apparent predictive importance of this variable relative to others. The solution is to transform all the candidate predictors in one's dataset into a common metric, a process known as *standardization*.

The most common type of standardization transforms continuous variables (whether measured as interval/ratio or ordinal-level variables) into z-scores. Z-scores have a mean of zero and a standard deviation of one. So, no matter how different their content (age, income, IQ, hours worked per week), after being z-standardized, the transformed variables will all have the same mean and the same spread.

Another type of variable creation occurs when one takes a variable that is continuous, such as age in years or income in dollars, and transforms it or recodes it into a set of discrete ordered categories, for example, creating categories with ages 0–10, 11–20, 21—30, and so on, up to ages 71–80. This "chunking" of previously continuous variables is known in DM as *binning* or *discretization* and, along with creating ratios and z-standardized predictors, it is one of the most common steps in preprocessing data prior to running a model.

At first impression, it would seem that changing a continuous variable such as age in years into a discrete variable such as age category implies a loss of information, a blurring of fine detail. That is true, but binning has the compensating advantage that it makes it much easier to discern and to model nonlinear relations between a predictor and an outcome variable. Let's give an example.

We will employ data from the American Community Survey to predict whether a person has health insurance using various demographic characteristics. We construct our particular data set to contain an equal number of cases of insured and uninsured individuals. Because uninsured people are a relatively small minority in the population (around 14%), we retain all the uninsured cases in the sample, but randomly sample from the more numerous insured individuals, to obtain a 50:50 split. We do so because in the presence of highly unbalanced outcomes classification algorithms often simply categorize all cases as belonging to the majority class to minimize the error rate in prediction. Balancing the data leads to both a more interesting model and a better test of predictive accuracy.

We run a logistic regression predicting health insurance status, coded as 1 if an individual lacks health insurance, and 0 if they are insured. Income, age, marital status, race, gender, home ownership, educational attainment, nativity, veteran status, labor-force status, and census region are entered as predictors, and it is important to stress here that age and income are entered into the model as continuous variables. Our model has a McFadden's pseudo-R^2 of .202 and a log-likelihood of -565007.947. Table 7.1 shows the confusion matrix (which tabulates predicted versus actual category of the outcome), and figure 7.1 is a visualization of the relative importance of independent variables to the prediction. Both displays can be generated automatically by SPSS after running a logistic regression.

The accuracy rate of the model overall is 71.4%, and the model works equally well at correctly classifying true positives and true negatives in terms of the outcome. According

TABLE 7.1   Confusion Matrix of Logistic Regression Using Balanced Data (SPSS)

	Predicted insured	Predicted uninsured	Precision
True insured	78,974	32,409	70.90%
True uninsured	31,242	79,788	71.86%

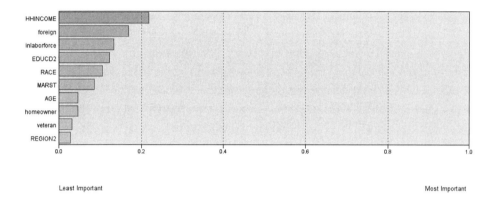

FIGURE 7.1

Predictor importance for logistic regression using balanced data (SPSS). Target: uninsured.

to our results, household income is the most predictive variable in our model, followed by nativity (a dummy variable for foreign-born individuals), labor-force status, and educational attainment. Age appears to be relatively unimportant in predicting health insurance coverage. This is rather counterintuitive, for we are aware that eligibility for certain health insurance programs (most notably Medicare) is age-based. Medicaid and SCHIP (the State Children's Health Insurance Program) are also available to individuals in part on the basis of age (and partly on the basis of income). According to our regression output (not shown), age has a mild negative relation to health insurance status. Perhaps the problem is that the relation between age and health insurance status is not linear; perhaps there are distinctly different probabilities of being insured for people in different age groups.

DISCRETIZING A CONTINUOUS PREDICTOR

Partition trees, otherwise known as decision trees or classification trees, are predictive algorithms which discover the most efficient way in which to separate cases with respect to classes of an outcome. They are described in detail in chapter 10, but right now we will focus on how they can be used to bin or discretize continuous variables so as to optimize prediction of an outcome.

To classify cases, partition trees split cases according to each value of each of the candidate predictor variables specified by the researcher, and find that split which best separates cases into classes of the outcome in question. Having found this optimal split, they proceed to repeat this procedure using each of the resulting groups, producing two more optimal splits. They repeat this process until they produce groups which are homogeneous in terms of the outcome, or until the researcher instructs the program to stop.

Typically, partition trees consider a large number of candidate variables when choosing where to split, but how many independent variables the algorithm uses is up to the researcher. If the researcher specifies only one continuous predictor, then the program will split only on this variable. This will, in effect, find breakpoints in the variable in terms of its relation to the outcome. So, if there are complex nonlinearities in the relation between a continuous predictor and a binary outcome variable, partition trees are excellent ways to find them. The "leaves" which result from the application of the partition tree in this manner will be "bins" of values of the predictor.

In our example, we are attempting to predict a lack of health insurance coverage, and we suspect that age might be highly predictive but that the relation between age and insurance status is not linear. We therefore use a particular form of classification tree known as CHAID (chi-squared automatic interaction detector), run in SPSS Statistics, to examine this relation. Results are summarized in table 7.2.

The tree has suggested a way to create optimal age groups for predicting health insurance status. The first age category produced contains persons aged 0–8; the second bin, persons 9–17; the third, 18–24, and so on. Examining how the probability of being uninsured across these age categories changes tells us how nonlinear the relation between age and insurance status is. In these data (which, remember, have been balanced in terms of the outcome) the relative probability of being uninsured is low for children.[1] Among young adults aged 18–30, however, the probability of being uninsured jumps substantially. We then witness a slow decline in this probability over the remainder of adulthood. In the oldest group (the lower bound of which SPSS has decided is 63 years old), the probability of being uninsured plummets.

In sum, the real relation between age and the probability of being uninsured is quite nonlinear, rising and falling across the age spectrum. Previously, when we entered age as a continuous variable in our logistic regression, we could capture only an average marginal relation between age and health insurance status which was completely incapable of mapping this complexity. As a result, age appeared to be relatively unimportant in predicting insurance status. This was, in short, a result of specification error. Moreover, because the relation between age and insurance status is driven by arbitrary statutory cutoffs for program eligibility, simply modeling this relation with quadratic or cubic terms for age is unlikely to be completely satisfying (though it will certainly be an improvement over the linear specification). We show, below, how optimally binning age into categories and including these categories as dummy variables can improve the predictive capacity of the model.

TABLE 7.2   Using a CHAID Tree to Optimally Bin a
Continuous Variable (Age) in SPSS

Node	Age group	% without health insurance	Number of cases
1	0–8	30.73	49,685
2	9–17	40.43	54,745
3	18–23	75.97	55,077
4	24–29	70.71	52,535
5	30–35	63.51	45,247
6	36–42	59.43	54,339
7	43–48	56.08	50,676
8	49–55	51.51	57,490
9	56–62	44.43	46,305
10	63+	7.87	54,548

But first, in table 7.3, we turn to a tree analysis of another relation between a continuous variable—household income—and health insurance. Once again, the program has determined cut-points in the continuous variable in terms of its relation with the outcome; cuts appear at $14,596, $23,000, $31,200, $40,000, and so on. But an inspection of how insurance status varies across these income groups indicates a linear (or at least monotonic) relation between household income and insurance. In the lowest two income groups, a relatively high proportion of individuals lack health insurance. This percentage drops as we move upwards in terms of income until we reach the highest-income category; the probability of lacking insurance for this group is a third of that for the lowest-income individuals. This implies that we would be unlikely to gain substantially in terms of predictive power by replacing a continuous specification of income with a set of income-group categories (though we ought to investigate this anyway), and in fact we are likely to lose predictive power. The point here is that binning ought not to be used indiscriminately. In situations in which complex nonlinearity is characteristic of the "true" underlying relation between a continuous predictor and an outcome, it will aid prediction. But if the underlying relation is indeed linear, it will not be helpful and is in fact inappropriate.

AN EXAMPLE USING SPSS STATISTICS

We just demonstrated how trees can be used to bin continuous variables, but readers should be aware that several DM software packages provide applications that can bin continuous variables more directly, without the user having to inspect and interpret a tree diagram (though the underlying mathematics is quite similar to that operating in

TABLE 7.3 Using a CHAID Tree to Optimally Bin Income in SPSS

Node	Household income ($)	% without health insurance	Number of cases
1	14,595 or less	63.81	52,014
2	14,596–23,000	65.18	52,163
3	23,001–31,200	63.65	52,259
4	31,201–40,000	61.20	53,355
5	40,001–49,997	56.38	48,617
6	49,998–61,400	51.59	53,983
7	61,401–76,000	45.35	52,216
8	76,001–96,990	38.30	51,713
9	96,991–133,500	31.33	52,257
10	Over 133,500	23.17	52,050

trees). They also enable the user to automatically create and save the new binned or discretized variable in the dataset, which is a considerable convenience. We demonstrate this by using SPSS Statistics 21 to create 9 bins from the variable for age, focusing once again on health insurance status as our outcome of interest.

The syntax for optimally discretizing is:

```
OPTIMAL BINNING
/VARIABLES GUIDE = uninsured BIN = AGE SAVE = NO
/CRITERIA METHOD = MDLP PREPROCESS = EQUALFREQ (BINS = 9)
   FORCEMERGE = 0 LOWERLIMIT = INCLUSIVE
LOWEREND = UNBOUNDED UPPEREND = UNBOUNDED
/MISSING SCOPE = PAIRWISE
/PRINT ENDPOINTS DESCRIPTIVES ENTROPY.
```

As shown in table 7.4, SPSS produces nine bins for age. The age groups produced here are broadly similar to those produced by the CHAID tree above. Young adults are no longer broken into two groups, but appear as one group aged 18–30. And the cut-point for the oldest group is now 64 rather than 63 (though still not 65, which is somewhat unexpected).

We would like to make note of the fact that if we specify a different dependent variable, the program is likely to generate very different age groups. Optimal binning produces categories of continuous variables which are optimal in terms of predicting a particular outcome. It is important to remember that optimal binning is not something done at the beginning of a DM project, with its resulting categories being usable for

TABLE 7.4   Age Categories Creating by Optimal Binning (SPSS)

	Age				
Bin	Endpoint		Number of cases by level of uninsured		
	Lower	*Upper*	*0.00*	*1.00*	*Total*
1	Unbounded	10	48,967	21,736	70,703
2	10	18	42,109	26,134	68,243
3	18	30	41,249	109,838	151,087
4	30	37	27,523	49,651	77,174
5	37	44	31,714	46,119	77,833
6	44	50	31,768	40,588	72,356
7	50	56	34,494	37,071	71,565
8	56	64	42,340	34,610	76,950
9	64	Unbounded	71,667	6,084	77,751
Total			371,831	371,831	743,662

NOTE: Each bin is computed as Lower ≤ Age < Upper.

predicting many different dependent variables. Each optimal binning is specific to one dependent or outcome variable.

Now that we have age in discretized bins, we can run a new logistic regression to see whether binning improved the model; as before, we present the confusion matrix (table 7.5) and predictor importance graph (figure 7.2). Our new logistic regression model has a McFadden's pseudo-R^2 of .259 and a log-likelihood of -486350.891, which both indicate a better-fitting model. The confusion matrix demonstrates that we have made some improvements in classifying both true positives and true negatives.

Most interestingly, we see in figure 7.2 (as compared to figure 7.1) that age is now by far the most important predictor of health insurance status; it is now more than twice as important as household income. The order of importance of the rest of the variables is largely unchanged, which suggests that age is not now describing some variance previously described by other variables. The binning of age has resulted in real model improvement, rather than a reallocation of "work" from other variables to age.

We have shown in this section how both classification trees and optimal binning can be used productively to discover nonlinearity in the relation between continuous predictor variables and a dichotomous outcome variable. We have also shown how detecting these nonlinear relations can result in an improvement in predictive capacity. Next, we turn to the relation between continuous predictors and continuous outcomes, and show how similar practices can also be useful in this situation.

TABLE 7.5 Confusion Matrix Predicting Health Insurance with Age Discretized

	Predicted insured	Predicted uninsured	Precision
True insured	82,914	29,181	73.97%
True uninsured	27,099	84,746	75.77%

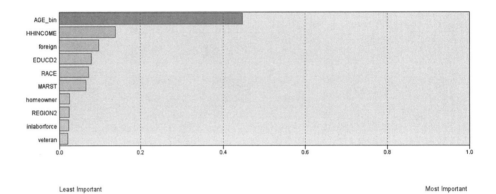

FIGURE 7.2
Predictor importance using binned age variable in SPSS. Target: uninsured.

CONTINUOUS OUTCOMES AND CONTINUOUS PREDICTORS

The same logic which worked in the case of a dichotomous outcome variable can be applied to continuous outcomes as well. Let's say we are trying to predict some continuously measured outcome like income using some other continuously measured attribute. If the relation between the two variables is linear, then standard linear regression can easily be used. If the relation is curvilinear, we may add quadratic, cubic, or other higher-order terms to approximate the relation. And if there are one or more clear breakpoints, we may model the relation quite well by fitting a spline.

Sometimes, however, two variables can be related in a manner that is more complicated. For example, consider the relation between occupational prestige and (log) income in figure 7.3. Though there is an overall upward trend in income as we move to higher values of occupational prestige, it is clear that there are breaks and discontinuities in this relation which are not being well captured by linear modeling. In figure 7.3 we have included a quadratic predictive line in the plot, but it largely follows the linear prediction.

That adding higher-order terms does not boost explanatory power much is confirmed by performing a regression (results in table 7.6). The linear term for occupational prestige alone accounts for about 14% of the variance in logged income. Adding a quadratic

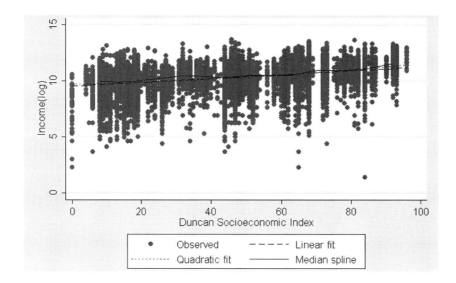

FIGURE 7.3

A scatterplot and fitted regression lines depicting the relation between personal income and occupational prestige in the 2010 American Community Survey (from Stata).

and then a cubic term boosts explanatory power by less than 1 percentage point. (The coefficients for these higher-order terms achieve statistical significance at $p < .001$, but this is primarily because we are using a dataset with over 340,000 cases. With this much statistical power virtually every variable will be statistically significant at standard alpha levels.)

Perhaps the problem is simply that there not enough inflection points in a cubic model, and fitting a spline might be more appropriate. In figure 7.3 we also show a fitted median spline with 10 equally spaced knots. But the spline does not differ much in path from the linear prediction.

Adding higher-power terms to this model does not boost predictive power because the relation is more complicated than this model allows. Also, adding the spline doesn't help because we don't know the number of inflection points in the relation between the variables and because these inflection points are probably not equally spaced. In this situation, we can take advantage of data mining techniques to help us do better.

When the relation between two variables is complicated in the manner we are seeing here, we can more productively model it by splitting our data into discrete bins of the explanatory variable, and then employing a set of dummy variables for these bins. But at which values of the Duncan socioeconomic index (SEI) ought we to make our cuts?

We use JMP's Partition function to do this for us, and use the k-fold cross-validation option (with five folds). This will enable us to judge whether we are overfitting the model.

TABLE 7.6   OLS Regression Models Predicting (log) Income from Duncan
Socioeconomic Index

	Model 1	Model 2	Model 3
SEI	0.0169***	0.0061***	0.0310***
SEI^2		0.0001***	−0.0004***
SEI^3			<0.0001***
Constant	9.523	9.692	9.455
R^2	0.143	0.147	0.149
RMSE	0.998	0.996	0.995

SOURCE: American Community Survey, 2010

***p < .001.

However, we are using a 10% sample of the 2010 ACS, which has about 340,000 cases. With this many cases we can build a very complicated model without overfitting.

Indeed, if we allow the model to run to the point where the validation R^2 begins to drop, the tree will split the data 79 times, forming 80 separate bins of SEI. Now, in this data there are only 81 distinct SEI values, which means that the program has created a separate bin for almost every separate value. This outcome is, however, a function of both prioritizing prediction over interpretability and of the extremely large size of our data. Large datasets bring the trade-off between interpretation and predictive accuracy into relief in a way that traditionally sized datasets simply do not. We want our model to *simplify* the data in a helpful manner—to summarize it. But in large datasets there is simply not much of a trade-off between complexity and accuracy. We will need to impose a bound on complexity at a point where interpretability begins to decline. This bound will be set rather arbitrarily, and so we decide to prune the tree back to 12 splits. At this number of splits, we have only sacrificed a tiny amount of predictive accuracy but have substantially improved interpretability.

The 13-group solution we settled on can be seen in figure 7.4 and table 7.7. As we saw before, the overall relation between occupational prestige and income is positive, but the increase is not monotonic. In the lower two-thirds of the range of SEI scores there is a pattern of increases and declines in income, suggestive of trade-offs between income and status. That this relation is characterized by a complex nonlinearity can be seen in figure 7.5.

Discretizing in this fashion boosts explanatory power by 35%, from R^2 = .1438 to R^2 = .1945. But is discretization helpful only because we are using only a single predictor? Will the gain in predictive power remain after the addition of relevant covariates, or will the additional variables be able to accomplish the work that discretizing performed?

We answer this question in table 7.8 by adding some standard wage-equation covariates. We begin first with the quadratic form of age. This addition boosts the proportion of variance explained substantially, but a gain is still visible between the model with a

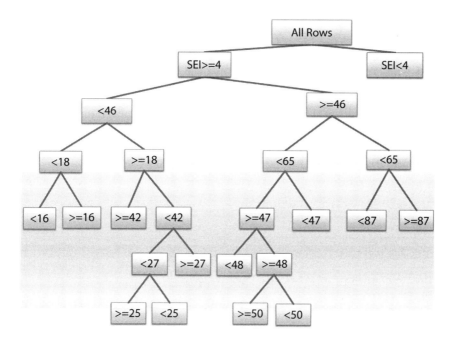

FIGURE 7.4
Using a partition tree to split Duncan socioeconomic index (occupational prestige) into thirteen bins.

TABLE 7.7   Mean Income by
Discretized SEI Category

SEI range	Mean income ($)
1–3	11,438.63
4–15	26,338.88
16–17	18,474.6
18–24	31,989.98
25–26	17,198.57
27–41	43,962.59
41–45	29,192.34
46	65,166.95
47–64	42,957.09
65–76	67,200.71
77–86	73,893.76
87–91	90,917.83
92–100	170,696.00

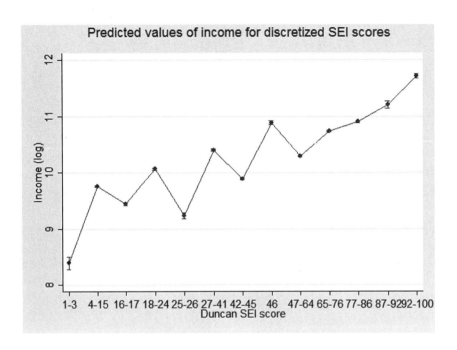

FIGURE 7.5

Predicted value of personal income for discretized Duncan socioeconomic index.

TABLE 7.8 Adding Discretized Variables Can Improve Prediction (Measured by R^2)

	SEI only		Add age		Add educational attainment		Add gender and race	
	Continuous SEI	Discretized SEI	Continuous SEI	Discretized SEI	Continuous SEI	Discretized SEI	Continuous SEI	Discretized SEI
R^2	.1438	.1945	.2544	.2916	.2912	.3211	.3371	.3559
Adj. R^2	.1438	.1945	.2544	.2915	.2911	.3210	.3370	.3558
RMSE	0.9987	0.9687	0.9320	0.9085	0.9088	0.8894	0.8788	0.8663

single linear term for SEI and the discretized form. Adding educational attainment boosts the R^2 in the linear-SEI model by 0.037, and in the discretized-SEI model by 0.030. The difference in R^2 remains—with the discretized model we explain about 3% more of the variance. Finally, we add dummies for gender and race, which further boosts the explanatory power of both models. The difference in R^2 between models has shrunk further, to about 0.018.

Is this a large difference? Does discretizing really matter that much? We contend that it does, for a number of reasons. First, differences in predictive power remain even after the addition of some of the most powerful predictors of income. Secondly, we have discretized with only a single variable, and this still improves our predictive accuracy substantially. But most importantly, discretizing has uncovered some suggestive features of the relation between income and occupational prestige which would be considered mere statistical noise in standard analyses. We would want to validate the general pattern with alternative measures of prestige, and with out-of-sample predictions, but it may be that though there is a global positive linear relation between prestige and income, there are small local trade-offs, where a more prestigious occupation pays somewhat less than a less-prestigious occupation.

BINNING CATEGORICAL PREDICTORS

We have previously seen how classification trees can be used to optimally bin a continuous variable in relation to some outcome we are trying to predict. Such a method works well in the case in which the relation between the predictor and the outcome is characterized by complex nonlinearity. Trees can also be used in a similar manner to create bins of categorical predictors. Let's say we have some nominal variable which has a relatively large number of categories—like a variable for occupation—which we would like to collapse into a much smaller number so as to be more parsimonious. Ideally, we would like to classify occupations into fewer categories in such a way that our model's predictive power is enhanced—or at least in such a way that we gain more from parsimoniousness than we lose in raw prediction. Traditionally, we would find some *theoretical* reason why certain occupations ought to be lumped together. We could then see to what degree this classification makes sense in a regression model. If one particular classification scheme did not work well, we could simply abandon it and try another that we think "makes sense."

Data mining suggests another possibility. What if we created our classification in a purely data-driven manner, that is, in such a manner that the categories maximize our ability to explain variance in the dependent or outcome variable, penalizing the model for the inclusion of additional parameters? We would then produce a binning of categories which is optimal in terms of the parsimony–prediction tradeoff.

To show what we mean, we draw again on our 2012 county-level election data. Our units of observation are counties, and each county lies in a particular state. Let's say we want to investigate the impact of states on predicting the vote share for Obama by county. We could include all 50 states as dummy variables in our regression model, but this is rather inelegant. Another option typically employed is to group states into larger categories on the basis of region (such as 9- or 4-category census region), or on the basis of some other characteristic (South/non-South, right-to-work vs. non-right-to-work, etc.). Those strategies might work for our purposes, but they are rather indirect ways of getting

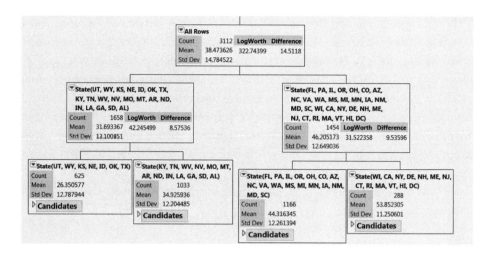

All Rows
Count   3112   LogWorth   Difference
Mean   38.473626   322.74399   14.5118
Std Dev 14.784522

State(UT, WY, KS, NE, ID, OK, TX,
KY, TN, WV, NV, MO, MT, AR, ND,
IN, LA, GA, SD, AL)
Count   1658   LogWorth   Difference
Mean   31.693367   42.245499   8.57536
Std Dev 13.100851

State(FL, PA, IL, OR, OH, CO, AZ,
NC, VA, WA, MS, MI, MN, IA, NM,
MD, SC, WI, CA, NY, DE, NH, ME,
NJ, CT, RI, MA, VT, HI, DC)
Count   1454   LogWorth   Difference
Mean   46.205173   31.522358   9.53596
Std Dev 12.649036

State(UT, WY, KS, NE, ID, OK, TX)
Count   625
Mean   26.350577
Std Dev 12.787944
Candidates

State(KY, TN, WV, NV, MO, MT,
AR, ND, IN, LA, GA, SD, AL)
Count   1033
Mean   34.925936
Std Dev 12.204485
Candidates

State(FL, PA, IL, OR, OH, CO, AZ,
NC, VA, WA, MS, MI, MN, IA, NM,
MD, SC)
Count   1166
Mean   44.316345
Std Dev 12.261394
Candidates

State(WI, CA, NY, DE, NH, ME, NJ,
CT, RI, MA, VT, HI, DC)
Count   288
Mean   53.852305
Std Dev 11.250601
Candidates

FIGURE 7.6

Using a partition tree to bin a nominal/categorical variable (state) in JMP Pro.

at what we really want: states in which the mean county-level vote for Obama is higher or lower, broken into optimal categories.

We create a partition tree in JMP by again selecting Analyze Modeling Partition. All we then do is select our dependent variable (Obama's vote share) and a single independent predictor (state). Since the state variable is characterized in JMP as categorical, the partition tree will test all possible ways of combining the states into two groups, and choose the one which creates two groups that are as different as possible in terms of the mean value of the dependent variable (Obama's vote share).

The first split, shown in figure 7.6, creates one group of states whose counties have a mean Obama vote share of 31.7% and another group of states with 46.2%. The first group contains the very reddest of the red states—Oklahoma, Texas, Utah, and Arkansas—and the second contains all of the blue states plus a number of solidly red states such as South Carolina and Mississippi. A second set of splits further subdivides the states into four groups, with mean county-level vote shares of 27%, 35%, 44%, and 53%, respectively. The second split on the "right" has separated the states into those which are reliably Democratic (such as Rhode Island, New York, California, and Hawaii) and more hotly contested "battleground" states (Florida, Pennsylvania, and New Mexico). Note, though, that this characterization does not tell the whole story—solidly blue Illinois, for instance, is in this "battleground" group, as is Republican stronghold Mississippi. The split on the "left," in the meantime, has separated the states into the very red (Utah, Kansas, Idaho) and the not-as-solidly red (Georgia, Kentucky, Indiana).

JMP permits you to build out a tree to maximize fit in a cross-validation sample, but here we are looking to do something a little bit different. We are trying to maximize prediction and parsimoniousness simultaneously rather than to prevent overfitting. In

TABLE 7.9   Binning States

Group	States	Mean Obama vote share
1	HI, DC	76.39%
2	RI, MA, VT	63.52%
3	DE, NH, ME, NJ, CT	55.12%
4	WI, CA, NY	51.22%
5	AZ, NC, VA, WA, MS, MI, MN, IA, NM, MD, SC	46.08%
6	FL, PA, IL, OR, OH, CO	41.22%
7	AR, ND, IN, LA, GA, SD, AL	36.96%
8	KY, TN, WV, NV, MO, MT	32.36%
9	ID, OK, TX	27.68%
10	WY, KS, NE	27.68%
11	UT	18.35%

TABLE 7.10   Effect of Binning Continuous Variables on R^2

Model	R^2	Adj. R^2	RMSE
State dummies	.3496	.3392	12.01
Data mining categories	.3448	.3427	11.98
Census region	.1637	.1615	13.53
Additional controls only	.5487	.5468	9.94
Additional controls + data mining categories	.6918	.6895	8.23
Additional controls + census region	.6586	.6563	8.66

JMP, this is done by building a tree bit by bit, examining fit statistics after each split. We examine the movement of the AIC (Aikake information criterion), which measures fit and penalizes a model for adding parameters. Because smaller AIC values indicate a better fit, we build out the tree as long as the AIC continues to fall. When it begins to rise again, we prune back the tree to the point where the AIC was lowest.

Doing so generates 11 categories of states, each with a different mean value for Obama's vote share. These 11 categories are presented in table 7.9 from largest to smallest mean vote share at the county level.

Clearly we have some outlier states on either side (Hawaii and Washington DC on the pro-Obama side and Utah on the anti-Obama side), which end up in rather small groups, and larger groups in the middle. And we should note that the states do cluster to some degree regionally. All New England states, after all, are in the second and third groups, while Southern Atlantic states appear in groups 5 and 7.

Table 7.10 compares the predictive accuracy of the grouping of states we achieved through DM with that obtained by using a received categorization like census region.

Our categorization has 11 categories and there are only 9 census regions, so it is informative to focus on a measure of model fit like adjusted R^2 (which penalizes a model for the inclusion of additional parameters) for a just comparison. We also compare our categorization against a model which includes a single dummy for each state (thus, one with 50 categories). The DM categorization vastly outperforms the census-region classification scheme, explaining more than double the variance in vote share. Using the state dummies explains more of the variance overall, but its adjusted R^2 is slightly lower. Thus, by using data mining, we are able to explain nearly as much of the variance in the dependent variable with a much more parsimonious model.

To further investigate this, we add a set of other highly predictive control variables,[2] in the bottom three rows of table 7.10. We do this to test the possibility that knowing the state a county is located in provides *no* information that is not ably described by other variables. Indeed, when we run a regression predicting Obama's vote share containing only the demographic control variables, we have explained quite a bit of the variance—54%. When we add the census region variables, we are able to explain nearly 11% more of the variance. Normally, this would be sufficient. We would look at the improved predictive power of the model that includes census region and conclude that regions matter in some sense. But in this instance we also have the "optimal" classification of states from data mining. Using this categorization is superior, even in a model with substantial controls: the adjusted R^2 rises from .65 to .68.

USING PARTITION TREES TO STUDY INTERACTIONS

Another use of partition trees is to identify interesting interactions between variables. Conventional regression modeling encourages us to think of the world as made up of a series of additive characteristics: one's probability of employment is a linear function of one's gender, race, educational credentialing, age, and past work history, for example. One's income is an additive function of age (squared), experience, and schooling.

Occasionally, we acknowledge that variables *interact* to produce outcomes. Perhaps the effect of education on income depends on one's gender. Or perhaps the effect of unemployment rate on the probability of incumbent reelection depends on whether or not the country is at war. For the most part, we handle interactions in precisely this manner: two-way interactions are as complex as we allow the world to appear in our models.

Partition trees enable us to look for interactions which are far more complicated. To understand why, we need to briefly indicate what it is that trees do (more detail is given in chapter 10). Tree algorithms divide cases in our data into two groups which are as homogeneous as possible in terms of the outcome. They do so by trying every possible value of every independent variable and finding the very best way to split the sample into subgroups. After making the first split, they repeat the process again and again, each time creating groupings which are increasingly homogeneous in terms of the outcome or dependent variable and increasingly different from each other.

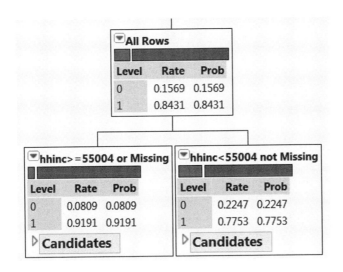

FIGURE 7.7
Tree of health insurance status—the first split of the
data.

Since various variables are selected in producing the cases which ultimately end up being grouped together in final "leaves," we can think of each leaf as defined by a complex interaction of terms. In this manner, trees help us discover complex interactions which we otherwise would have difficulty identifying.

We demonstrate this using data from the 2010 American Community Survey. We grow a tree using as a dependent variable an indicator of having health insurance coverage, and use race, citizenship, gender, household income, age, educational attainment, employment status, and marital status as independent variables. We use one-at-a-time splitting to grow out a modest-sized tree. Unlike in the prior section, we have not balanced the data on the outcome, and we have applied a population weight. The resulting conditional probabilities therefore constitute estimates of population quantities.

In figure 7.7 we see that in the root node (all cases), about 84.3% of all cases have some form of health insurance, and about 15.7% do not. The tree finds its first split on income. Those in households with combined income of at least $55,000 per year are about 92% insured; in lower-income households the insurance rate is only about 78%.

We can follow these two branches further (figure 7.8). Among the wealthier group, the tree continues to discriminate according to health insurance status. A second split is made in income at about $85,000. Among the relatively lower-income group (incomes between about $55,000 and $85,000), citizenship is most predictive of insurance; nearly half of noncitizens in this relatively high-income range lack access to health insurance, according to these data. This is very different from U.S. citizens in the same income group, over 90% of whom are covered by insurance. This highlights an important

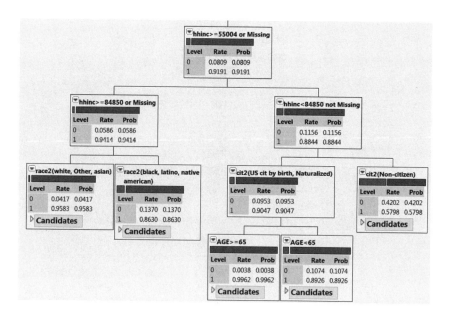

FIGURE 7.8

Further splits of the data among those with incomes greater than $55,000.

interaction between income and citizenship within upper-middle-income households. Among citizens at this income level, there is a split at age 65: almost 100% of the older group have insurance. Among those with incomes over $85,000, whites, Asians, and "other race" individuals are insured at nearly 95%, but blacks, Latinos, and Native Americans at only about 86%.

Following the right-hand branch (not displayed) containing those with incomes below $55,000, we find that first of all age is the most important predictor of insurance status. Those eligible for Medicare, aged 65+, are virtually universally insured. Nonseniors next split again at the age of majority. Only about 12% of children in households with incomes of less than $55,000 per year are uninsured, but nearly a third of such working-aged adults are. However, among children, citizenship is highly predictive of insurance: only about 10% of American citizens in this income bracket lack insurance, while nearly half of noncitizen minors do. Among working-age adults, we find splits again in income (at $30,000), citizenship, and employment status.

In all, we have grown out a tree with 13 leaves. These leaves contain differing proportions of the sample, and have vastly different outcomes in terms of health insurance, as described in table 7.11.

It is important to note that partition trees do not simply select the variables that best distinguish between who is insured and who is not; they do so in the way that best sorts all the *cases* into such bins. Thus they take into account the *proportion of cases* that fall into groups defined by the leaves. A split which divides the data very cleanly into catego-

TABLE 7.11 Leaves of the Tree

Leaf	Household income	Age	U.S. citizenship	Race	Employment status	% insured	% of cases	% of all uninsured
1	$85,000	All	All	White, Asian, other	All	95.84	23.58	6.25
2	$85,000	All	All	Black, Latino, Native American	All	86.28	5.04	4.41
3	$55,000–85,000	65+	Yes	All	All	99.62	2.02	0.05
4	$55,000–85,000	<65	Yes	All	All	89.26	15.31	10.48
5	$55,000–85,000	All	No	All	All	57.99	1.16	3.11
6	<$55,000	65+	All	All	All	99.05	8.61	0.52
7	<$55,000	<19	Yes	All	All	89.74	12.63	8.26
8	<$55,000	<19	No	All	All	53.48	0.54	1.60
9	$31,000–55,000	19–64	Yes	All	All	79.72	11.45	14.81
10	$31,000–55,000	19–64	No	All	All	45.65	1.48	5.13
11	$31,000	19–64	Yes	All	Yes	68.18	13.57	27.53
12	$31,000	19–64	Yes	All	No	43.74	2.08	7.46
13	$31,000	19–64	No	All	All	35.40	2.52	10.38

ries of outcome, but splits off a very small portion of the data into one group, is less likely to be made than one which generates two groups with more similar mean values of the outcome but creates two relatively large groups. Another important side note is that groups which have low insurance rates can be very small, so the majority of the uninsured are in groups with middling levels of insurance. For example, low-income employed citizens of working age are uninsured at a rate of about 32% and account for 27.5% of all those who lack insurance.

Can we use these results to improve predictive modeling? In table 7.12 we show a number of logistic regression models predicting health insurance coverage. Remember that in these data more than 80% of the cases have health coverage, so that the breakdown of the dependent variable is very lopsided. In this sort of situation, as we have indicated earlier, a model can *appear* very efficient at correctly classifying cases simply by predicting a positive outcome for all cases. That is, a model can do a good job on a fit statistic that identifies the percentage correctly classified simply by assigning all cases to the majority outcome (insured, in this example).

Therefore, a good model will have to do better than this—it will have to be more subtle, and do a decent job of distinguishing true from false positives. We therefore inspect a number of measures of model fit. The pseudo-R^2 is actually not that bad a measure for capturing how much a better a model does than random guessing in this instance, for it identifies how much better a model is than the null model. The AIC and BIC statistics

TABLE 7.12   Effect of Adding Leaf Dummies to a Predictive Model

	Regression model	Pseudo-R^2	AIC	BIC	% correctly classified	Sensitivity	Specificity	Area under ROC curve
1	Component variables[1]	.1492	204,421.9	204,538.8	87.30%	98.40%	15.13%	0.7745
2	Leaf dummies only	.1749	196,559.1	196,686.7	87.06%	97.65	18.25	0.7957
3	Component variables + leaves	.2030	189,596.5	189,777.2	87.29%	98.40%	15.10%	0.8182
4	Additional control variables only[2]	0.0546	227,415.8	227,596.6	86.66%	100.00%	0.00%	0.6675
5	Controls + component variables	.1791	197,291.8	197,578.9	87.48%	98.29%	17.27%	0.7943
6	Controls + leaves	.2111	189,788.6	190,086.3	87.38%	98.29%	16.45%	0.8177
7	Controls + components + leaves	.2395	182,801.2	183,205.2	87.81%	98.03%	21.45%	0.8342

[1] Age, household income, race, citizenship, employment status

[2] Gender, educational attainment, school attendance, region, marital status

SOURCE: American Community Survey 2010

factor into the analysis the desirability of both prediction and parsimoniousness. As we said above, using the percentage correctly classified as our criterion of a good model is misleading in this instance because of how imbalanced the data are in terms of the outcome. Here we really want to examine the *specificity* of the model: the percentage of those without insurance who are correctly classified as such. The area under the ROC (receiver operating characteristic) curve also measures how much better a model does than random guessing.

First, we run a model which includes "naive" versions of the variables used by the partition tree above. That is, we include only age (as a continuous variable), household income (also continuous), race (five separate groups), citizenship status (three groups: citizen by birth, naturalized citizen, and noncitizen), and employment status. This model does not perform badly at all, in fact. The area under the ROC curve suggests that it does 55% better than random guessing, and it correctly classifies 15% of the uninsured. This is, in part, a testament to the help provided by the partition tree, given that the tree selected the variables we used here, indicating that they are probably quite important. We compare this with a model which includes only dummy variables for each of the 13 leaves created by our partition tree (actually, 12 leaves, using the largest group as a reference). Note that these are not dummy variables as we are accustomed to thinking about them. They are defined by an intersection of five characteristics, two of which are measured continuously (but split into groups) and the rest of which are categorical measures.

Further, we do not use all possible combinations of these variables in the analysis, but only the particular groups identified above. Group 1, for instance, is identified only on the basis of income and race; it includes all white, Asian, and "other race" individuals in households that make over $85,000 per year, irrespective of citizenship, age, and employment status. But citizenship, age, and employment status are explicitly involved in the distinctions between other groups. Specifically, group 1 is distinguished from group 2 according to categories of race, and from all other groups by a breakpoint in income.

The model which contains only these "leaf" dummies performs somewhat better than using the "component" variables—the untransformed main effects. When we combine these two variable sets, we do even better (except in terms of specificity). The differences in predictive accuracy are not large, however.

Next, we test a model which contains only some additional variables (gender, educational attainment, region, and marital status) which were not selected by the partition tree. We want to test whether the predictive advantage provided by the leaf variables is something which could be performed by simply including more independent variables in the model, ones which are perhaps only mildly correlated with the component variables. These variables are, by themselves, of some predictive value, though not a lot (yielding a pseudo-R^2 of .05). Results from this model are displayed to establish a new baseline. We can see by examining the sensitivity and specificity that the logistic model has here, in the absence of better information, simply classed all cases as belonging to the dominant outcome class.

In models 5–7 we add the variables used in models 1–3 above. The control variables, when added to the component variables, bring us to about the same predictive accuracy that we had when we just used the leaf dummies. Does this mean that the leaves are no better than adding controls? Model 6 tells us that this is probably not true. The leaves contribute substantially to predicting the outcome on top of the controls, and do a better job than the component variables themselves (model 5) in terms of all measures of fit.

Finally, we present a model in which the controls, leaves, and components are all included. This model has the greatest predictive accuracy of all, in terms of all measures of fit except for sensitivity. The sensitivity is highest in model 4 simply because it assigned all cases to the positive outcome (thus capturing 100% of true positives). The predictive accuracy is not hugely higher here, but that we are able to gain an advantage by using interaction terms generated from a partition tree is significant, especially considering that the lopsided nature of the outcome presents challenges to any classification model. Further, we should note that the classification tree was allowed to split only 12 times in this data; if grown out fully, it would have split into far smaller groups. The predictive power of the interaction terms would probably have been improved somewhat had we continued splitting.

The weakness of this tree method is, once again, the interpretation of the final model. When partition trees are used to build interaction terms such as those in this analysis, regression model output cannot be read in the same straightforward manner as a conventional model. In simple terms, "variables," which are typically interpreted as measures of socially salient forces, are no longer doing the "acting" (Abbott 2001). We cannot say, "A 10% change in income is related to a 2% increase in the odds of having insurance." Instead, we can say that being a member of a group identified by a particular conjunction of characteristics is related to an increase in the odds of having insurance. That is, we allow social structure to gather people in complex ways into groups that experience differing outcomes.

Secondly, in model 7, where we have included leaf variables along with the components from which the leaves were generated, interpreting the coefficients on *either* the leaves or the main effects is challenging. We cannot even use the methods typically used for interpreting interaction terms (see e.g. Brambor, Clark, and Golder 2006; Jaccard and Turrisi 2003). For example, consider interpreting the coefficient β_2 in the following equation characterizing model 7:

$$\log\left(\frac{p}{1-p}\right) = \alpha + \beta_2 G_2 + \sum_{j=3}^{12} \beta_j G_j + \beta_{13}\, income + \beta_{14}\, black + \beta_{15}\, latino + \beta_{16}\, asian$$
$$+ \beta_{17}\, nativeamerican + \beta_{18}\, otherrace + \gamma X + \delta Z + \varepsilon$$

β_2 is the effect of being in group 2 (relative to being in group 1) on the odds of having insurance.[3] However, this group is defined relative to group 1 by race (black, Latino, and Native American vs. white, Asian, and other). It is the racial difference among those making at least $85,000. However, other racial groups enter into the analysis as separate controls (all measured against the reference group, white). Income is also a separate variable measured continuously. So the effect on health insurance of the racial difference among high earners is net of income and race. Clearly, making sense of this is tricky. And the group difference is *simplest* in this particular case, since groups 1 and 2 are only one split away from each other. Groups 1 and 10, on the other hand, are six splits apart, and vary in terms of income, citizenship, race/ethnicity, and age group.

The interpretation is challenging because of the inclusion of both leaf dummies and their components in the same model. Picking one or the other set of these variables eases interpretation substantially. For the purposes of maximizing prediction, though, including all of the information in these variables is helpful.

SUMMARY

We do not live in what Andrew Abbot (2001) calls a "general linear reality." Rather, outcomes are generated by the complex interaction of social processes for which our variables are usually just convenient shorthand. Even our standard manner of coding interactions between variables is not really sufficient for capturing the complexity of how attributes interact in the world. Regression models are just that—models—and they assist us precisely through the simplification they impose upon the world, indicating average relations of great importance.

Still, in some ways we can do better, and we have indicated in this section how data mining tools like partition trees can allow us to do so. Partition trees in particular can detect how variables interact—and an important variant on the partition tree is named after this precise quality: chi-squared automatic interaction detection (CHAID). Further, leveraging this interaction-detection capacity can assist us in improving predictive capacity—after all, partition trees frequently outperform logistic regression at classification tasks. We have shown here that using even a small amount of the interaction-detecting power of partition trees can improve the performance of regression models at prediction.

Data mining methods can be used to create new variable transformations—optimal binning and the creation of complex interaction terms. In some ways, this can be seen as making our variable or feature set more complex (but more accurate). Next, we move on to a set of techniques for reducing the complexity of our feature set while preserving the overall structure of the data: methods of variable extraction.

8

EXTRACTING VARIABLES

PRINCIPAL COMPONENT ANALYSIS

When we have data of high dimension, that is, data that are very *wide* (lots of attributes or predictors), we sometimes want to find ways of reducing their dimensionality. We have already discussed *feature selection* methods like stepwise regression, LASSO, and VIF regression. These methods are certainly options when we want to decrease the dimensionality of predictor variables in terms of their relation with an outcome. Feature selection tools are all "supervised" methods, in that one particular dimension of the data (the outcome, target, or dependent variable) is privileged, and we select variables that are interesting for how they relate to this privileged variable.

But we do not always have one variable which we are particularly interested in. Sometimes we simply have a mass of data and we want to discern patterns in these data. It could be that a good bit of what is important in a large set of variables could be boiled down and expressed cogently and simply by a handful of summary attributes. It is for precisely this sort of situation that the time-honored techniques of principal component analysis (PCA) and its close relative, factor analysis, were developed.

Consider, in our county-level 2012 election dataset, three variables: median income, the percentage of the population with a college degree or higher, and the percentage of the labor force in professional or managerial occupations. Though these are clearly three distinct concepts, we would not be surprised to find them interrelated. After all, most people in professional or managerial occupations are college graduates, and both college

TABLE 8.1 Correlation Matrix

	Median income	% higher ed.	% prof./managerial
Median income	1	–	–
% higher ed.	0.690	1	–
% prof./managerial	0.585	0.788	1

graduates and those in such occupations tend to have higher-than-average salaries. To examine their interrelations, we can produce a correlation matrix (table 8.1) and a three-dimensional scatterplot (figure 8.1), the latter courtesy of JMP.

This provides a confirmation of the interrelation of these measures at the county level, for they are all ways of indicating the relative affluence of a county. Now, one *could* reduce dimensionality by simply using one of these three attributes and assuming that it adequately expressed the concept of affluence. But consider that the variables are not *perfectly* intercorrelated. Clearly, they express similar but not identical things about the counties. We could instead create a fourth attribute that expresses most of the variance in these three variables, performing exactly the same amount of dimensionality reduction but by pulling information from all three measures.

We do this by finding the *first principal component* of these three variables. But what exactly does this mean? Consider a correlation matrix, as in table 8.1. A correlation matrix is the standardized form of the variance-covariance matrix; a variance-covariance matrix describes interrelations among the variables in a manner that does not correct for the variances of the variables themselves.

From any set of variables one can derive a variance-covariance matrix of dimensionality $p \times p$, where p is the number of variables under consideration. For this matrix one can determine a set of exactly p special vectors known as *eigenvectors,* which when multiplied by the covariance matrix return themselves times a given scalar known as an *eigenvalue.* These eigenvectors represent straight lines which, when projected through the p-dimensional data cloud, most efficiently describe the variance in the data.

Each eigenvector has its own eigenvalue, and the relative sizes of the eigenvalues tell us the relative importance of each of the eigenvectors in terms of describing the variance of the data. That is, the eigenvector with the largest eigenvalue describes the largest share of the variance in the data. The one with the next-largest eigenvalue describes the largest share of *remaining* variance after the variance described by the first eigenvector has been removed; and so on.

It is important to note that this means that all the eigenvectors are at right angles to each other, meaning that they are uncorrelated with (or *orthogonal to*) each other. What they tell us is rather interesting. Consider the three-dimensional scatterplot in figure 8.1. We could rotate the data-cloud around its centroid (central point) such that a line which minimizes the distances between it and the data points themselves lies along the x axis.

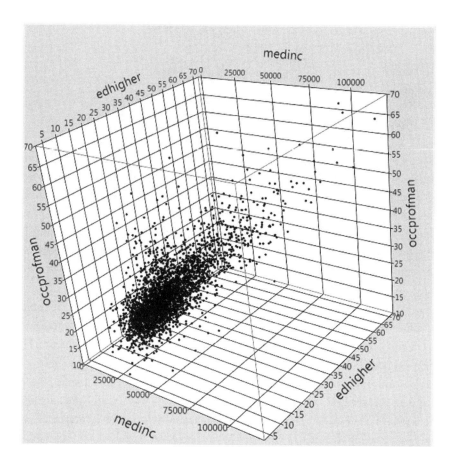

FIGURE 8.1
A three-dimensional scatterplot produced by JMP Pro.

The vector which described this line would be the eigenvector with the largest eigen-value, and the y and z axes would represent the other two eigenvectors. For this three-dimensional data cloud, the x axis would be the first principal component, and the y and z axes the second and third principal components.

When we perform a PCA of our three variables using JMP, we can visually inspect the relations between the data, the variables, and the principal components by producing three *biplots*. These are simply scatterplots with the principal components forming the axes (figure 8.2).

Both the top and middle plots have component 1, the first principal component, as the x axis. The fact that the data cloud is spread out horizontally clearly demonstrates that most of the variance in the data occurs along this dimension—79.3% of it, to be exact (table 8.2). We can also see that the vertical variance is slightly more pronounced in the top-left plot. This is because the vertical dimension here is the second principal component, which describes more of the variance, intrinsically, than does the third.

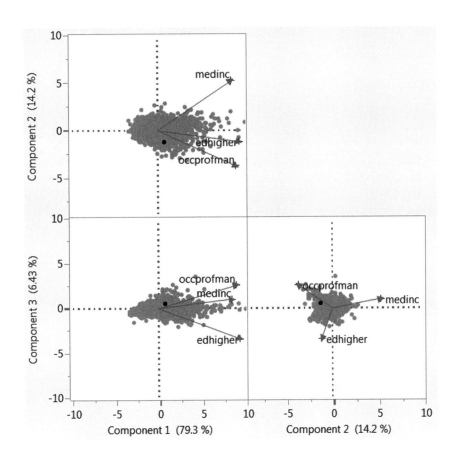

FIGURE 8.2
Biplots of principal components (JMP Pro).

TABLE 8.2   Components, Eigenvalues, and Loadings

	Eigenvalue	Variance described	Loading		
			Median income	*% higher ed.*	*% prof./mgr.*
PC1	2.37	79.3%	0.85	0.93	0.89
PC2	0.43	14.2%	0.52	−0.12	−0.37
PC3	0.19	6.4%	0.11	−0.34	0.26

TABLE 8.3 Regression of Obama Vote-Share on Principal Components

	Model 1	Model 2	Model 3
Median income ($1,000s)	−0.225 (0.029)	—	—
% higher ed.	1.148 (0.052)	—	—
% prof./mgr.	−0.728 (0.061)	—	—
PC1	—	1.855 (0.159)	1.855 (0.159)
PC 2	—	—	−1.159 (0.375)
PC3	—	—	−11.116 (0.558)
Intercept	48.42	38.44	38.44
RMSE	13.69	28.44	13.69
R^2	.148	.034	.148
Adj. R^2	.147	.036	.147

The shadowy gray dots in figure 8.2 represent individual cases, and we can see that the point cloud has been rotated such that its dimension of greatest variance lies along the axis defined by the first principal component. The arrows show how each of the measured variables relates to the three principal components. We can see that all three variables are closely correlated with the first principal component. Numbers called *factor loadings* tell us how correlated each of the contributor variables is with each of the three principal components. Note that all of the correlations between the variables and the first principal component are higher than *any* of the bivariate correlations between the variables we saw in table 8.1. The first principal component provides, then, a good summary of what these three measures have in common, without privileging any of the variables.

As a summary measure, the first principal component will serve as an excellent method of reducing analytic complexity. We can demonstrate this by regressing the percentage vote for Obama first on the three component variables (model 1 in table 8.3) and then on simply the first principal component (model 2). We then add the other two principal components (model 3). Median income has been divided by 1,000 to ease interpretation.

Note that though two of the independent variables have *partial* correlations with the outcome (vote share for Obama) that are negative, the principal component has a strong positive relation. This demonstrates the use of principal components in getting rid of interpretive difficulties generated by correlated predictor variables' being included in the same model. Each of the predictors individually has a *positive* bivariate relation with Obama vote share, but the relation with the outcome was strongest in the case of the variable measuring the percentage of the adult population with higher degrees. Thus, when we hold percentage of the population with a college degree constant, the effects of the other two variables become negative. In such a model, we need to carefully specify that the relation between, for example, median income and vote share is negative *only* after we control for the density of college graduates. If we were interpreting each variable as reflecting underlying affluence, though, we would (mis)interpret the evidence as being mixed. Collapsing common information into a single principal component leads us to be able to show a more straightforward positive relation between these aspects of social hierarchy and the vote share for Obama.

In table 8.3, we note that moving from model 1 to model 2, when predicting the vote for Obama, reduces the R^2 by 77%. But how could this be, if this component itself describes 78% of the variance among the three predictors? The answer is, first, that the principal component was not identified with reference to the outcome variable but describes only relations among the three predictors. Secondly, none of the predictors is highly correlated with the outcome. The correlations with Obama's vote share are: for percentage with college degrees, $r = .298$; for median income, $r = .102$; and for percentage in professional or managerial occupations, $r = .107$. In fact, Obama vote share is more highly correlated with the *third* principal component ($r = -.329$) than with the first ($\rho = .1929$) or with any of the predictors on their own. Simply put, *affluence* is positively correlated with Obama vote share, but the relation is weak. PCA actually helps reveal, in this case, that the majority of the explanatory work being done by the three variables in question was *not* being done by what they most share in common.

Finally, note that the measures of fit (RMSE, R^2, and adjusted R^2) are identical in models 1 and 3. This is because the three principal components together contain all of the information in the original measured variables.

To truly demonstrate the model-simplifying property of PCA, we need to begin with more variables. We gather 22 predictors of Obama vote share and perform a PCA (table 8.4). A regression of vote share on all 22 variables yields an R^2 of .5826. However, the model is quite complex, and many of the variables are intercorrelated. We can use PCA to reduce the dimensionality of the data, this time using Stata's PCA command.

We can examine the decreasing value of the eigenvalues by calling a scree plot after the analysis (figure 8.3). We can see that the number drops quickly at first, and flattens out at about five. This tells us that five components together describe most (about 68.5%) of the variance in the 22 variables. However, to be careful we will include two more components—seven in total.

Regressing vote share on these seven components yields an R^2 of .4338, which represents about 75% of the initial variance explained in the full model, yet with far fewer variables. Because all the principal components are on the same scale (i.e. normally distributed, with a mean of 0 and a standard deviation of 1), regression coefficients can be directly compared. In table 8.5 we can see that components 1, 2, 3, and 5 have positive relations with Obama's vote share, and the most powerful are components 2 and 3. These components relate positively to population density and the percentage of a county's population that is black (respectively), and negatively to such variables as percentage of seniors and percentage of minors in the population (respectively).

One of the useful things about PCA is a consequence of the fact that the components themselves are uncorrelated. Because of this orthogonality, the R^2 of a regression on all

TABLE 8.4   Results of a Principal Component Analysis

Component	Eigenvalue	Proportion of variance	Cumulative variance
1	5.56	0.253	0.253
2	4.75	0.215	0.469
3	2.15	0.098	0.567
4	1.53	0.070	0.637
5	1.05	0.048	0.685
6	0.97	0.044	0.729
7	0.91	0.041	0.770
8	0.83	0.037	0.808
9	0.73	0.033	0.841
10	0.65	0.029	0.871
11	0.54	0.025	0.896
12	0.44	0.020	0.916
13	0.36	0.016	0.932
14	0.30	0.014	0.945
15	0.28	0.012	0.957
16	0.26	0.012	0.968
17	0.20	0.009	0.978
18	0.17	0.007	0.986
19	0.14	0.006	0.992
20	0.07	0.003	0.995
21	0.07	0.003	0.998
22	0.04	0.002	1.000

NOTE: $N = 3,114$; 22 input variables

components is a sum of the R^2s from regressions on each of the components individually. Each component describes a unique portion of the variance in the outcome variable, even though (and in fact because) the outcome was not involved in the PCA itself. Table 8.5 tells us that component 2 describes over 21% of the variance in Obama's vote share by itself, and that substantial portions of the variance are also described by components 3, 6, and 7. Many of the components are basically unrelated to the outcome variable, which is to be expected given that the outcome was not used in the generation of the components.

This leads us to the chief drawback of PCA: the interpretation of the individual components themselves. The components describe unique portions of the information contained in all of the variables, but it is not guaranteed, in a multidimensional context like this one, that most or even any of the variables will load highly onto only one of the components. In this case, many of the variables load only moderately onto any of the compo-

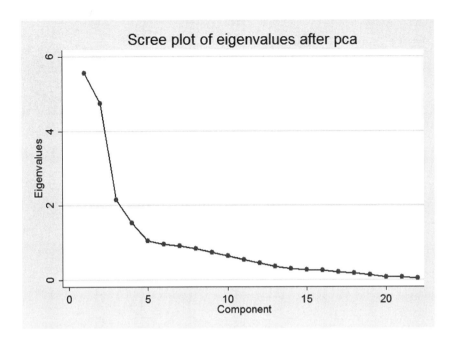

FIGURE 8.3
Scree plot showing eigenvalues of components from a principal component
analysis.

nents, and load similarly onto two or three. Thus, interpretation of the "meaning" of a
component when PCA is performed with many variables is often not straightforward.

The key point is that the primary use of PCA is reduction in dimensionality itself,
forming a more parsimonious model. This can come at the cost of easy interpretation.
If we want to reduce dimensionality while improving interpretability, a better strategy
would be to perform factor analyses or principal component analysis on subgroups of
variables, as we did with the PCA of median income, educational attainment, and percentage in professional or managerial occupations which began this section. This leads
to more interpretable summary variables being generated. However, if separate groups
of theoretically associated variables are used to generate separate factors, most likely
these factors would themselves be associated. As a result, they would not describe *separate* components of variance in the dependent variable, and their intercorrelation would
itself need to be examined as a part of the overall analysis.

SUMMARY

In this section we have focused on the most common method of variable extraction,
principal component analysis. This method is not intrinsically a DM method, but it is
frequently used by data miners to make complex datasets more tractable. It is a rigorous

TABLE 8.5 Results of Principal Component Analysis, and Regression Using Principal Components, in 2008 County-Level Election Data

	Principal Component Analysis				Bivariate correlation with Obama vote share	Regression of vote share on components	
	Positively loading variables	Negatively loading variables	% variance in covariates	Eigenvalue		Coeff. (SE)	% of variance explained
PC1	% < HS ed., % poverty	Median income, % prof./mgr.	25.31	5.56	0.089	0.560*** (0.084)	0.76
PC2	% immigrant, pop. density	% age 65+, % just HS	21.59	4.74	0.463	3.152*** (0.091)	21.44
PC3	% divorced, % black	% age < 18, % Latino/a	9.79	2.15	0.343	3.467*** (0.136)	11.75
PC4	% age < 18, household size	% age 65+, % Latino/a	6.96	1.53	-0.071	-0.859*** (0.161)	0.48
PC5	% same-sex couples, % Asian	% young adult, % black	4.81	1.05	0.073	1.052*** (0.194)	0.53
PC6	% young Adult, % white	% black, % age 65+	4.40	0.96	-0.216	-3.267*** (0.203)	4.67
PC7	% evangelical Protestant, % exactly HS	Male unemployment, female unemployment	4.14	0.91	-0.189	-2.940*** (0.209)	3.58

***p < .001.

way of summarizing the majority of shared variance among a large group of variables with a much smaller number of measures. We have demonstrated here that just 7 principal components can perform about three-quarters as well as the 22 separate variables from which they were derived in predicting Obama's 2012 county-level vote share. There is, of course, a trade-off here of accuracy for parsimony, and which is more important depends on what you are seeking from your model.

INDEPENDENT COMPONENT ANALYSIS

Independent component analysis (ICA), originally conceptualized by computer scientist Pierre Comon (1994), is descended from and quite similar to principal component analysis. The differences between the two techniques are driven by the types of problems they were initially devised to solve and that they are best suited for. Both techniques, that is, *may* be used as data-reduction or simplification tools, to detect basic data structures in complex multivariate data. Both techniques may also be used to solve an *unmixing* problem—that is, to sort out independent signals that are jumbled together in observed data. PCA can be used in the second situation, but is far more appropriately employed in the first (data reduction), for which it was designed. ICA can be used in the first sort of situation, but was designed for, and is at present the premier technique for, the second purpose (unmixing signals).

ICA was designed as a method of *blind source separation*, the classic case of which is the "cocktail party problem." Let's say we have three people talking at cocktail party, and we are recording their conversation with three microphones placed at random in the room. Each of the microphones will generate a recording which is a mixture of the three speakers, and we want a method of pulling apart the three recordings so as to isolate, as much as possible, the individual voice of each speaker. In this situation, we can make a crucial assumption of the statistical *independence* of the sound waves emitted by the three individual speakers. Leveraging this assumed independence permits ICA to perform superbly at this sort of disaggregation problem.

ICA is thus distinguished from PCA by its use of statistical independence, instead of uncorrelatedness, as its guiding principle for separating out data into components. But how do independence and uncorrelatedness differ? Basically, independence is a much stronger condition. For two variables to be uncorrelated it is required only that they have no *linear* relation to each other. They may, however, have a distinct *nonlinear* relation. Orthogonality, or uncorrelatedness, is a necessary but insufficient condition for independence.

Now, if two variables are uncorrelated *and* normally distributed, then they are by definition independent. And since PCA extracts components which are Gaussian, the distinction between uncorrelatedness and independence is, for PCA, moot. ICA, however, assumes that the basic structure of the data consists of elements which are non-Gaussian; indeed, ICA has been described as *non-Gaussian factor analysis*.

This is an important point to emphasize to potential users of ICA. All methods should be used in situations where they are appropriate to the task at hand, and for the most part that is the case if the assumptions which guide the methodology seem reasonable for the real-world situation we are analyzing. ICA makes sense to use if and only if we think that the underlying components of the data are continuous but not normally distributed— indeed, if they are *maximally non-Gaussian.* In practice, non-Gaussianity has to do with *kurtosis*—the "peakedness" of the distribution of the components in question. ICA extracts components that are either highly peaked (*leptokurtic*) or very unpeaked (*platykurtic*). So, if one has reason to believe that the basic elements underlying the data in question are structured by basic elements which are either highly concentrated about the mean or particularly unconcentrated (or, more likely, a mixture of both platykurtic and leptokurtic components), then ICA is ideal. Conversely, if one is convinced that the basic elements are normally distributed, then ICA should be avoided in favor of PCA or factor analysis.

ICA works according to the following steps.

1. *Specification of the number of independent components to be extracted.* With ICA, the researcher must specify how many basic elements or dimensions they believe underlie the data at hand. This researcher involvement is more important than with PCA or factor analysis. In the latter cases, programs typically generate as many factors or components as there are variables used in the analysis, and the researcher decides after the fact (after analyzing a scree plot or using some other criteria) how many will be retained. ICA, by contrast, will only extract the number of components that the researcher stipulates beforehand. In blind-source-separation situations, the number of independent signal sources is typically known, so this limitation is not a problem. But in social science situations, where often the number of basic elements or components is unknown, it is more problematic. Additionally, to the best of our knowledge, counterparts to the scree plot or the percentage of variance explained have not been developed for ICA.

2. *Whitening of the data.* The program proceeds to produce a set of components which are not correlated, as is done in PCA. In this sense, PCA is the first stage of ICA.

3. *Finding the decorrelation rotation of the components which is maximally non-Guassian.* Maximal nonnormality is determined in one of two ways. The first finds components whose kurtosis varies (either positively or negatively) from the kurtosis of a normal distribution. The second makes use of a statistical quantity called *negentropy,* which is the difference in entropy relative to what would be expected in a normal distribution with the same variance.

AN EXAMPLE OF ICA USING R

ICA has not been incorporated into any of the major commercial statistical software programs, like Stata, SPSS, and SAS (although, with strong enough mathematical chops, one could program ICA for Stata or SAS). However, some programs that implement ICA have been written for R (and for MATLAB). Here we show how to implement ICA using an R package called fastICA (Marchini, Heaton, and Ripley 2012).

As with PCA, we make use of the 2012 county election data. We retrieve the fastICA package from R, and load the program into working memory:

```
install.packages("fastICA")
library(fastICA)
```

Next, we column-bind the variables from which we would like to extract independent components, and store them in matrix *X*. Here we select 21 separate variables measuring various demographic and socioeconomic characteristics of the counties and form them into a 3114 × 21 matrix.

```
X<- cbind(lnpopdens,agelt18, age1834, age65over, perwhite,
    perasian, perblack, perlatin, edhigher, edhs, edlhs,
    unempmale, unempfem, perpov_q, imdens, divorce2per,
    samesexper, evprot10, hhsize, occprofman, medinc)
```

The fastICA program is executed by the following code:

```
ica1<-fastICA(X, 5, alg.typ = "parallel", fun = "logcosh",
    row.norm = TRUE, maxit = 200, tol = 0.00001, verbose =
    TRUE)
```

Let's trace exactly what it is we are doing here. We are generating an object called "ica1" by performing the function fastICA on object *X*, our matrix of 21 variables. The next option tells fastICA to generate five independent components (the choice of which number, in this case, is rather arbitrary since we are not grounded by a priori knowledge or theory). Next, we have selected `alg.typ = "parallel"`, which means that the program will extract the components simultaneously; had we instead specified `"deflation"`, the components would have been extracted one at a time. There is not a lot of guidance on this decision, and if all one is trying to do is to extract independent components from data then it doesn't seem to matter all that much. In our analyses, components selected with parallel and sequential extraction are equally unrelated, and are moderately correlated with each other.

Next, there are a series of options which bear on the speed of convergence. ICA is an iterative algorithm which seeks to generate uncorrelated components which are maximally non-Gaussian. But there are two different ways to maximize non-Gaussianity, specified through the `fun` option. We can select either an exponential function (`fun = "exp"`) or the log of the hyperbolic cosine (`fun = "logcosh"`). Both will work well, according to the developers of ICA, but in our experience `logcosh` is a bit faster. Next, we need to choose whether the rows of the data matrix ought to be normalized prior to analysis. Selecting TRUE leads to slightly faster convergence. The next two options more directly control the number of iterations which occur before the program is allowed to

```
> ica1<-fastICA(X, 5, alg.typ = "parallel", fun = "exp", row.norm=FALSE, maxit=200, tol=0.00001, verbose=TRUE)
Centering
Whitening
Symmetric FastICA using exponential approx. to neg-entropy function
Iteration 1 tol = 0.2260052
Iteration 2 tol = 0.03040553
Iteration 3 tol = 0.004389073
Iteration 4 tol = 0.001747418
Iteration 5 tol = 0.0008245586
Iteration 6 tol = 0.0002008048
Iteration 7 tol = 5.819656e-05
Iteration 8 tol = 1.502786e-05
Iteration 9 tol = 3.911512e-06
> |
```

FIGURE 8.4

Independent component analysis output in R, displaying model convergence.

settle on results. First, we choose the maximum number of iterations to perform. And secondly, we choose the tolerance, which is a statistical quantity of fit. In general, convergence is fairly quick using fastICA, so we advise setting maxit relatively high. It should be looked at more as a safeguard than anything else. Instead, one should control the quality of convergence with the tolerance parameter. Higher values of tolerance will lead to faster convergence but will be less reliable. So we advise setting tol quite low. In our data, even if we set tol to something absolutely miniscule (like `tol = 0.000000000002`), convergence occurs after only 32 iterations, although with a larger dataset or more input variables it would take longer. Finally, as with many R commands, there is a `verbose` option. Choosing `TRUE` will let you know how many iterations occur before convergence, and what the tolerance is at each step.

We run the command, and get the output shown in figure 8.4. This tells us only that we achieve convergence in nine iterations, even with a low tolerance. As is typical with R, the immediate output is uninformative. But we can look at the structure of the object we generated (ica1) in figure 8.5.

Note that the object has a number of components (appearing here as $X, $K, etc.). The most immediately relevant are the rows labeled $A and $S. $A contains weights for each variable from which the factors were extracted, but to view it in a manner that is understandable it needs to be transposed.

The rows shown in the R output in figure 8.6 relate to our original variables; the columns, to our five components. The independent components, like principal components, are formed as a linear combination (specifically, a weighted sum) of these variables. Row variable 1 is, here, the natural log of population density. We can see that it is negatively related to all five components (reading across the first row of figure 8.6 we see only negative loadings). Row variable 5 is the percentage of county population that is non-Hispanic white; reading across this row reveals that this variable is positively related to all but the second component. We can produce a scatterplot matrix (figure 8.7) that will demonstrate the independence of the components:

```
pairs(ica1$S)
```

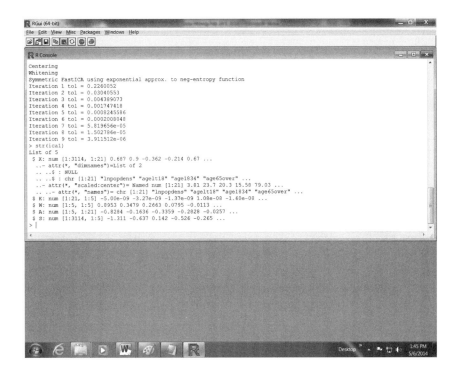

FIGURE 8.5

Independent component analysis output in R, displaying elements stored in the object ica1.

```
> icax<-t(ica1$A)
> icax
             [,1]          [,2]         [,3]          [,4]          [,5]
 [1,] -8.283974e-01 -1.635510e-01  -0.33586791 -2.828321e-01   -0.02569168
 [2,] -7.534602e-01  1.188017e+00   0.81876368 -3.412732e-01   -0.26775500
 [3,] -6.857371e-01  7.673276e-01  -2.36287292 -1.042139e+00   -0.03683924
 [4,]  2.048622e+00 -8.168581e-01   0.54752415  9.015014e-01    0.26740844
 [5,]  3.896963e+00 -1.275983e+01   2.80395509  1.343995e+01    2.37669696
 [6,] -1.084192e+00  3.871865e-01  -0.68739616 -6.672089e-02    0.41238990
 [7,] -1.789888e+00 -1.192614e+00  -0.80462510 -1.391951e+01   -2.86030378
 [8,] -1.511812e+00  1.248646e+01  -0.55644999  1.157924e+00   -0.54341440
 [9,] -4.994147e+00 -6.564257e-01  -5.45941235  1.192229e+00    3.85955798
[10,]  3.222079e+00 -2.055457e+00   4.66016941  6.636984e-02   -1.49410152
[11,]  2.199088e+00  2.957579e+00   1.29134600 -2.508304e+00   -4.12948385
[12,]  6.391428e-01  2.044565e+00   0.01991776 -1.601425e+00   -0.80343201
[13,]  2.916598e-01  4.057088e-01   0.02993627 -1.595181e+00   -0.97189036
[14,]  3.150933e+00  1.318655e+00  -1.92242399 -2.538748e+00   -1.84009937
[15,] -2.282504e+00  3.608501e+00  -1.13242145  1.399252e-01    0.49048434
[16,]  6.986458e-01  6.074155e-01  -1.01934678 -3.223424e+00   -1.77173634
[17,] -6.764998e-02 -7.919631e-03  -0.05714206  7.658156e-03    0.03281129
[18,]  2.933898e-01 -1.625769e+00  -1.70527143 -2.081538e+00  -15.93016197
[19,] -7.096410e-02  1.109367e-01   0.04352250 -5.177998e-02   -0.04362304
[20,] -2.866001e+00 -7.831559e-01  -3.50091146  1.137107e+00    2.95849352
[21,] -1.025127e+04 -8.270563e+02 357.06189755  3.213813e+03 3855.12223523
> |
```

FIGURE 8.6

Loadings of variables (rows) on components (columns) from independent component analysis (using R package fastICA).

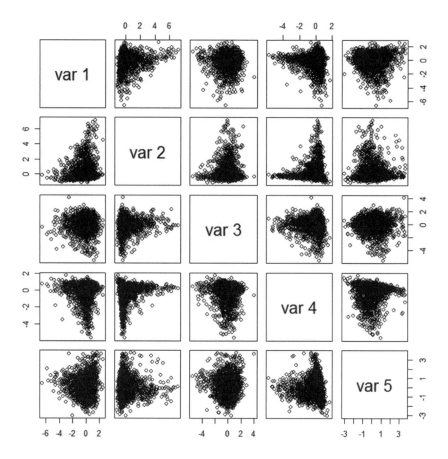

FIGURE 8.7
Scatterplot matrix of independent components (in R).

In component S are stored the actual values of each component for each case. It will be a bit easier to look at this if we turn S into a series of five variables:

```
comp1<-ica1$S[1:3114, 1]
comp2<-ica1$S[1:3114, 2]
comp3<-ica1$S[1:3114, 3]
comp4<-ica1$S[1:3114, 4]
comp5<-ica1$S[1:3114, 5]
```

Now we can use these variables as predictors in a regression predicting Obama's vote share in given counties (table 8.6). The regression begins in the column labeled (1) with the first independent component, and then adds the rest one at a time. It is important to recall that the dependent variable was not a member of the variable set from which the independent components were extracted, so any variance in this dependent

TABLE 8.6 Regression of Obama Vote Share on Components from Independent Component Analysis

	(1)	(2)	(3)	(4)	(5)
Comp 1	−5.0855***	−5.085***	−5.085***	−5.085***	−5.085***
	(0.2496)	(0.238)	(0.238)	(0.215)	(0.214)
Comp 2	–	4.214***	4.213***	4.213***	4.213***
		(0.238)	(0.238)	(0.215)	(0.214)
Comp 3	–	–	0.035 (0.238)	0.035 (0.215)	0.035 (0.214)
Comp 4	–	–	–	5.667***	5.667***
				(0.215)	(0.214)
Comp 5	–	–	–		−1.255***
					(0.214)
Constant	38.4431	38.443	38.443 (0.238)	38.443 (0.215)	38.443 (0.214)
	(0.2496)	(0.238)			
R^2	.1177	.1984	.1984	.3446	.3517
Adj. R^2	.1174	.1979	.1977	.3437	.3507

***p < .001.

variable explained by the independent components is due either to random chance or to their relation to the original variables in the set. It also bears keeping in mind that a regression model using this full set of predictors (i.e. before doing ICA) had an R^2 of .5855.

A few things are immediately apparent from this analysis. First, the full set of five independent components has just over half of the explanatory power of original variable model. Thus, though we have performed substantial data simplification, it is at the price of considerably lowering our model's predictive power. Second, the fact that the variables are unrelated to each other is immediately made apparent by the fact that, as with PCA, regression coefficients do not alter at all when additional components are added. Indeed, if they did change, this would imply substantial correlation among the variables. But linear regression, of course, can only give us hints as to whether or not the components are *correlated*, not whether they are independent.

Third, there is something strange going on with the standard errors in this analysis. Within models, they are exactly the same for all components (and the intercept). And they are very similar across models. This is probably because the components are maximally non-Gaussian. As nonnormal variables (which are similarly nonnormal), they confound the very attempt to calculate a standard error, which assumes normality. Finally, the constant term does not alter at all from one model to the next. In fact, it is equal to the mean of the dependent variable for the full data. (Yes, the mean vote for counties was 38.44% for Obama. Obama won handily in more populous counties and lost the very sparsely populated ones, and population is concentrated in a relatively small number of counties.) This is because the data were normalized before we extracted components. Therefore, all of the components have means quite close to zero. That the constant term remains at the population mean is therefore true by definition.

SUMMARY

Variable extraction methods are used to reduce the number of variables, prior to undertaking an analysis, through discovering a small number of uncorrelated components or factors that summarize a larger number of measured variables. In contrast to the data-reduction methods discussed earlier (such as stepwise regression), which pick out the most important predictors from among a longer list of candidate predictors, variable extraction methods attempt to summarize all of the available variables. More precisely, variable extraction decomposes the covariance matrix that describes the relations between measured variables. PCA and ICA both attempt to summarize the covariance matrix with fewer orthogonal eigenvectors or components.

These are *unsupervised* methods: they do not involve a dependent variable. Instead, they summarize the relations between all attributes, predictors, or independent variables. Unfortunately, there is a trade-off between simplification and accuracy. The extracted components rarely account for the entirety of the covariance embodied in the larger number of measured variables. Moreover, even when extracted components do summarize most of the covariance among predictors, it does not follow that a model that uses those extracted components to predict a dependent variable will necessarily provide good predictions. In fact, in the examples shown above, we repeatedly found that the original variables taken as a group performed better in terms of predicting a dependent variable than the components extracted from them. Nevertheless, both PCA and ICA techniques are used by data miners, especially in situations where there are so many measured variables (very large P) that the analyst has little choice but to summarize them by extracting a smaller number of components. Data miners would describe this extraction process as reducing the dimensionality of data while preserving its original structure or pattern.

9

CLASSIFIERS

In data mining, *classifiers* are programs that predict which category or class of a dependent variable individual observations fall into. For example, we previously classified individuals according to whether or not they have health insurance, making use of several demographic characteristics. In some types of classification algorithms, classification involves developing a predictive statistical model, using a set of independent variables or attributes to predict each individual's value on an outcome or dependent variable or *target*. That prediction, in the form of a probability that a given case will fall into a certain category or class, is then used to *classify* which category any given observation is assigned to.

Other types of classification algorithms do not employ a predictive model of this type but instead use nonparametric methods to decide what class of an outcome variable each observation falls into. But all types of classification involve *supervised learning*: using a training dataset that contains cases for which one already knows the correct classification of each observation in order to develop some kind of predictive rule. That rule can then be applied to a dataset where one does not know the category or class of each case, in order to classify these new cases.

In the following sections we give examples of several different classifiers used by data miners. Computer scientists have developed numerous algorithms for classifying. They vary according to their processing speed and accuracy; moreover, some work better for certain datasets than for others. Practitioners don't usually know in advance which classifier will work best for their data, so it is not unusual to try several classifiers and compare their accuracy on test datasets, or even to combine the predictions derived from different classifiers into one, in what is known as *ensemble learning*. Combining multiple classifiers into one ensemble can often yield a result that is more accurate than the best of the individual classifiers.

K-NEAREST NEIGHBORS

The *k*-nearest neighbors (KNN) classifier is a nonparametric method of classification. As a classifier, it is quite simple and intuitive. Imagine that we have a set S of data points whose membership in one of two classes we would like to estimate. For these points we have information about their values on other variables, X. This means, among other things, that we can locate each of the data points in S in a multidimensional space defined by these input variables X. For each member of S we can identify its *nearest neighbors*— nearest in terms of having similar values on X—among the other data points. We can then assign each data point S_i to the class to which most of its nearest neighbors belong.

For instance, we might have data describing a group of three- and four-year-old children. From these data, we know some things about all of the children: their household income, their parents' educational attainment and labor-force status, and the population density and median household income of their census tract, and so on. In this situation, we might use KNN classification to predict the preschool status of a child simply by assigning that child the preschool status of the other children who are most similar to that child in terms of the family and neighborhood measures. Essentially, what we are doing in this technique is taking a case, looking around it at other, similar cases, and using these cases to guess at its class membership.

This technique can be used for more than just binary classification. It can be employed for multicategory classification as well (though the probability of a "tie" increases with the number of categories), or for predicting the value of a continuous outcome. In this latter case, it calculates a measure of centrality from the neighbors (most commonly the mean or the median) and applies it as a prediction for the case in question. KNN regression is thus quite similar to local smoothing and kernel-based techniques such as local linear regression (Altman 1992).

There are a few preliminary questions one encounters before performing this technique. First, how many neighbors should one choose? This choice can be very consequential, for cases can be assigned to different categories depending on whether, for instance, three nearest neighbors are "polled" rather than seven. In an early formulation, Cover and Hart (1967) argued that using just one neighbor can be sufficient and even preferable. However, Hastie and Tibshirani (1996) suggested that whether a single neighbor is optimal is highly dependent on the number of features used to determine distance. The radius employed to search around a case increases with the number of predictors employed, drawing more distant cases in as possible nearest neighbors.

A solution to the problem of how many neighbors to use involves, not surprisingly, yet another nonparametric technique. One can use cross-validation to select the best value of k. Specifically, we split the data randomly into three parts: training, validation, and test data. We generate estimates using several different values of k in the training set; then select the best value of k by employing the validation set to see which k yields the most accurate classification; finally, we evaluate fit in the test dataset.

A second preliminary issue is determining the criterion for deciding which data points are closest—that is, what type of distance one will use to determine which points are "nearest." Most commonly, KNN techniques use Euclidian, Manhattan (city-block), or Minkowski distance, though other types of distance (Mahalanobis, for instance) could be employed.

Third, and related to the prior two matters, is the matter of "vote counting." That is, after we choose k, and determine how to measure distance, we will get, for each data point, a set of k other data points which provide information for class prediction. These k points are in essence "voting" on the membership or class of the target case. But since these k points might not agree, how should we tally these votes? Ought we to count them all equally? Or ought we to regard the votes of the closer data points as more informative? Generally, the practice is to weight votes inversely to the distance from the observation in question (Dudani 1976). Doing so, incidentally, to some degree mitigates how consequential the choice of k is. That is, when we increase k, we are increasing the size of the space around the data point where we are searching for information about class membership, and in doing so we increase the chance that we will make an error because we might "cross over" from a space in which one class is dominant to that in which the other is dominant. This is particularly important for boundary cases (that is, the cases in one class which are most similar to cases in the other class). But weighting by inverse distance downplays the importance of cases which are further away and increases the influence of cases which are closer.

A final preliminary matter which is consequential is the number of predictor variables which are made use of in determining distance—the X's discussed earlier. It would seem, intuitively, that choosing as many predictor variables as possible would be ideal since it would give us more information about which cases are "really" similar rather than just similar on a small number of rather arbitrarily chosen characteristics. However, it turns out that having too much information can be a problem. Increasing the number of features or predictors increases the dimensionality of the search space and therefore the search space's overall size (think about moving from a circle surrounding a point to a sphere with the same radius around that point). By doing so, we end up increasing the number of "neighbors" which are equidistant from the point in question (the one we want to classify). With a large enough number of features, we end up with a search space described by an n-sphere (that is, a sphere in n dimensions, where n is the number of features), the surface of which is occupied by a large number of data points which "tie" in terms of distance from the point at the center. In this situation the KNN method is fatally compromised by the curse of dimensionality (Hastie and Tibshirani 1996).

Having a large number of features, then, necessitates some method of dimensionality reduction—either feature extraction or feature selection (or even a combination of the two). Principal components or random projection could be used to collapse the dimensionality of the space. Or we could draft stepwise, LASSO, or stagewise to select the dimensions which are most consequential.

KNN, though it has been around in various forms for decades, has never found a home in the social sciences (for an exception, see Qian and Rasheed 2010), though it has been used in applied settings such as facial recognition, text categorization, biology, and credit application screening.

K-NEAREST NEIGHBORS USING SPSS MODELER

Programs for running a KNN classifier have been written for MATLAB and R (package knn). SPSS's data mining package, Modeler, also has a KNN routine, and it is this we demonstrate below. We demonstrate its predictive capacity using data from the American Community Survey and using KNN to predict health insurance status.

Modeler is a very accessible system, developed for use by applied data miners—people in business, marketing, and so on. Like some other recent applications (RapidMiner, for instance), its format has the user construct "streams" of analyses. Each stream consists of a series of connected "nodes," each of which represents a series of operations carried out on the data. Double-clicking a node icon opens a window with node-specific options. These windows are quite similar to those in SPSS Statistics, and options are altered largely through pointing and clicking rather than through syntax.

We randomly sampled 6,000 cases from our larger dataset, because Modeler, like many other data mining programs, can run quite slowly when performing complex operations on very big data. Additionally, we balanced the data on the outcome when we sampled, so that we drew a 6,000-case sample divided evenly into cases with and without health insurance. We did this to remove from the program the temptation to simply assign all cases to the majority category (a strategy which, incidentally, would yield a not-unrespectable 13% error rate).

In the Modeler program we pass the data file through a Type node in which we choose the target variable and clean up the levels of measurement of other variables. Next, we partition the data into a 50% training set and a 50% test set, because cross-validation is absolutely necessary to use with KNN classification. Finally, in this stream we set a KNN node (figure 9.1).

The KNN routine has a fairly large number of options built into it, lending it a fair amount of flexibility. After double-clicking the node, a window opens which allows you to choose, in the Objectives tab, whether you want to use KNN simply to find the nearest neighbors of each case or as an actual classifier. Since we want the latter, we select "Predict a target field." Next, the program asks whether we care most about getting the project done quickly, being very accurate, or a combination of the two, or whether we want to customize the model. The first three options allow the user three different methods for

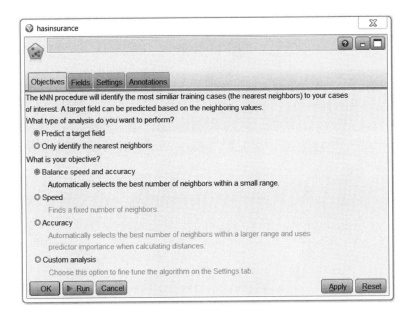

FIGURE 9.1

The *k*-nearest neighbors classifier in SPSS Modeler.

the model to choose default settings. We strongly encourage users to simply click "Custom analysis" and move on to the settings themselves.

Next, in the Fields tab, we chose our model (figure 9.2). Here we are predicting health insurance coverage using census region, age, race, gender, citizenship status, educational attainment, marital status, household income, and employment status as predictors.

In the Settings tab (figure 9.3) are a number of subsections which enable parameter-setting. Under Model, you choose whether you want to use partitioned data to cross-validate results, and set your partition variable. You can also choose whether you want to build separate models for different sets of cases. This means you could run separate classifications for men and women, for example, or split the data into randomized subgroups and run separate classifications routines for each. This latter option will drastically increase the amount of time it takes for the operation to run. You may want to simply run separate routines manually on separate datasets, as Modeler can have any number of datasets "open" at once.

Next, under Neighbors, we set values for *k*. The speediest route is to supply the program with a fixed *k*. But one can also choose a range, and the program will choose the value that minimizes the validation error rate. This involves running multiple KNN analyses, and so increases operating time substantially. However, it is more important to get *k* right, and selecting either too high or too low a value of *k* will decrease the predictive accuracy of the model. We set the lower bound to 3 and the upper bound to 25 to enable the program quite a bit of flexibility in choosing the best value of *k*.

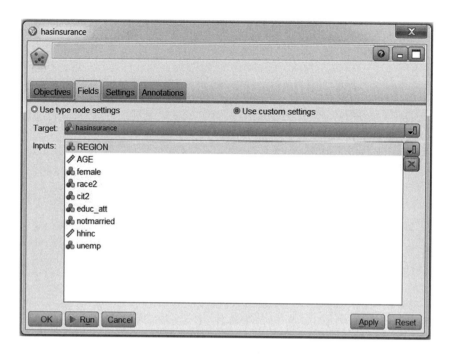

FIGURE 9.2

K-nearest neighbors classifier input in SPSS Modeler.

In this tab you also choose the distance metric you will use, and whether or not features are weighted. The program can calculate either Euclidian distance or city-block (Manhattan) distance; we prefer Euclidean. We also choose to weight predictors by their importance, meaning that the predictors which are most important in predicting group membership overall will be relied upon more in calculating distances to potential neighbors.

Next, under Feature Selection, you choose whether or not you want the program to select features, to decide on which particular predictor variables to use. If you have even a middling number of features—15 or 20, perhaps—using some method of eliminating redundant or unhelpful features is probably a good idea. We do not face this situation, and so we elect to not perform feature selection.

The settings for Cross-Validation include parameters which can only be altered if feature selection is *not* being performed. They allow the researcher to perform *k*-fold cross-validation, and to set a seed for randomly assigning cases to folds so that the analysis can be replicated. We are using random holdback cross-validation, so this is unnecessary (and in fact the program will not allow you to choose *k*-fold cross-validation if you have already entered a validation variable). Finally, we run the model by clicking Run.

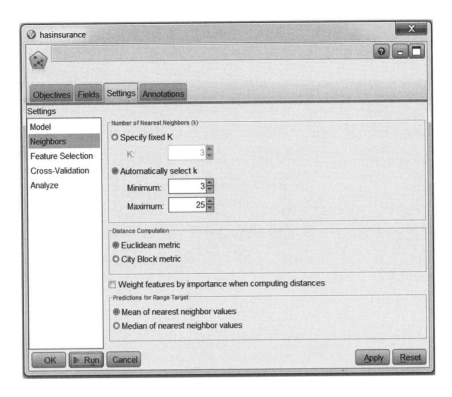

FIGURE 9.3

Parameter specification for k-nearest neighbors classifier in SPSS Modeler.

The "model nugget" produced by Modeler shows us how the error rate varied with k (figure 9.4). It began relatively high, around 30.0%, when k was 1 or 2, and dropped—quickly at first, and then more slowly—until k reached 20 (about 27.5%). After this point the error rate began to rise again. Two things are important to note in this instance. First, the error rate shows a curvilinear relation with k. That the error rate rises fairly consistently after $k = 13$ is important, for it lets us know that we probably did not simply identify a local minimum. Secondly, we should note that the error rate varies somewhat but not drastically. For most data this will probably be the case, which indicates that mistakes in choosing k are not necessarily of massive practical consequence. Here the range in the error rate is less than 4 percentage points. On the other hand, this does show that by selecting a wide range of possible values of k it is often possible to do better in terms of prediction.

By adding an Analysis node to the stream, we can investigate how well the model has worked. The KNN classifier performs admirably, correctly classifying 74% of the training data and 75% of the test data. We note also that it has decent predictive capacity for both true positives (those with insurance) and true negatives. In the training data, the model

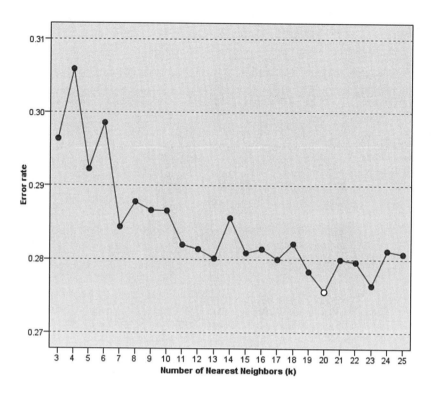

FIGURE 9.4

A graph of error rate by value of *k* in *k*-nearest neighbors classification (SPSS
Modeler).

sensitivity is 71.5% and the specificity is 76.2%. Comparable numbers for the test data
are 70.6% and 78.1%.

Modeler calculates "propensity scores" for its classifications that indicate how sure the
program is in its prediction. In the Confidence Values Report (figure 9.5), we see that
Modeler is correct in 100% of the cases when it is 90.9% sure of its prediction in both
the training and test data.

How does KNN stack up against other predictive models in our data? Table 9.1 compares it against four other methods: logistic regression, partition trees, support vector
machines, and a neural network. The answer seems to be: fairly well. The other models
do a better job of predicting true positives, and KNN does a better job of predicting true
negatives.

We have begun our discussion of classification tools—a huge field in data mining—
with a discussion of the nonparametric *k*-nearest neighbors classifier. This classifier
performs quite well on our American Community Survey data in predicting health insurance coverage, though it is not obviously superior to other classifiers. We continue, in the
next section, to analyze other classification algorithms.

Results for output field hasinsurance

Comparing $KNN-hasinsurance with hasinsurance

'Partition'	1_Training		2_Testing	
Correct	2,175	73.75%	2,273	74.5%
Wrong	774	26.25%	778	25.5%
Total	2,949		3,051	

Coincidence Matrix for $KNN-hasinsurance (rows show actuals)

'Partition' = 1_Training	0.000000	1.000000	$null$
0.000000	1,077	326	10
1.000000	410	1,098	28
'Partition' = 2_Testing	0.000000	1.000000	$null$
0.000000	1,240	342	5
1.000000	405	1,033	26

Performance Evaluation

'Partition' = 1_Training	
0.000000	0.413
1.000000	0.392
'Partition' = 2_Testing	
0.000000	0.371
1.000000	0.448

Confidence Values Report for $KNNP-hasinsurance

'Partition' = 1_Training	
Range	0.5 - 0.955
Mean Correct	0.73
Mean Incorrect	0.633
Always Correct Above	0.909 (2.82% of cases)
Always Incorrect Below	0.5 (0% of cases)
90.56% Accuracy Above	0.727
2.0 Fold Correct Above	0.876 (68.18% of cases)
'Partition' = 2_Testing	
Range	0.5 - 0.955
Mean Correct	0.737
Mean Incorrect	0.634
Always Correct Above	0.909 (3.41% of cases)
Always Incorrect Below	0.5 (0% of cases)
90.78% Accuracy Above	0.727
2.0 Fold Correct Above	0.883 (68.18% of cases)

FIGURE 9.5

Output from *k*-nearest neighbors classifier in SPSS Modeler.

TABLE 9.1 Comparing *K*-Nearest Neighbors to Other Classifiers

	Accuracy (training)	Accuracy (test)	Sensitivity (test)	Specificity (test)
K-nearest neighbors	73.8%	74.5%	70.6%	78.1%
Logistic regression	72.19%	73.1%	73.6%	72.3%
Support vector machine	79.25%	72.93%	73.6%	74.4%
Neural network	72.74%	72.89%	72.60%	73.2%
Partition tree	75.82%	73.45%	75.61%	71.1%

NAIVE BAYES

The naive Bayes classifier is a very straightforward, apparently simple classifier which has proven remarkably successful in applications such as spam filtering and document classification. It is more than 40 years old, and until quite recently, it was used in most applications of information retrieval (Lewis 1998). It works on the unrealistic assumptions that (a) the contributions of all predictor variables to the overall prediction or classification are equally important, and (b) the effects of the predictors are independent of each another. These unrealistic assumptions, which give "naive" Bayes its name, allow it to be quite computationally efficient, and to require very little training data for the development of parameter estimates. And despite the unrealistic assumptions on which it is based, it often performs quite well in comparison to more complicated, computationally intensive algorithms (Rish 2001; Zhang 2004).

In any classification problem there are an outcome class we are trying to predict and a set of input variables which we use to build this prediction. We are, then, estimating the probability of the class given the input variable(s). Bayes's theorem famously rewrites this classification problem as:

$$p(Y = y | X = x) = p(Y = y)p(X = x | Y = y)/p(X=x)$$

That is, the probability of the outcome given the input(s) is the product of the probability of the outcome and the probability of the input(s) given the outcome, divided by the probability of the inputs. And if there are multiple variables in a vector X, we simply multiply conditional probabilities. We can do this for each category of Y, and then assign each case to that class of Y for which the estimated probability (or "posterior probability") is highest. A naive Bayes classifier uses training data to estimate the values of the parameters on the right-hand side of the above equation, and applies these estimates to test data for classification (Lewis 1998).

Naive Bayes differs from regression in two important ways. First, it does not treat any one of these predictors as more important than any other—which is essentially what coefficients in a logistic regression model do, by acting as weights by which each variable's value is multiplied. Second, whereas regression models estimate *partial effects* of variables—the independent average marginal impact of each variable when the values of all others are held constant—naive Bayes permits the conditional probabilities of the predictors to be entirely independent of each other.

AN EXAMPLE IN RAPIDMINER

Routines for performing naive Bayes classification have been written for R (the command naiveBayes in the larger package e1071) and MATLAB. There is an application for it in SPSS Statistics Server, and macros for its use have been written for SAS and Python.

In this worked example we will build a naive Bayes classifier using the free software package RapidMiner (easily downloaded from http://rapidminer.com/). Much like SPSS

Modeler discussed above, RapidMiner operates through the user-friendly streams-and-nodes format. The reader should note, though, that the naive Bayes algorithm is not contained in the version of RapidMiner which is downloadable from the website indicated above. Adding it is free, but it must be downloaded separately via RapidMiner's extensions marketplace. Look for the extensions marketplace under the Help menu when the RapidMiner program interface is opened.

We use data from the American Community Survey to predict health insurance status. The data were randomly sampled and balanced so that insured and uninsured individuals each comprise 50% of the cases. As we have discussed already, balancing the data on the outcome is often a good idea when performing a test of a classifier. Doing this removes from the classifier the temptation to take the easy way to minimizing the error rate by simply classifying all cases as belonging to the dominant class.

Several preliminary steps need to be undertaken in order for the naive Bayes classifier to run smoothly in RapidMiner. Firstly, although naive Bayes can in theory handle continuous predictors (calculating the conditional probability from a Gaussian distribution), in our experience RapidMiner works better, and much faster, if continuous predictors are discretized ahead of time. Secondly, Rapidminer by default reads all variables with numeric values as continuous variables. In other words, categorical variables and dummy variables need to be recoded from numbers into string variables (with string values) for RapidMiner to be able to read those variables correctly.

After discretizing continuous variables and creating string values, we designate 70% of our data to train the model and 30% to test it. We then run the naive Bayes model. In RapidMiner, this appears onscreen as shown in figures 9.6 and 9.7.

The confusion matrix (table 9.2) indicates that the model has an overall accuracy of 72.42% in the test data. This suggests that it is competitive with other classifiers, such as *k*-nearest neighbors, which we have investigated previously.

RapidMiner also gives us estimates of probability distributions, in a "model distribution table" (table 9.3). These are, the reader will remember, the probability of the attribute given class membership, not the other way around (which is why the probabilities do not sum to 100). They should be read as follows. The probability that a case is *white* given that it is *insured* is .732, and the probability that it is *white* given that it is *not insured* is .513. Whites thus constitute the majority of both insured and uninsured people, but they are overrepresented among the insured. By contrast, the probability of *black* given *insurance* is .099, and the probability of *black* given *no insurance* is .125. This indicates that African Americans are overrepresented among those lacking health insurance.

If we choose, we can estimate from this distribution table the likelihood that an individual with a given mix of characteristics will be insured or not insured. For instance, consider a person who is black, is single, has a bachelor's degree, lives in the Central U.S. Region, is not Hispanic, is not foreign-born, owns his or her home, is not a veteran, is employed, is age 27, and lives in a household making $70K a year. We can multiply the baseline probability of the outcome by the probabilities of these attributes reported in the

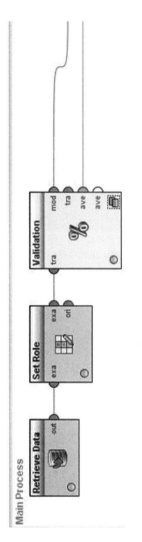

FIGURE 9.6

Constructing a naive Bayes stream in RapidMiner (first frame).

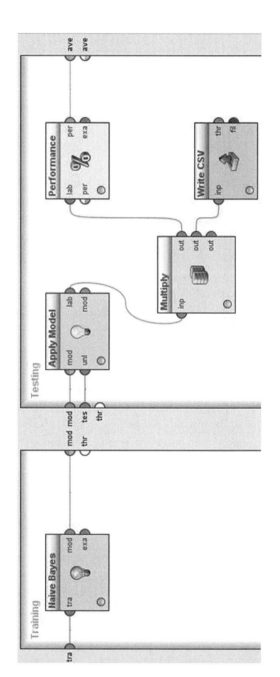

FIGURE 9.7

Constructing a naive Bayes stream in RapidMiner (second frame).

TABLE 9.2 Confusion Matrix from Naive Bayes Classifier

	True insured	True uninsured	Accuracy
Predicted insured	83,239	33,278	71.44%
Predicted uninsured	28,256	78,326	73.49%
Total accuracy rate			72.42%

TABLE 9.3 Model Distribution Table from Naive Bayes Classifier

Attribute	Parameter (X)	Pr(X)|Insured	Pr(X)|Uninsured
Race	White	0.732	0.513
Race	Black	0.099	0.125
Race	Asian	0.048	0.052
Race	Native American	0.007	0.016
Race	Hispanic	0.112	0.291
Race	Other	0.001	0.002
Marital status	Single	0.388	0.492
Marital status	Married, spouse present	0.449	0.310
Marital status	Married, spouse absent	0.012	0.029
Marital status	Separated	0.013	0.030
Marital status	Divorced	0.080	0.120
Marital status	Widowed	0.058	0.019
Education	Less than high school	0.331	0.344
Education	High school	0.209	0.306
Education	Some college	0.171	0.203
Education	Associate's degree	0.059	0.050
Education	Bachelor's degree	0.144	0.076
Education	Graduate degree	0.088	0.022
Region	Pacific	0.154	0.186
Region	Mountain	0.070	0.082
Region	Central	0.396	0.400
Region	Northeast	0.187	0.120
Region	South Atlantic	0.192	0.213
Hispanic	No	0.888	0.709
Hispanic	Yes	0.112	0.291
Foreign-born	No	0.962	0.805
Foreign-born	Yes	0.038	0.195
Homeowner	Yes	0.761	0.553
Homeowner	No	0.239	0.447
Gender	Female	0.523	0.468

(continued)

TABLE 9.3 (continued)

Attribute	Parameter (X)	Pr(X)|Insured	Pr(X)|Uninsured
Gender	Male	0.477	0.532
Veteran status	No	0.911	0.970
Veteran status	Yes	0.089	0.030
Employment status	Not employed	0.510	0.318
Employment status	Employed	0.490	0.682
Age	Under 10	0.132	0.058
Age	10–18	0.113	0.070
Age	18–30	0.111	0.295
Age	30–37	0.074	0.134
Age	37–44	0.085	0.124
Age	44–50	0.085	0.109
Age	50–56	0.093	0.100
Age	56–64	0.114	0.093
Age	64+	0.193	0.016
Household income	Under $34,300	0.240	0.426
Household income	$34,300–50,000	0.135	0.190
Household income	$50,000–70,900	0.172	0.169
Household income	$70,900–106,000	0.205	0.127
Household income	Over $106,000	0.247	0.087

table above twice: once given insurance, once given lack of insurance. In both cases the probabilities are also multiplied by the prior probability of the outcome (.50 for both having and not having health insurance, given that the data are balanced):

$$\text{Likelihood of being insured} = .50 \times .099 \times .388 \times .144 \times .396 \times .888$$
$$\times .962 \times .761 \times .477 \times .911 \times .490 \times .111 \times .172 = .00000298$$
$$\text{Likelihood of being uninsured} = .50 \times .125 \times .492 \times .076 \times .400 \times .709$$
$$\times .805 \times .553 \times .532 \times .970 \times .682 \times .295 \times .169 = .000005175$$

From this calculation, we can surmise that this type of individual is more likely to be uninsured than insured. To make better sense of this information, we can turn these likelihoods into probabilities:

$$\text{Probability of being insured} = 0.00000298/(0.00000298 +$$
$$0.000005175) = 0.3583 = 35.83\%$$
$$\text{Probability of being uninsured} = 0.000005175/(0.00000298 +$$
$$0.000005175) = 0.6416 = 64.16\%$$

In other words, this type of individual is roughly two times more likely to be uninsured than insured, and naive Bayes would assign them to the uninsured class.

We have seen that naive Bayes can be an efficient, accurate, and informative classifier. It compares quite well with more complex algorithms, and is much more readily understood than many other classifiers, which work more as "black boxes." We move now from one of the simplest classification algorithms to arguably the most complex: the support vector machine.

SUPPORT VECTOR MACHINES

Support vector machines (SVMs) are another type of classifier. The SVM algorithm was developed in the early 1990s by Bell Laboratories researcher Vladimir Vapnik (Boser, Guyon, and Vapnik 1992), and presented in modern form in 1995 by Vapnik and his colleague Corrina Cortes (Cortes and Vapnik 1995). Initially developed as a binary classifier, the SVM framework has since been extended to multicategory classification, regression, clustering, anomaly detection, and even feature selection. However, binary classification remains its most common usage, and we focus on this application in what follows. SVMs have come to be standard fare in fields such as image and text classification and character recognition, and have proven extremely useful in the biomedical sciences for protein classification and cancer detection. However, only recently have they made a limited appearance in the social sciences, in fields such as finance (Gavrishchaka and Banerjee 2006), demography (Kostaki et al. 2011), and marketing (Cui and Curry 2005).

To understand what an SVM does, first consider a set of points in space which are of two categories. SVMs, like other classifiers, seek out a principle which will separate these points into groups with as little error as possible. If our points exist in two-dimensional space, this separator will be a line; in three dimensions, a plane. In higher dimensions, the separator will be a hyperplane. Since SVMs are almost always searching for a classifier in high-dimensional space, they typically seek to describe the hyperplane (or *decision surface*) which will best discriminate between our two groups. Think of a multidimensional space filled with red and blue dots, where the colors are not completely mixed up; rather, there are regions with mainly blue dots and other regions with mainly red dots, and "borders" where one color gives way to the other. The decision surface is an *n*-dimensional plane capable of separating, as much as possible, the blue-dot from the red-dot regions. The question is, where ought this decision surface to be placed?

Unlike regression techniques or many other machine-learning techniques like naive Bayes classifiers or neural networks, SVMs do not use all the available data points to figure out how to separate out the data. Instead, they only use the most troublesome points—the ones closest to the "border" and the separating hyperplane—to decide how to make the discrimination. Data points are, of course, each described by a *set* of coordinates and are therefore *vectors*. The vectors of each category which are closest in space to those of the other category, and which are utilized by the SVM to find the decision surface, are called the *support vectors*.

Now, an infinite number of decision surfaces could be traced or woven between these crucial cases, so we need to choose the one which works best—the one that is optimal. What principle of optimization ought to be used? We can describe, mathematically, the distance between a point and a line. With SVMs, we choose the decision surface for which the distance between it and the support vectors is largest. So imagine a plane set between those red and blue dots that are closest to the boundary, and which maximizes its distance from those two sets of dots. This gap or distance between the support vectors and the decision surface is called the *margin*; SVMs seek the decision surface which maximizes the margin.

So far, then, SVMs are not all that different from more familiar methods. The SVM traces a surface through multidimensional space which describes, efficiently, the relation between attributes and group membership, and so is not really all that different in principle from logistic regression. SVMs are only fundamentally different insofar as they make use of a crucial subset of cases rather than all of them (which renders SVMs more efficient), and because SVMs are maximizing, rather than minimizing, the distance between key points and the line the hyperplane is tracing.

But so far we have assumed that the information we have about our cases or points—our collection of features or variables—will allow us to draw a line or plane or hyperplane through the points which efficiently separates them out into discrete groups. That is, we have assumed that our groups are *linearly separable*.

But often this is not the case. We may, for example, have situations in which one category (or color of dots) are entirely surrounded by those in a different category. If this is true, there is no *linear* separator which can be imagined which would separate the cases out into their respective groups. As long as we are restricted to the n-dimensional space defined by our inputs (the *input space*, in SVM parlance), any classifier will fail to correctly classify a large percentage of cases.

This is where the novelty of SVMs emerges. SVMs interpret this classification difficulty as owing purely to restricted dimensionality. If we could project our data into a higher-dimensional space, we would be able to separate the cases. This hypothetical higher-dimensional (or even infinite-dimensional) space, in which the cases are linearly separable, is referred to as the *feature space*. And mapping the input space into the feature space is merely a matter of applying a mathematical function to the data to appropriately transform them into a higher-dimensional space.

The difficulty is that the characteristics of this feature space are not actually known to us, so it is not generally possible to know the exact mathematical function we need. But it turns out that this does not actually matter. All we need to do is define a *kernel function* which will approximate it (which SVM developers refer to as the *kernel trick*). There are many such kernel functions, and generally SVM programs will provide the user with a few options as to which kernel to use. The best kernel for the job is not something we can typically know ahead of time (unless you are very good at mapping data into higher dimensions in your head), so the choice can only really be made through trial and error.

Statistics File

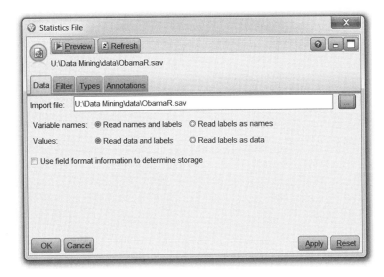

FIGURE 9.8
Uploading data for a support vector machine analysis in SPSS Modeler.

One difficulty with such a maneuver is that it is quite likely to overfit the data. That is, projecting the data into high-dimensional space may result in a good linear separation of the particular data at hand, but it has achieved separation by leveraging a particular constellation of support vectors, and this constellation might be peculiar to those particular data. Therefore, it is essential to perform cross-validation when SVMs are employed, either through holding back a portion of the data to test the SVM model on or through *k*-fold cross-validation. That will tell you whether the SVM model works when applied to other data—whether it can be *generalized*.

SUPPORT VECTOR MACHINES IN SPSS MODELER

Because SVMs have not been around all that long, and because their use is still restricted to specialized tasks, they have not been incorporated into most of the commercial statistical packages. SVM programs are available in R and MATLAB, as well as in a number of data mining suites. SPSS has also incorporated it into its Modeler data mining program, which we present a demonstration of below.

To run an SVM in Modeler, we first need to select some data. Modeler is able to read a number of different types of data files, such as Excel files or text files. Our data are already in an SPPS .sav file, so we select the Sources tab of the Nodes palette and choose Statistics File. A node then opens up onscreen, which we double-click to select the data file we want. (To browse for the file on your computer, click the blue button with three dots in it, to the right of the Import File text box, as shown in figure 9.8.)

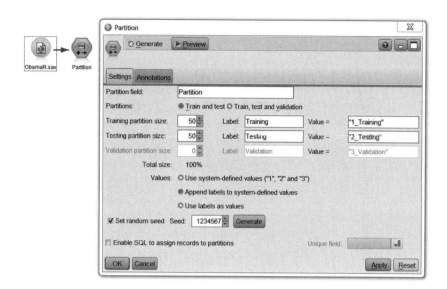

FIGURE 9.9
Partitioning data prior to a support vector machine analysis in SPSS Modeler.

We choose the county-level 2012 election dataset, which we have altered to include a dummy variable which is coded 1 if 50% or more of a county's vote went to Obama and 0 otherwise. Our data are already preformatted, for the most part. This is not strictly necessary, since Modeler allows you to create new variables or to transform those that exist. It also allows you to sample your cases or to exclude a subset of them. But data preparation is somewhat easier and more straightforward in a standard statistical program like SPSS or Stata, especially if you have to make a lot of changes, and so we suggest getting your data ready first before loading it into Modeler. You will still need to check that all of the variables are coded correctly as continuous, categorical, and so on. This can be done manually, or automatically by clicking Read Values in the Types tab in the Statistics File node window.

Next, we partition the data into two sections. This must be done in a separate node, rather than being selected as an option within the procedure window as in JMP. In the Nodes palette, select the Field Ops tab and then click Partition. This calls up the Partition window, displayed in figure 9.9. Modeler allows you to create training, test, and validation portions, or just the first two, and to choose what portion of the data to include in each. We include only training and test portions, as our data have only 3,114 cases.

Among our 3,114 counties, the breakdown of Obama votes was about 25% for and 75% against (the 25% of counties that Obama won are the most heavily populated). Many classifiers have difficulty with data which is lopsided in terms of the outcome, tending to hedge their bets by assigning all or most cases to the majority group. To see whether this matters for SVMs, we run analyses with both balanced and unbalanced data. Data balancing is quite

ObamaR.sav   Partition   Balance   No Targets

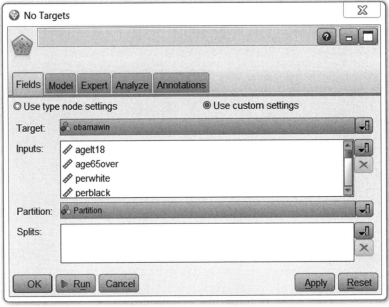

FIGURE 9.10
Building a support vector machine analysis stream in SPSS Modeler.

simple in Modeler. Simply click the Record Ops tab, and then choose Balance. Modeler balances by reducing a given category of cases (by randomly sampling cases) or by augmenting another (by duplicating cases). You will need to select a formula which tells Modeler what cases you want to alter (such as "Obamawin = 1") and then a factor by which to multiply the cases to reach your desired number. We multiply Obamawin = 0 cases by 0.4 and Obamawin = 1 cases by 1.54 in order to balance the data (more or less) on the outcome. You can choose, here, whether you want to balance the data only in the training set or in the test and validation sets as well. Sampling the data in the training set only is helpful if you want to use the test set to generate propensity scores (which Modeler can easily generate). Since we do not want to do so, we balance in both sets.

We are now ready to run an SVM. This is found under the Modeling menu as SVM. After adding it to the stream, you will need to build your model (figure 9.10). Start by identifying your target variable, and then choosing the predictors you want in the model, and the partition variable (generated automatically if you have created the Partition node). Next, choose the specifics of the SVM you want to run. This is done by choosing the Expert tab in the SVM window. You can unlock the option keys by setting the Mode

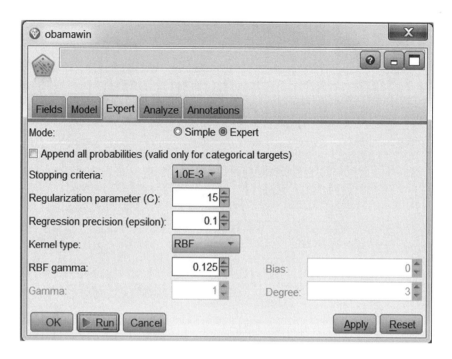

FIGURE 9.11

Setting support vector machine parameters in SPSS Modeler.

to Expert within this tab (figure 9.11). This will enable you to choose the kernel type, the gamma parameter (if you have a nonlinear kernel), the regularization parameter C, the precision parameter, and the stopping rule.

The stopping rule tells Modeler when you want it to decide that your model has converged. Its default is set fairly low, but if you want to be sure to reach a global minimum, you can enter a lower number. If you want speedier convergence, raise the stopping value. But Modeler runs fairly fast with data of this size, so we advise sticking with the default.

Modeler allows you to use four different kernels—the radial basis function (RBF), the polynomial, the sigmoid, and the linear function. Linear kernels do not project the data into higher-dimensional space, so if this fits pretty well, then you simply have data that doesn't need to be mapped to a feature space to be classified. The other kernels all have their strengths, and we suggest that you try each one, along with different values of the model parameters, in order to get the best separation without overfitting.

Once you have chosen a kernel, it is time to tune the model parameters. For any of the four kernel types, you can set the regularization parameter (C) and the regression precision (epsilon). The latter matters only for modeling continuous outcomes (in which Modeler is performing an SVM regression); it tells the program what size of error it

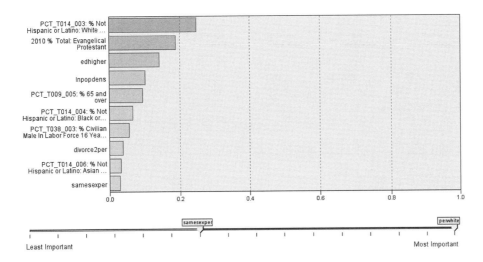

FIGURE 9.12
Predictor importance from a support vector machine in SPSS Modeler. Target:
obamawin.

should find acceptable. The former is consequential for the trade-off between accuracy
in the training data and overfitting. Higher values of C result in more accurate classification, but can reduce the model's ability to generalize to the test data. For RBF, polynomial, and sigmoid functions, there is also a gamma parameter. Like C, larger values of
this parameter result in more accuracy at the price of potentially overfitting. If we choose
the polynomial kernel, we can set the degree of the polynomial kernel (the default is 3).
Finally, for both polynomial and sigmoid kernels, one can set a bias parameter, which is
similar to a constant term in regression.

Which of these ought to be set? The program offers some guidance, but within these
parameters it is difficult to say before the fact. The researcher really can just experiment
with different settings, and choose the ones that are optimal.

Run your model by clicking Run. A "nugget" appears, which is the node which contains the results of the model you have run. Unfortunately, not a whole lot is available in
terms of output from an SVM in Modeler. If you have selected Calculate Predictor Importance in the Analyze tab within the SVM window, the contributions of the different variables to the separator will be shown (figure 9.12).

What we see here is that the most important variable in predicting Obama vote is the
percentage of the county which is non-Hispanic white. After this, in rapidly declining importance, are percentage evangelical Protestant, proportion with a bachelor's or higher, population density, and proportion 65 or older. Modeler is not particularly well documented, unfortunately, when it comes to describing what its generated statistics (like Predictor Importance)
precisely mean or how they are calculated; but the meanings are pretty intuitive.

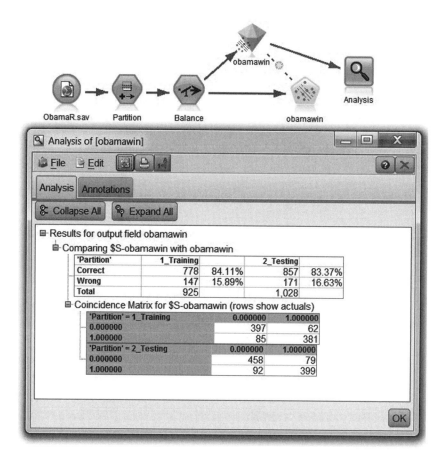

FIGURE 9.13

Support vector machine output in SPSS Modeler.

To look at fit statistics, choose the Output and select the Analysis node (figure 9.13). Within this node, in the Analysis tab, click the box for Coincidence Matrices. This will give you percentages correctly categorized in the training and test datasets, as well as confusion matrices for both which you can use to calculate model sensitivity and specificity.

We ran models on the 2012 election data using different kernels (altering the parameters for optimal performance), and for comparison ran the same models using logistic regression, partition trees (CART in Modeler), and neural networks. For a further comparison, we ran the models using both balanced and unbalanced data. The results are presented in tables 9.4 and 9.5.

In the unbalanced data, SVMs slightly outperform the other three classifiers in the training data, but are less obviously superior in the test data. This does not mean, however, that the models are necessarily overfitted. After all, they achieve superiority in the

TABLE 9.4 Comparing Support Vector Machine Performance to Other Classifiers Using Unbalanced Data

	Accuracy (training)	Accuracy (test)	Sensitivity (training)	Sensitivity (test)	Specificity (test)
SVM (RBF kernel)	89.8%	88.9%	66.45%	60.72%	96.03%
SVM (polynomial kernel)	97.03%	85.95%	89.67%	67.06%	90.78%
Linear SVM	87.82%	88.14%	60.64%	58.06%	95.73%
Logistic regression	88.3%	88.02%	62.5%	59.21%	95.27%
Partition tree	86.73%	84.98%	65.80%	59.51%	91.39%
Neural net	87.62%	88.32%	59.35%	58.30%	95.88%

TABLE 9.5 Comparing Support Vector Machine Performance to Other Classifiers Using Balanced Data

	Accuracy (training)	Accuracy (test)	Sensitivity (training)	Sensitivity (test)	Specificity (test)
SVM (RBF kernel)	83.84%	84.11%	80.77%	82.12%	85.97%
SVM (polynomial kernel)	88.52%	81.54%	89.38%	77.64%	85.41%
Linear SVM	84.21%	81.57%	84.64%	82.06%	81.08%
Logistic regression	83.32%	83.25%	81.87%	80.91%	85.71%
Partition tree	80.6%	77.76%	90.81%	84.53%	71.55%
Neural net	85.16%	82.40%	88.84%	86.33%	78.63%

training set but are competitive and for the most part better in the test set as well. In these data, only the polynomial kernel SVM seems overfit; the RBF kernel outperforms all competitor classifiers in the test data (though not substantially).

The unbalanced data consist disproportionately of negative outcomes, and in such cases classifiers tend to fail mostly by misclassifying positives. So a measure of model sensitivity (the percentage of positives which are correctly classified) is essential to examine. In particular, it is crucial to examine sensitivity in the test set. And it is here that SVMs show their superiority. With the exception of the linear SVM, which doesn't take advantage of mapping the data into a higher-dimensional space, the SVMs are better than the other methods at finding successes, and the "overfit" SVM is particularly good at it. SVMs are after all not using all of the data, but only borderline cases, to achieve optimal classification. As a result, they are less prone to err by assigning most cases to the majority category.

When we turn to the balanced data, we find that the SVM with the RBF kernel is slightly better than logistic regression and neural nets at overall accuracy. Once again, the polynomial SVM appears to be slightly overfitted. The radial basis function SVM is slightly superior to competitor classifiers in terms of sensitivity, but the partition tree and the neural network modestly outperformed it on sensitivity. That SVMs did not vastly outperform their competitors here could be a function of the data (they could be linearly separable, giving SVMs no real advantage) or of the particular implementation in Modeler (which is not particularly flexible in terms of parameter adjustment). On the other hand, the competitor algorithms are also quite good at classifying data in many circumstances.

We suggest that researchers try out the SVM in social science research settings, and use them where they outperform other classifiers. SVMs may be used to generate propensity scores, for instance; these may be helpful or unhelpful for your purposes. Modeler's implementation of SVMs is not particularly useful in terms of providing us with information about the relation of the features to the outcome—it tells us little about the model it is building for classification. But in general, the very strength of SVMs—their ability to map the data into high-dimensional space via a kernel function—renders them rather opaque. In this respect they are similar to neural nets; the kernel transformation is not exactly a black box, but neither is it transparent. Nonetheless, SVMs should be explored for their usefulness, having already proven themselves highly adept at classifying complex data in many practical settings.

OPTIMIZING PREDICTION ACROSS MULTIPLE CLASSIFIERS

We have reviewed a number of classification algorithms, and many other methods of classification have been developed. (A couple of these—partition trees and neural networks—will be covered in detail in subsequent chapters.) What is more, researchers have developed many variations on each method. The natural questions at this point are: Which one is best? Which one should I use? Is there one which is unambiguously more accurate? Does it depend on the data, and if so, are there any hard and fast rules (or even helpful rules of thumb) for choosing a classifier if I know something about the data?

Unfortunately, the answer is: Not really. Or rather, it depends, but not on characteristics of the data per se. We argue instead that the choice is better thought of as a practical matter. Also, which classifier is best is sometimes more a matter of the *other things* that the classifier does while it is classifying. For example, we will spend quite a bit of time on partition trees, not because they are necessarily powerful at classification tasks (though they often are) or because their results generalize well to external samples (though they frequently do), but because they are quite flexible. Investigating the structure of the tree itself permits us to learn quite a bit about the relation between the outcome and the predictor measures, and it tells us things about them that logistic regression does not necessarily tell us. Neural networks, especially when combined with visualization software such as JMP Pro, can also be used to help us learn about complex nonlinear relations. At this point, *k*-nearest neighbors classifiers and support vector machines do not provide us with all that much information about predictors themselves, though they are (arguably) better at some complex classification tasks.

But there is another answer to this question, which is that we don't have to choose one best method. It is quite possible to combine the results of several classification algorithms into one final result. The problem is to do this in such a way that builds on the relative strengths, rather than the relative weaknesses, of the various classification techniques (Xu, Kryznak, and Suen 1992). By combining methods, one may be able to obtain a classification which is even more powerful than any one technique alone. But this result is not guaranteed, and perhaps this is not even the best rationale for classifier combination. A second rationale is that combining classifiers helps to reduce the potential that idiosyncratic results from the eccentricities of any one classification method will drive the final classification decision. Combining classifiers is more likely to give a "smoother" result, one that perhaps generalizes a bit better. In this sense, combining classifiers becomes a bit more akin to bagging (or random forests) than to boosting in its logic.

COMBINING CLASSIFIERS IN SPSS MODELER

In SPSS Modeler, combining classifiers is quite easily accomplished by using the Auto Classifier node. This is a single node that allows the user to pick several different classifiers and the parameters which govern how they will be selected and combined. In using this node, the temptation will often be to simply use default settings for each type of classifier used. We counsel against this. Instead, we suggest that you carefully tune each separate model so it is optimal before classification. As always, using data mining tools carefully and judiciously is preferable.

We begin by selecting, once again, our American Community Survey data, which we will use to predict health insurance coverage. We make sure, in the Type tab (Field Ops palette), that the variables are assigned the correct level of measurement, and then we partition the data 50%:50% into training and test sets (Partition tab, Field Ops palette). Then, in the Modeling palette, we select Auto Classifier.

After selecting the outcome, predictor, and partition variables, we proceed to set up our classifiers. We suggest that rather than going first to the Model tab, you click on Expert and get right into specifying the classifiers and their settings. Doing so presents you with a screen like that shown in figure 9.14. The program automatically chooses one of eight separate classifiers for you, each with default settings. You will need to edit this screen to include the models you want. It is important to note a few things which ought to guide this decision. First, you can have multiple versions of a single classifier, each with different parameter settings. Can't decide whether you want an SVM with a radial basis function or a sigmoid kernel? Never mind—include one of each. You can decide if you want to include all the results, or only the best ones, in your final prediction. Secondly, remember that more models means extra data processing. This in turn definitely means more time, and unfortunately also means a higher likelihood of the program's

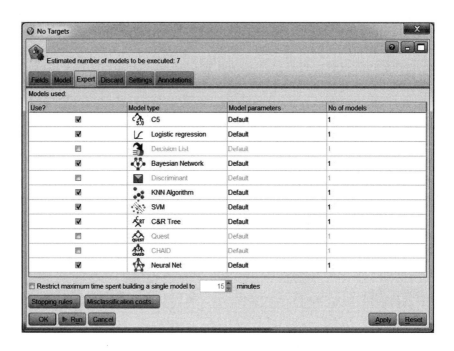

FIGURE 9.14

Selecting classifiers for optimization using the Auto Classifier node in SPSS Modeler.

freezing up or crashing. It is advisable to perform a brief experiment around this, before simply trying everything all at once. This is also a benefit of having already experimented with the individual models, incidentally.

We are going to select five models—one logistic regression, one KNN, one SVM, one partition tree (here called a C&R tree), and one neural net—and adjust the settings of each. Now, we go back to the Model tab (figure 9.15) and adjust the rules for combining results. First, select how many of the models you would like to use. If you are building a large number of models, some of them might be very inaccurate, and you may not want to use them. We set the "Number of models to use" field to 4, which means that we will be dropping the results of one model. And we rank by overall accuracy (the other option is number of fields), so that we will keep the four most accurate models. Further, we choose to rank by accuracy in the test portion rather than in the training set, so that we can select the combination of models which best generalizes to external data.

But how do we determine which model is the most accurate? This depends on settings for costs, revenue, and weight. Each new observation or record "costs" the model a certain amount to attempt to classify, and the model is rewarded with "revenue" if it gets the classification correct. Finally, we can set a weight variable, which gives more importance to the classification of some cases than to others—for example, ones which "represent" many persons in a population rather than relatively few.

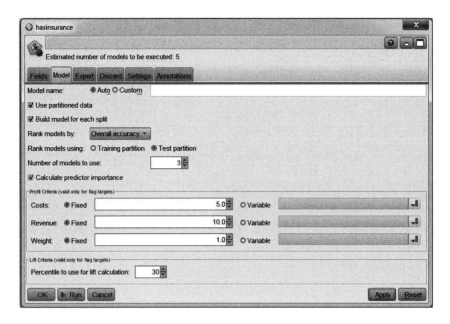

FIGURE 9.15

Setting accuracy determination parameters in Auto Classifier node.

In the Discard tab one can choose a floor for model inclusion. This means that models that fail to attain a certain researcher-chosen minimum level of accuracy get discarded even if they are one of the "top" models. One can in fact choose multiple floors—percent accuracy, total profitability, or area under the ROC curve, for instance. We opt to omit only very poorly fitting cases, where the accuracy is less than 60% and the area under the ROC curve is lower than 0.65.

Finally, choose the method for combining "votes" from different models (Settings tab, figure 9.16). Remember that the models calculate not only a predicted category for each case but also a confidence in this categorization. One can choose, then, to go with the model with the highest confidence for each case; or the program can do simple majority voting; or it can perform confidence-weighted voting. Consider this similar to the voting procedure in KNN classification. Voting can be problematic if there are an even number of models which will inform the decision, but Modeler here provides a choice of what to do in case of a tie: random selection or highest confidence. We opt to use confidence-weighted voting.

The model runs each of the five models in question and computes the accuracy of each. It then discards the least accurate, which in this case was the logistic regression. Next, it takes the predicted values for the test and training sets from each of the remaining models, and combines them by giving them each a vote weighted for that model's estimated confidence. This combination procedure results in new set of predicted values that are essentially best guesses from the four best models.

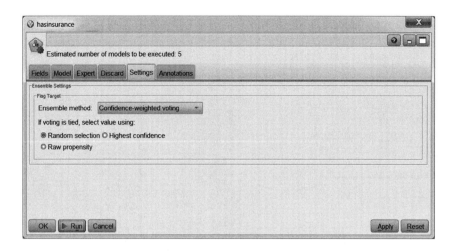

FIGURE 9.16

Choosing methods for combining predictions from multiple classifiers.

TABLE 9.6   Comparing Performance of Optimized Combinations of
Classifiers to Individual Classifiers

	Accuracy (training)	Accuracy (test)	Sensitivity (test)	Specificity (test)
Logistic regression	72.19%	73.06%	73.91%	72.27%
K-nearest neighbors	75.14%	72.53%	72.76%	72.77%
Support vector machine	78.60%	72.70%	74.90%	72.02%
Neural net	72.63%	73.75%	76.16%	71.52%
Partition tree	75.35%	73.19%	75.61%	70.95%
Combination of classifiers	79.72%	75.71%	75.95%	75.48%
Combined classifiers with preprocessed variables	80.94%	76.63%	76.98%	76.31%

As table 9.6 indicates, the combination of classifiers does indeed outperform any of the individual classification routines. Moreover, it outperforms all individual classifiers in both training and testing data, and it does so while striking a balance between correctly classifying true positives and true negatives. These results demonstrate that there is something to be gained by combining classifiers, as long as one does so carefully. After all, a combination of five bad models is likely to do worse than any one good model (though it would probably do better than any one of the five bad models on its own). On the other hand, though the improvement is noticeable, it is not, in this case, dramatic. There are two reasons for this. First, each of the individual models is already doing a fairly good job (consider that random guessing would result in a 50% error rate in this case). Secondly, we are making use of fairly broad predictor variables in this model (region, age, labor-market status, household income, gender, race, citizenship, school attendance, and marital status). Quite simply, our predictors do not offer the classifier raw material for a better prediction. This is an important point to underscore. Data mining is an intelligent method of leveraging raw computational power, but it is not in and of itself a solution for bad data, insufficient information, or measurement error. Data mining can probably improve prediction even with bad data, but a better way to improve prediction remains the same as it was in the twentieth century—get better data.

However, we actually can do better by feeding into each of the classifiers some variables which we have already optimized (see table 9.6 again). We draw here on the "leaf" variables (discussed earlier, under Using Partition Trees to Study Interactions, pp. 108–115), as well as the income and age groups from which they were generated, from the classification tree used earlier to generate complex interactions. By using these variables in addition to those we were previously using, we are able to further nudge up predictive accuracy. This is interesting because we used a classification tree as one of our component models, and it would in theory have found not simply the groups we generated from our small partition tree but indeed more fine-grained groups. Nonetheless, feeding the entire algorithm these groups improves overall predictive power.

10

CLASSIFICATION TREES

PARTITION TREES

Developed by Breiman and colleagues (1983), the classification tree (also known as CART, CHAID, decision tree, or partition tree) is in some ways the paradigmatic data mining tool: simple, powerful, computation-intensive, nonparametric, and utterly data-driven. It is first and foremost a classifier, using input characteristics to create a model which sorts cases into categories with different values on an outcome of interest. And it doesn't matter whether the outcome variable or the input variables are dichotomous, categorical, or continuous; partition trees can handle all of them, and deal with them in more or less the same manner. However, partition trees are most straightforward when used with a dichotomous outcome, so we'll focus on this.

As classifiers, partition trees have two advantages over more traditional tools like logistic regression. First, they are oriented toward predicting the outcome variable rather than accurately estimating parameters for the predictors. Second, they are not constrained to estimate only average relations. Instead, they develop a highly complex and specific set of classification decisions that work differently over different parts of the data.

How do they work? Partition trees begin with all of the data, and focus on an outcome variable designated by the researcher. The researcher also specifies a set of predictor variables potentially helpful for the classification task. A partition tree splits the sample at each value of each input variable. Each time, it calculates how effectively this split has separated out cases into different categories of the outcome variable. It chooses the variable and the split which have done best at this separation task, resulting in two subgroups (or *descendant nodes*) which are much more homogeneous than the sample as a whole (the *root node*). The process is repeated on each of the descendant nodes, resulting in four groups, and then on their descendants, and so on. Classification trees continue in this manner until either completely homogeneous groups of observations are attained or some other specified stopping point is reached.

The procedure is very similar with multicategory outcomes. In this case, the partition tree attempts to split the data into subsets which are as homogeneous as possible, which means that eventually, given enough splits, it will produce nodes in which one or another category clearly predominates. Initial splits will work toward this end, but no split is likely to result in a perfectly homogeneous node. This goes, of course, for dichotomous outcomes as well.

For continuous outcomes, the procedure cannot separate out cases into homogeneous categories. Instead, it creates subgroups in which values of the outcome variable are as similar as possible (resulting in large differences in means *across* subsets). Thus, given successive splits, it creates subsets of the data in which the variance on the dependent variable is significantly reduced.

Because they are so data-driven, trees contrast dramatically with classical statistical techniques which prioritize hypothesis testing. The tree method does not result in anything akin to a regression coefficient; it does not tell you whether a variable is a "significant" predictor of the outcome, net of other predictors. For this reason, much of the social science community has greeted partition trees tepidly at best, though there have been a few uses by social science researchers (see e.g. Ruger et al. 2004; Weerts and Ronca 2009). Trees are widely used in fields like clinical epidemiology and ecological modeling.

Trees are of value for researchers for at least three reasons. First, they tend to be better at producing accurate predictions than, say, regression. Given enough data and enough independent variables, they will tend to produce a better-fitting model. Secondly, there are no limits on the number of independent variables that can be entered into a model; degrees-of-freedom problems are not relevant here. Thirdly, as we detailed earlier (pp. 108–114), classification trees are extremely good at finding interactions and nonlinear relations. Regression models can only handle nonlinear forms if they are prespecified by the researcher, and interactions in regression tend to be limited to two or at most three variables. In contrast, partition trees generate complex interactions automatically. They are thus a powerful tool for exploratory research.

One drawback of partition trees flows directly from these strengths. It is through their flexibility and complexity that trees can generate a more accurate predictive model. But a tree grown on a large dataset and making use of many variables will of necessity be very large and intricate, making interpretation quite difficult. What the tree gains in discriminating or predictive power it loses in parsimony.

Partition trees, when run to their conclusion, continue splitting the data until only very homogeneous *terminal nodes* (or "leaves") remain, with very few cases or observations in each. However, a researcher can specify a stopping rule to prevent this from going too far. For example, a minimum size split can be set; then the tree will not split a node if either resulting node would have less than a certain number of cases in it. Stopping rules are important, because our goal is typically not simply to classify the particular data we happen to be looking at but to develop a model that will predict well generally. But even with stopping rules in place, a partition tree runs a high risk of overfitting the model—producing a model which is overly influenced by the peculiarities of the data with which it was built and which has little external validity. To guard against and test for overfitting, cross-validation should be performed. When random holdback is performed, the training data are used to build a tree, and the test data are then "dropped" down the tree. If the data are divided into three sections, the training set is used to grow a tree, and this tree is then calibrated or fine-tuned using the validation set. Branches which particularly contribute to overfitting in the validation set are eliminated (*pruned*), resulting in a model which is more likely to be generalizable. Finally, the test set is dropped down the fine-tuned tree, for an independent test of the accuracy of the model. Alternatively, *k*-fold cross-validation can be performed.

AN EXAMPLE IN JMP PRO

Partition trees have been around for quite a while, and routines for them have been written for R, SPSS Modeler, SPSS, Stata, and MATLAB, among other software packages. We demonstrate trees using JMP's Partition routine, which we like for its ease of use, its flexibility, and the quality of visualization JMP provides.

We demonstrate the operation of classification trees using data from the American Community Survey. We selected a subsample of this data containing only adults aged 25–65 who have been married at least once. Within this group, we substantially oversampled individuals who have been married three or more times. We will use trees to sort out these "serial marriers" from others in the data.

We open the Partition setup platform (figure 10.1) by selecting Analyze Modeling Partition. We choose as the response (the field is labeled "Y, Response") a dummy variable coded 1 if a person has been married three or more times and 0 otherwise. Next, we choose a set of predictors (field "X, Factor"): age, total personal income, educational attainment, race, occupational prestige, gender, region of the country, and citizenship/birthplace status (U.S.-born citizen, naturalized citizen, or noncitizen). Third, we choose a portion of the data to hold back in order to validate the model. We have lots of cases here—over 100,000—so we don't have to use *k*-fold cross-validation (though there is no reason in principle not to). Instead, we set the validation portion to 0.33, which holds back a third of the data for validation. Figure 10.1 shows what we have before launch.

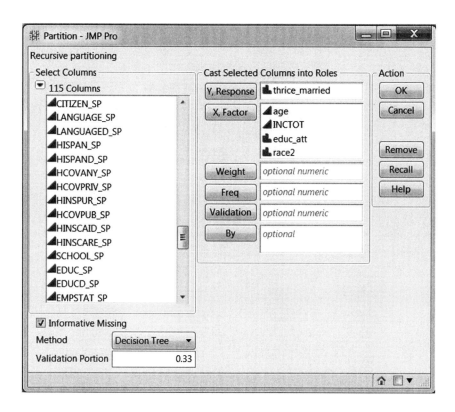

FIGURE 10.1
Launching the Partition platform in JMP Pro.

We click OK, and the Partition launch platform opens. We'll make a couple of modifications to customize what we see. We want to see the numerical proportion of cases in each node that are in each category of the outcome (1 or 0), so from the menu (red triangle) in the top-right corner we select Display Options Show Split Prob. This shows us that all 114,528 of our cases are in a single node (the root node) and that 41.8% are "serial marriers" (remember, we have oversampled this group, so proportions will not reflect population quantities). Now we are ready to make the first split of the data, by clicking the button that says Split.

The partition tree has split the data into two nodes (figure 10.2). The node on the left contains only people aged 43 and older; the other contains those younger than 43. In this example, only one of the resulting nodes (the one on the right) is more homogeneous than its parent; the other node is *less* homogeneous. But overall, across both nodes, homogeneity has been increased (or, to use tree parlance, *entropy has been reduced*), and it is this that the procedure is attempting to accomplish.

If we want to know where a node will be split next, we click the triangle next to Candidates at the bottom of each node. This shows the logworth statistic for each variable (that

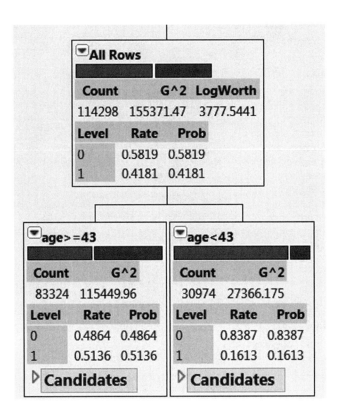

FIGURE 10.2

The first split of the data using JMP Pro's partition tree.

is, for the value or level of this variable which best splits the data); JMP will choose the variable with the largest logworth statistic. This feature is helpful because it allows us to compare variables at each stage, indicating which are most useful for classifying the data.

After a few more splits, we have a somewhat better picture of what distinguishes serial marriers. We follow first the left-hand branch (figure 10.3), which finds further differentiation among those 43 and older. The first split in this group is made in terms of nativity (the variable cit2), with native-born Americans more than twice as likely to be married three or more times than immigrants (regardless of immigrant citizenship status). Among the native-born, the model then splits in terms of educational attainment. Individuals with a bachelor's degree have a substantially lower rate of serial marriage than their less credentialed fellows. Among immigrants, a split is made according to race; Asians appear particularly unlikely to marry many times.

Following the right-side branch (figure 10.4), which splits among those younger than 43, we find another split according to age at 35 years. Those younger than 35 are very, very unlikely to have been multiply married (and recall that we have substantially oversampled the thrice-married). Among those 35–42, the tree splits again according to educa-

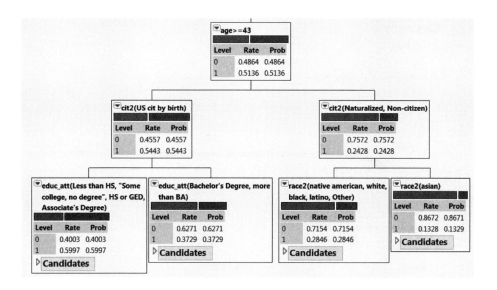

FIGURE 10.3

Following the left-hand branch of a partition tree (JMP Pro).

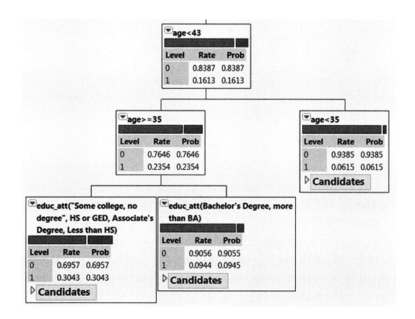

FIGURE 10.4

Following the right-hand branch of a partition tree (JMP Pro).

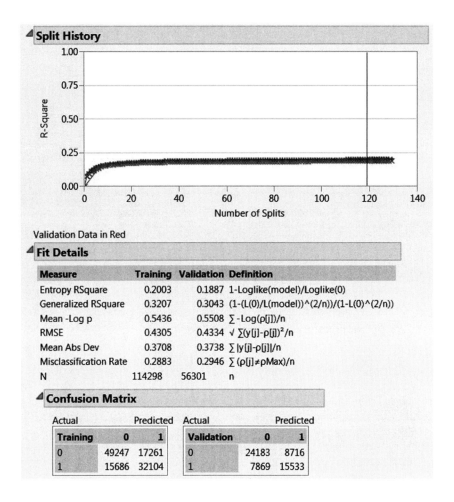

Split History

Validation Data in Red

Fit Details

Measure	Training	Validation	Definition
Entropy RSquare	0.2003	0.1887	1-Loglike(model)/Loglike(0)
Generalized RSquare	0.3207	0.3043	(1-(L(0)/L(model))^(2/n))/(1-L(0)^(2/n))
Mean -Log p	0.5436	0.5508	$\sum$ -Log(p[j])/n
RMSE	0.4305	0.4334	$\sqrt{\sum(y[j]-p[j])^2/n}$
Mean Abs Dev	0.3708	0.3738	$\sum$ |y[j]-p[j]|/n
Misclassification Rate	0.2883	0.2946	$\sum$ (p[j]≠pMax)/n
N	114298	56301	n

Confusion Matrix

Actual		Predicted	Actual		Predicted
Training	**0**	**1**	**Validation**	**0**	**1**
0	49247	17261	0	24183	8716
1	15686	32104	1	7869	15533

FIGURE 10.5
Partition tree output in JMP Pro.

tional attainment, and once again the college-educated are less likely to have been involved in three or more marriages.

JMP also computes a running fit statistic, which it calls R^2. In reality this is McFadden's pseudo-R^2, which shows how much the current model has improved over the null model or initial root node. This measure has at this point risen to .138 in the training data and .135 in the validation data.

We have a lot of cases here in each node, and can keep making individual splits if this is what we want to do. But instead, we will jump ahead and grow the whole tree. We do so by clicking Go.

JMP has grown the tree. We can see (figure 10.5) that it has split the data 116 times, and this has pushed the McFadden's pseudo-R^2 up to .189 in the validation set. JMP also shows us the split history in terms of model fit. This shows separate improvement curves for the training set and validation set; the training line is slightly above the validation line, because the predictive power is always higher in the training set than in the validation set. Also note, though, that these two curves are very close—the sheer size of the dataset in comparison to the number of features has ensured that we did not overfit by very much. This window also shows corrections for overfitting. Note the black vertical line at 116, which is the number of splits in the final tree. The tree was stopped here because the validation R^2 is higher here than it was 10 more splits out. In other words, JMP performed these extra 10 splits, calculated the R^2, and chose the smaller tree by pruning the larger tree back for optimal prediction in the validation set.

To get more measures of fit, we click the red triangle next to "Partition for thrice_married," and then click Show Fit Details. Under Fit Details, JMP gives us a number of statistics, and, helpfully, the formulas it uses to compute these statistics. It provides two R^2 formulas, which it calls the "Entropy R^2" and the "Generalized R^2" (McFadden's and Cox and Snell's formulas, respectively). It also provides the root mean squared error, the mean absolute deviation, and the misclassification rate.

This is a good place to note how partition trees decide what "class" a case ought to belong to. We have already discussed how the partitioning algorithm will grow a tree out until some stopping point is reached. This will result in a collection of terminal nodes (or "leaves"), all of which contain cases from both classes of the outcome. Predicted class membership is decided by simply classifying every case as belonging to the outcome class of the majority of cases in its terminal node. The misclassification rate is simply a measure of the proportion of cases incorrectly assigned by this procedure.

JMP Pro also allows the researcher to produce receiver operating characteristic (ROC) curves, which are particularly useful tools for assessing the performance of a classifier like a partition tree (figure 10.6). They plot sensitivity (or true positive rate) by 1 − specificity (or the false positive rate), thus demonstrating how good the model is overall at predicting what class the cases fall in.[1] The area under the ROC curve is an excellent measure of predictive accuracy: an area of 0.5 tells us that the model is no better at classification than random guessing, and higher values indicate the degree to which the model aids in classification.

All of this gives us a pretty good idea of how well this model fits the data. But what can the tree tell us about predictor variables? At this point, we encounter a trade-off between predictive accuracy and easy interpretability. We have grown a tree which has correctly classified about 70% of the cases in the dataset, a substantial improvement over random guessing. But in order to do so, we have generated a very complex tree— one made through 116 separate splits. JMP will permit us to look at the tree in its entirety (in the output window, using the red triangle in the top-right corner, select Display Options Show Tree). Partition trees are entirely transparent, so it is quite simple to make sense out of any one *part* of the tree. But this is unsatisfying; what we usually want is some sort of summation of what a model is telling us, some way to grasp the results of

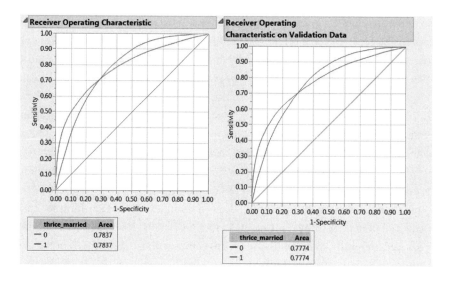

FIGURE 10.6

The receiver operating characteristic curve as a measure of partition tree model fit.

the model in its entirety, and this is not easy given the immensity and complexity of a tree grown on large data. It is important to stress, though, that what makes partition trees so predictive is the very subtlety and complexity that renders them difficult to fully understand.

One way to examine the results of the tree is to examine the content of the leaves themselves, which we can do in JMP by examining the Leaf Report (red triangle Leaf Report). This report defines each leaf by listing all the splits that went into its construction (and which constitute, in essence, highly complex interaction terms—see pp. 108–115), and tells us the breakdown of the leaf in terms of outcome categories. For example, a leaf in which thrice-married individuals are represented in one of the highest proportions contains those who are:

· U.S. citizens by birth
· Not college-educated
· 50 or older
· "Other" race, Native American, or white
· Residing in the West South Central census division (Texas, Louisiana, etc.).

By contrast, a leaf in which serial marriers are virtually absent contains people described as:

· age 43–51
· U.S. citizen by birth
· bachelor's degree or higher

Validation Data in Red

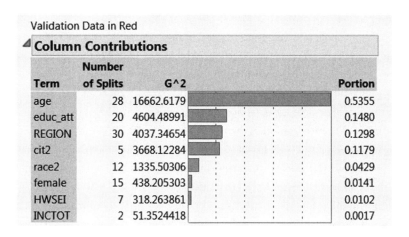

Column Contributions

Term	Number of Splits	G^2		Portion
age	28	16662.6179		0.5355
educ_att	20	4604.48991		0.1480
REGION	30	4037.34654		0.1298
cit2	5	3668.12284		0.1179
race2	12	1335.50306		0.0429
female	15	438.205303		0.0141
HWSEI	7	318.263861		0.0102
INCTOT	2	51.3524418		0.0017

FIGURE 10.7
Predictor importance in partition tree model.

- living in New England or the Mid-Atlantic States
- male

In a small, manageable tree with a small number of splits, this would be very effective for helping us "get" the tree. But this tree has 116 separate leaves, each made though several spits. Still, examining all the leaves can help us get a sense of overriding logic of the splits.

Perhaps the best path to understanding how the tree was built is to look at what JMP calls the *column contributions* (red triangle Column Contributions). This generates a chart which compares the input variables in terms of how much they contributed to making the leaves more homogeneous than the root node (figure 10.7).[2] In tree parlance, this is how much they contributed to *entropy reduction*, which is measured through the G^2 statistic. Variables which were utilized more frequently by the tree for splitting the data will on the whole have higher G^2, but this is not all that matters. Earlier splits, which sorted out larger portions of the data, will matter more for G^2 than later splits. So, in the figure, note that the region variable was used to make more splits than the educational attainment variable (30 vs. 20), but that educational attainment has a higher G^2 value. This is because many of the more consequential, early splits were made using educational attainment; it "explains more" of what separates out serial marriers from those who are not serial marriers among ever-married individuals.

So what is the tree telling us about what separates the serial marriers from the rest of married people? First of all, and not particularly surprisingly, age makes by far the most important contribution; it is used to make 28 separate splits, and many of these occur early in the tree. Of course, we know that this is simply about *exposure*—people who have been alive longer have been "exposed to the risk" of marriage for longer, and are thus more likely to have been married multiple times. We are, of course, presuming that most of the splits involving age leave more serial marriers in the older group; this can be confirmed by scroll-ing through the whole tree and examining all of these splits. We also see that educational attainment makes an important contribution. A look at the detail of the tree informs us that those with higher educational attainment are far *less* likely to have married multiple times, which is understandable given that those with higher education tend to marry later and have a lower risk of divorce. Next, we see that region of the country is used in a lot of splits; serial marriage is more common in the regions of the South and Southwest than in places like New England and the West Coast (despite the stereotype about California as a divorce capital). Finally, our variable for citizenship and nativity is tapped quite a few times, and in most of these splits the foreign-born are particularly *unlikely* to be serial marriers.

But unfortunately, though we can easily produce a summary of what variables matter in building the tree, the direction of the relation between an important variable and the outcome is not so easily expressed. Trees will kick out nothing so clear as a regression coefficient for expressing the strength and direction of a given relation. This is simply not what trees are particularly good for; if it is average relations you are interested in, we suggest you return to tried-and-true logit and probit models. In a tree, really the best you can do is what we do above: note important variables, and then examine the tree and report what happened in most of the splits involving them.

SUMMARY

Partition trees are powerful tools for classification and prediction. Their strength in prediction is supplemented by the transparency of their results and an easy comprehen-sibility of their underlying algorithm. They are computationally intensive, but not par-ticularly complicated; indeed, they work by performing a whole lot of relatively simple calculations. They are easy to employ, and to use with cross-validation procedures. Fur-thermore, they can tell us which variables are most important in generating predictions; their drawback is that they don't tell us precisely *how* a given variable matters.

Trees are widely used and popular, and have spawned a number of more complicated variants. Below, we examine two of these "super-trees": boosted trees and random forests.

BOOSTED TREES AND RANDOM FORESTS

Let's say that you think that the partition tree is an interesting way of looking at and clas-sifying data, but that it's just too *simple*. Isn't there a way we can take the strengths of the partition method, but intensify it so as to truly take advantage of the ability of a computer to churn through massive numbers of calculations? If you feel this way, statisticians have developed an answer to your prayers. In fact, they have developed many, but we will focus here on two: boosted trees and random forests. Both of them can be thought of as parti-tion trees on steroids, beefed up in terms of complexity and intensity of calculation. We will explain what they are, and then describe how they can be run in JMP Pro.

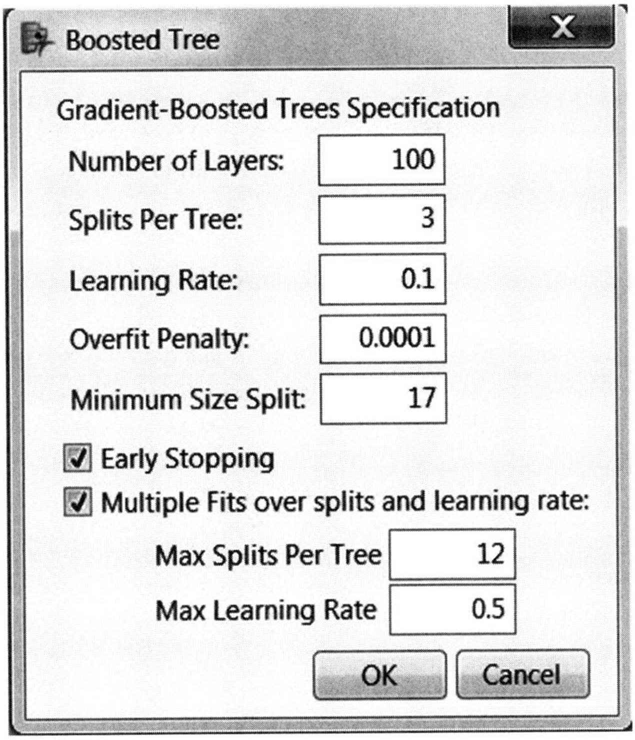

FIGURE 10.8
Boosted Tree platform in JMP Pro.

BOOSTED TREES

A boosted tree makes use of a number of smaller trees to learn from early classification mistakes and, hopefully, build an even more accurate model. First, it grows one tree with a small, prespecified number of splits. It then calculates a predicted probability and a residual for each case in the dataset. Cases are reweighted according to these residuals, such that misclassified cases receive more weight than correctly classified cases (a process called *boosting*). Another small tree is then grown using these reweighted cases, and the procedure is repeated a given number of times until a final model is generated. Boosted trees are, then, iterative models which are capable, in theory, of learning from mistakes and becoming gradually more precise over time.

To run a boosted tree in JMP, open the Partition launch platform (Analyze Modeling Partition). Near the bottom-right corner of this window, click on Method and select Boosted Tree. Then populate the rest of the window as you would a partition tree and click OK. This will open the Boosted Tree launch platform (figure 10.8), which enables the user to customize the boosting process.

First, we choose the number of *layers*. This is the number of small trees that will be additively fit to the data. JMP defaults to 50; more layers gives the program more opportunities to learn and improve, and will result in a more accurate model. However, it will also increase the amount of work the computer has to do and the amount of time the program will take to run. For large datasets like the one we are using, this can result in very long running times, and the program can easily crash if the computer doesn't have enough RAM.

Secondly, we choose the number of splits per tree. More splits in any tree will lead the tree to be more accurate, as it will generate smaller and more precise terminal nodes (remember, the tree discussed earlier used 116 splits and did not overfit). So, once again, in general, more splits are better. But, as before, more splitting exponentially increases the number of calculations the computer needs to perform, and can increase the amount of time required.

Next, we specify the *learning rate*. This is a number that ranges between 0 and 1; higher values imply that the program should be more confident in its initial conclusions, while lower rates instill more caution. Thus, a high learning rate speeds up the calculations involved but at the cost of overfitting; lower rates slow down convergence but yield more accuracy.

There are two more parameters which also act as safeguards against overfitting in JMP's Boosted Tree platform. The *overfit penalty* ensures against having any cases with predicted probabilities equal to zero; higher values will result in less overfitting. Researchers can also specify a *minimum size split*; this will prevent the program from splitting any node with below a specified number of cases in it. In large datasets such as the one we are using, it is unlikely that these will be utilized, but in small datasets they could be very important.

The two final options, which are either on or off, are called "Early Stopping" and "Multiple Fits over splits and learning rate." Early stopping, if enabled, cues the program to stop the additive boosting process if further boosting fails to improve fit on the validation data. "Multiple Fits over splits and learning rate" cues the program build *a separate boosted tree* for every possible combination of splits and learning rates specified by the researcher. (The lower bounds of these quantities are set in the Splits and Learning Rates boxes already described; the upper bounds are set below the checkbox in the "Max Splits Per Tree" and "Max Learning Rate" fields.) This permits the boosted tree program to try various combinations of these parameters in order to find the one that maximizes fit. Turning it on increases the chances of finding the "best model," but it *significantly* increases run time.

We choose, for our analysis, to grow a tree with 100 layers (twice the default). We employ early stopping, but we also set minimum and maximum values of both splits per tree and learning rate, and allowed JMP to choose the values of these parameters which worked best in correctly classifying cases in the validation set. Splits per tree ranged from 3 to 12, and learning rate ranged from 0.1 to 0.5. In contrast to the partition

Model Validation-Set Summaries

The fit below was the best of these models fit.

N Splits	N Layers	Learning Rate	Entropy RSquare	Misclassification Rate	Avg -Log p	RMS Error	Avg Abs Error
3	100	0.1	0.1876	0.2946	0.5513	0.4339	0.3853
4	100	0.1	0.1896	0.2960	0.5507	0.4340	0.3833
5	100	0.1	0.1941	0.2908	0.5474	0.4321	0.3794
6	100	0.1	0.1941	0.2919	0.5473	0.4322	0.3783
8	100	0.1	0.2020	0.2886	0.5420	0.4297	0.3756
10	100	0.1	0.2029	0.2873	0.5419	0.4296	0.3743
3	100	0.2	0.1956	0.2931	0.5466	0.4321	0.3755
4	100	0.2	0.2010	0.2878	0.5423	0.4298	0.3740
5	100	0.2	0.2044	0.2860	0.5404	0.4290	0.3718
6	100	0.2	0.2031	0.2856	0.5410	0.4293	0.3704
8	100	0.2	0.2019	0.2878	0.5426	0.4299	0.3717
10	100	0.2	0.2033	0.2875	0.5420	0.4295	0.3703
3	100	0.4	0.2017	0.2877	0.5416	0.4292	0.3696
4	100	0.4	0.2065	0.2849	0.5391	0.4284	0.3686
5	100	0.4	0.2069	0.2844	0.5389	0.4282	0.3677
6	100	0.4	0.2052	0.2853	0.5404	0.4287	0.3679
8	89	0.4	0.2047	0.2865	0.5399	0.4286	0.3676
10	77	0.4	0.2050	0.2860	0.5405	0.4286	0.3671

FIGURE 10.9

Fit statistics for multiple boosted trees in JMP Pro.

tree, which produced results immediately, with these specifications the boosted tree program took about eight minutes to complete, mostly because we asked the program to grow many separate boosted trees.

Figure 10.9 shows the results for all 18 of the trees we grew at different settings of splits and learning rate. For all but the final two boosted trees, all 100 specified layers were produced; for the final two, early stopping kicked in because adding more layers was leading to worsened fit. The routine ended up choosing a boosted tree model with a relatively low number of splits per tree (5) and a relatively high learning rate (0.4). Given that the boosted tree stopped adding layers at our specified maximum (even with our selected tree), there is a chance that fit could have been improved slightly more if we had specified more layers.

The output from a boosted tree (figure 10.10) is quite similar to that of a "regular" partition tree. The primary difference is that the cumulative validation graph shows multiple measures of fit, and graphs them not against the number of splits in a given tree but rather against the cumulative number of layers or trees fit. We can see rapid initial improvement in prediction accomplished by early trees, followed by a long period of slower, steady progress. After boosted trees, column contributions, ROC curves, and lift curves can also be generated. Leaf reports are not available.

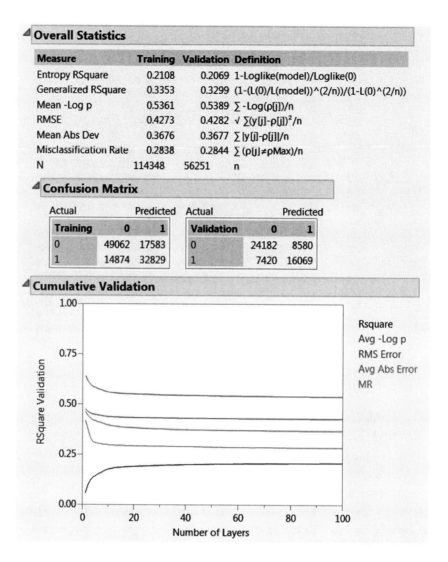

Overall Statistics

Measure	Training	Validation	Definition
Entropy RSquare	0.2108	0.2069	1-Loglike(model)/Loglike(0)
Generalized RSquare	0.3353	0.3299	(1-(L(0)/L(model))^(2/n))/(1-L(0)^(2/n))
Mean -Log p	0.5361	0.5389	$\sum$ -Log(p[j])/n
RMSE	0.4273	0.4282	$\sqrt{\sum(y[j]-p[j])^2/n}$
Mean Abs Dev	0.3676	0.3677	$\sum$ |y[j]-p[j]|/n
Misclassification Rate	0.2838	0.2844	$\sum$ (p[j]≠pMax)/n
N	114348	56251	n

Confusion Matrix

Actual Training	0	1
0	49062	17583
1	14874	32829

Actual Validation	0	1
0	24182	8580
1	7420	16069

Cumulative Validation

Rsquare
Avg -Log p
RMS Error
Avg Abs Error
MR

FIGURE 10.10
Boosted tree output in JMP Pro.

The column contributions (figure 10.11) show us how important each input was to the classification process. Since this tree is different from a standard partition tree, in that a large number of small tree-layers was grown, each on its predecessor's residuals, there is a chance that the relative contribution of the inputs is different from what we saw above. And indeed, this is the case. Though the top two inputs in the partition tree (age and educational attainment) remain the top two inputs here, we see that the input for race is now more important than region. Occupational prestige, which barely played any role at all previously, was tapped most often here to make splits. And the contributions of citizenship and nativity have declined relative to the other inputs.

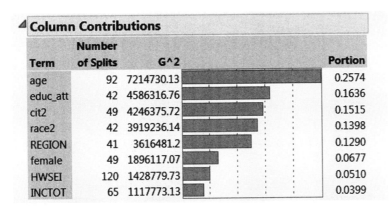

Column Contributions

Term	Number of Splits	G^2		Portion
age	92	7214730.13		0.2574
educ_att	42	4586316.76		0.1636
cit2	49	4246375.72		0.1515
race2	42	3919236.14		0.1398
REGION	41	3616481.2		0.1290
female	49	1896117.07		0.0677
HWSEI	120	1428779.73		0.0510
INCTOT	65	1117773.13		0.0399

FIGURE 10.11
Predictor importance from boosted tree model.

JMP also allows researchers to view individual layers. Since each layer is small, it can be easily viewed in its entirety. Trees can be shown with various degrees of detail; to see as much information as is depicted in figures 10.12 and 10.13, click red triangle > Show Trees > Show Names > Categories. Here we have chosen two layers (layers 8 and 63) at random for demonstration purposes; showing the full 100 layers would be impractical. These two trees make quite different splitting decisions, the first using educational attainment, age, and occupational prestige, and the second using age, income, and citizenship status.

RANDOM FORESTS

A *random forest* (or *bootstrap forest*) makes use of a technique through which a potentially infinite number of random samples can be generated from a finite dataset. Bootstrapping is computationally intense: we sample our data *with replacement* (this is key), thus generating as many separate randomly generated datasets as we require. Since the initial data are randomly collected from a population, by resampling from this sample it is "as if" we are resampling the population, with the (strong) caveat that cases not included in the initial sample have no chance of inclusion in any of the bootstrap resamplings (while those who *were* included initially have equal probabilities of being included, or not, in resamplings). Bootstrapping thus enables statistical analysts to get at least partially around the problem of having a single sample when standard (also known as *frequentist*) statistical theory presumes repeated resampling. For this reason, it is most frequently used as a creative way of getting more "robust" standard errors.

Random forests utilize bootstrapping to grow a large number of separate trees (hence the term *forest*), each on a different randomly selected portion of the data (sampled, of course, with replacement). In addition, forests sample a portion of the predictor variables

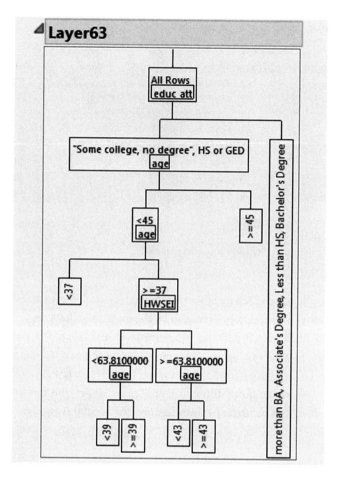

FIGURE 10.12
One layer of a boosted tree.

used to generate splits in a tree. This guarantees that each tree generated will be substantially different. After this, all of the trees are combined and averaged. The purpose is similar to that of cross-validation: it reduces the possibility of overfitting, and increases the likelihood of generalizability.

To run a bootstrap forest, open the Partition launch window as before, and in the Method box, select Bootstrap Forest. All else is the same. When you click OK, the Bootstrap Forest launch platform opens (figure 10.14), allowing parameters to be adjusted. First, we select the number of trees which will be grown to generate the forest. As you may expect, growing more trees will generally lead to a more accurate, generalizable model, but will also increase running time.

We are now able to adjust parameters which set the sampling rates of cases and variables (or, if you like, columns and rows). First we set the "Number of terms sampled per

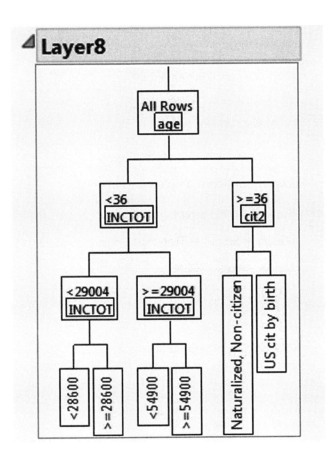

FIGURE 10.13
Another layer of a boosted tree.

split." This refers to the number of independent variables which are used in each tree; the bootstrap forest randomly samples the independent variables as well as the cases (or, if you like, it samples both the rows and the columns of the data matrix). Using more columns allows each tree to be more complicated, but of necessity they will also be more similar, thus surrendering some of the benefit of growing and averaging a large number of varying trees. Next, we set the "Bootstrap sample rate." This indicates the size of the bootstrapped sample to be created from the data (relative to the size of the original sample). A value of 100, for instance, will generate a bootstrap sample equal in size to the original data. Now, this number does not indicate the *proportion* of the data used in the bootstrap sample, for we are sampling with replacement and thus some cases are likely to be selected more than once. This number can, then, be larger than 100. In general, larger samples will lead to more accuracy but also to increased run-time.

"Minimum Splits Per Tree" and "Minimum Size Split" are precisely what they appear to be: they work to set bounds on the complexity of the model, and are guards against

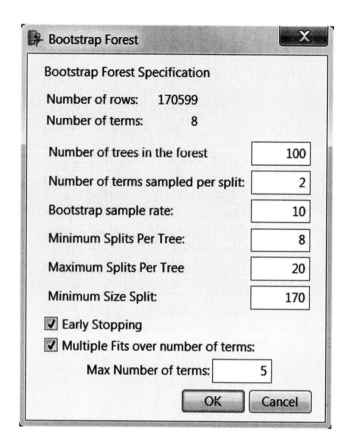

FIGURE 10.14
Bootstrap Forest launch platform in JMP Pro.

oversimplicity and against overfitting, respectively. As with boosted trees, "Early Stopping" cues the program to stop generating more trees if additional trees do not improve validation fit. Finally, "Multiple Fits over number of terms" will, if checked, create a *separate forest* for various values of number of terms, starting at the number specified in "Number of terms sampled per split" and going up the number entered in "Max Number of terms." This option allows more comprehensive modeling, but dramatically increases run-time.

We grew a forest with 100 separate trees (twice the default) and chose a bootstrap sampling rate of 10%. We checked "Multiple Fits over number of terms" and allowed the number of terms to vary between 2 and 5, which led to the program's producing four separate forests of 100 trees each (figure 10.15). Because of this latter choice, the program took four minutes to execute. It settled on five terms per tree as the ideal. Once again, note that at this optimal value the forest contained only 29 trees, which means that early stopping was engaged. However, it is possible that sampling more terms could have improved model fit.

Model Validation-Set Summaries

The fit below was the best of these models fit.

N Terms	N Trees	Entropy RSquare	Misclassification Rate	Avg -Log p	RMS Error	Avg Abs Error
2	36	0.1579	0.3019	0.5725	0.4420	0.4123
3	100	0.1739	0.3001	0.5612	0.4373	0.3989
4	43	0.1813	0.3014	0.5565	0.4357	0.3905
5	29	0.1830	0.2986	0.5549	0.4349	0.3883

FIGURE 10.15

Optimizing a random forest model in JMP Pro by choosing the number of terms sampled.

The fit statistics and other relevant output from a random forest in JMP is depicted in figure 10.16. JMP will automatically produce overall fit statistics, a similar cumulative validation chart to that produced with a boosted tree (except that the *X* axis charts the number of trees in the forest rather than the number of layers in the tree), and a confusion matrix. It will also produce statistics for each individual tree.

By using the red triangle at the top left of the full output window (not displayed), we can see a "small tree view" for each individual tree in the dataset. We can also get such helpful information as column contributions, ROC curves, and lift curves. Predicted probabilities can be generated as well.

Examining the Cumulative Validation graph in figure 10.16, it is interesting to note that the fit statistics do not uniformly improve as the random forest grows more trees. In contrast, the cumulative validation graph for the boosted tree model demonstrated rapid initial improvement in fit, followed by slow but continual progress. This difference is due to the difference in what these two methods are actually doing. Boosted trees are designed to learn from previous mistakes, leading to a closer and closer fit (but with a chance of overfitting). Random forests, on the other hand, grow individual trees sequentially but independently of each other; what one of its individual trees does is entirely a function of the inputs and cases it randomly samples, not of what an earlier tree has done. Therefore, though in the long run the validation statistics will improve (as a larger and larger number of trees are grown and averaged), the progress is not guaranteed in the short run.

The column contribution statistics (figure 10.17) are very similar, in relative terms, to those of the initial partition tree. Age, educational attainment, region of the country, and nativity are again the variables tapped most frequently to split the data. Note, though, that the *number* of splits made here is huge. This is because in the settings for the random forest, we set only a *minimum* number of splits that the model can make per tree; it allows for no maximum. Therefore, most of the trees in this forest are quite elaborate, with many splits each.

It is fair to ask, at this point, which of the three tree variants performs the best. Boosted trees and random forests are variants on the partition tree, but each is far, far

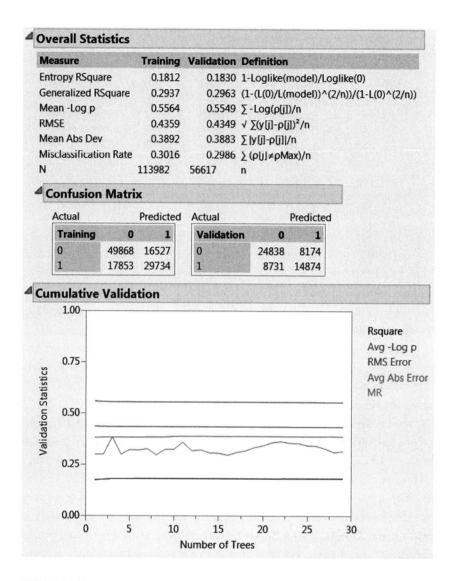

Overall Statistics

Measure	Training	Validation	Definition
Entropy RSquare	0.1812	0.1830	1-Loglike(model)/Loglike(0)
Generalized RSquare	0.2937	0.2963	$(1-(L(0)/L(model))^{(2/n)})/(1-L(0)^{(2/n)})$
Mean -Log p	0.5564	0.5549	$\sum -Log(p[j])/n$
RMSE	0.4359	0.4349	$\sqrt{\sum(y[j]-p[j])^2/n}$
Mean Abs Dev	0.3892	0.3883	$\sum |y[j]-p[j]|/n$
Misclassification Rate	0.3016	0.2986	$\sum (p[j]\neq pMax)/n$
N	113982	56617	n

Confusion Matrix

Actual		Predicted	Actual		Predicted
Training	**0**	**1**	**Validation**	**0**	**1**
0	49868	16527	0	24838	8174
1	17853	29734	1	8731	14874

Cumulative Validation

Rsquare
Avg -Log p
RMS Error
Avg Abs Error
MR

FIGURE 10.16

Output from a random forest in JMP Pro.

more computationally intensive and elaborate. Does all this extra work produce results in terms of increased predictive accuracy? Table 10.1 compares these models using various measures of fit, and the answer it provides is that yes, both the boosted tree and the random forest are superior at out-of-sample classification. But do they improve results substantially? This is up to you to decide. We lean toward the answer that it depends on how important it is that you be as accurate as possible. If your classification problem is not particularly consequential, but you have huge amounts of data and variables to churn through, you may want to save yourself the huge increase in run-time and just build a

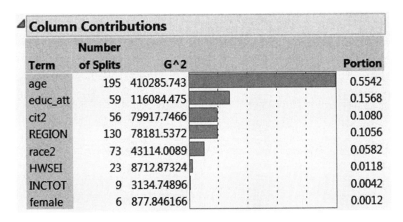

Column Contributions			
Term	**Number of Splits**	**G^2**	**Portion**
age	195	410285.743	0.5542
educ_att	59	116084.475	0.1568
cit2	56	79917.7466	0.1080
REGION	130	78181.5372	0.1056
race2	73	43114.0089	0.0582
HWSEI	23	8712.87324	0.0118
INCTOT	9	3134.74896	0.0042
female	6	877.846166	0.0012

FIGURE 10.17

Predictor importance from a random forest model.

TABLE 10.1   Comparing the Performance of a Partition Tree, a Boosted Tree, and a Random Forest

	Partition tree	Boosted tree	Random forest
McFadden's Pseudo-R^2 (validation)	0.189	0.2069	0.181
Root mean square error (validation)	0.433	0.428	0.435
Misclassification rate (training)	0.288	0.283	0.301
Misclassification rate (validation)	0.292	0.284	0.299
Area under ROC curve (validation)	0.778	0.783	0.752
Sensitivity (training)	0.653	0.688	0.625
Sensitivity (validation)	0.649	0.684	0.630
Specificity (training)	0.753	0.736	0.751
Specificity (validation)	0.750	0.738	0.752

single tree. But if you have a high-impact problem (such as sorting cancerous from noncancerous cells), maybe you will want to wait a bit longer and be more sure.

Boosted trees and random forests harness the basic logic of trees, but combine them with boosting and bootstrapping processes in an attempt to improve model accuracy and generalizability to independent samples. Given the right data and settings, they can outperform their parent, the partition tree, but in our experience do not *always* do so. Moreover, they surrender much of the advantage of the partition tree—its transparency—by substantially increasing complexity. The sheer work it would take to examine each of a large number of trees produced by boosting or in forests is overwhelming (though not in principle impossible). They are more exclusively *predictive* models than their parent— not as helpful for understanding what goes into the classification process. But if these methods confound attempts at interpretation, what we discuss next is even more difficult in this regard. We move next to discussing the "black-box" method *par excellence,* the neural network.

11

NEURAL NETWORKS

Artificial neural networks (ANNs; *neural networks* or *neural nets* for short) are machine-learning tools which are inspired, as the name suggests, by the operation of biological neurons. To get a very general, abstract notion of how ANNs operate, consider the basic functioning of a neuron. Neurons have dendrites which gather input information from other neurons. This information is combined, and when some threshold is reached the neuron "fires." In this fashion, the neuron channels information to other neurons. Additionally, *networks* of neurons are capable of "learning" based on previous errors.

Artificial neural networks work in similar fashion. They gather information from a set of inputs (a dataset with a given set of independent input variables). Each input variable is assigned a weight at random, and the information from all variables is then gathered together through summation, and transformed via some nonlinear function into the value of an outcome. Both input and output variables can be continuous, categorical, or binary.

An example of a neural net such as that described above appears in figure 11.1. We have specified a model with eight inputs, or independent variables. Information from these variables is combined in the circle displaying a smoothed-S shape (representing the hyperbolic tangent function), and used to predict the output variable.

This will help us introduce some neural network terminology. The eight rectangles on the left are the *input nodes* or *input layer*—independent variables which transmit information to the model. The circle represents the *hidden layer* of the neural net, which weights, sums, and transforms information from the inputs. Finally, the rectangle on the right is the *output layer*, the predicted probability of the outcome.

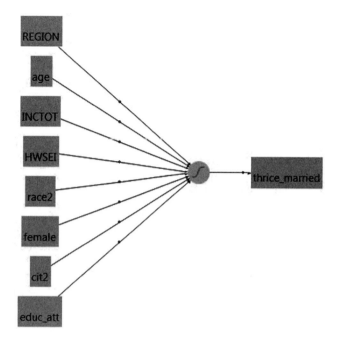

FIGURE 11.1
A simple neural network (image from JMP Pro).

This is a simple neural net, which for all intents and purposes is a logistic regression. Generally, neural networks improve upon logistic regression by adding complexity through multiple hidden nodes. A more typical neural net appears in figure 11.2. The hidden layer now consists of *four* hidden nodes. Each variable in the input layer is connected independently to each hidden node, which in turn is connected to the response variable.

To understand why this is important, let's consider what the neural net does when it passes information from inputs to a single hidden node. Each input node represents a single variable, which has a finite set of values of a given distribution (binomial, normal, etc.). As each variable passes its information to the hidden node, it is assigned a weight, which is analogous to a regression coefficient. The weighted values are then added, along with an intercept term, and the result is transformed via a specified function. This produces an output value.

It is important to elaborate here that the weights referred to above are initially *randomly chosen* by the neural net platform. They are then adjusted iteratively as the model progresses through the data to correct for prediction mistakes. The same process occurs in *each hidden node*. That is, in each node, *different* randomly chosen weights are applied to each variable and then iteratively adjusted. Thus, the number of predicted values of the dependent variable generated in each hidden layer is equal to the number of hidden

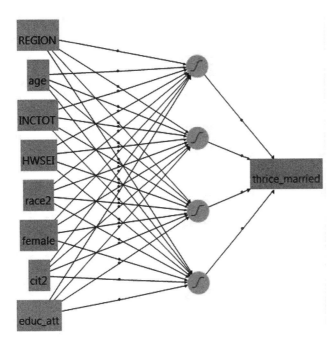

FIGURE 11.2
A neural network with multiple hidden nodes.

nodes in that layer. These predicted values are *also* assigned a random weight, and *these* weighted values are *also* iteratively adjusted and combined to produce single predicted probability of the outcome.

It is possible, in addition, to have more than one hidden layer. JMP allows the building of models with two hidden layers, and experts generally agree that for most problems two hidden layers are sufficient. The second layer simply uses the first hidden layer as an input layer and performs the same process of weighting, combining, and transforming as the first hidden layer performs on its inputs.

The weighting-and-iterative-correction process requires a bit of elaboration. Remember that the weights assigned in each hidden node are analogous to regression coefficients. In fact an intercept term is added as well, so it is entirely accurate to think of each hidden node as essentially performing a nonlinear regression. Neural nets choose regression coefficients in a manner much more similar to logistic regression, which uses maximum-likelihood estimation, than to OLS regression. Just like maximum-likelihood, the neural formula starts out with a randomly chosen "guess" at the best value and adjusts after this.

However, unlike logistic regression, it does not do this using all of the data, but instead goes observation by observation. In this way, the neural net is able to learn from predictive "mistakes" it makes as it works through the training dataset in order to fine-tune its parameters. Now, it has to simultaneously adjust a very large number of parameters, and it does so by moving, in a complicated process, from the output node "upstream" to each of the hidden nodes, and thence to each of the input nodes, adjusting each weight along the way. Through this process, the net "trains itself" to better guess at the predicted value based on the data that came before.

One of the advantages of the neural network is that it handles nonlinearity much better than ordinary regression techniques, especially given enough hidden nodes. And it is able to handle them without specified input from the researcher. The researcher does not need to manually input interaction terms or transformed terms (squares, log transformations, etc.); the model will more or less map them itself.

But this is not to say that neural nets are fully automated. There are numerous model parameters which, to optimize prediction, need to be toggled by the researcher through multiple runs of a given neural net, as we will see in a minute. Tuning a neural net is very much a "trial-and-error" process.

Another advantage of this technique is enhanced predictive capacity. Neural nets are generally superior to regression models (or, in theory, even classification trees) at generating accurate predictions. Like classification trees, they also handle both continuous and categorical outcomes perfectly well.

But like all techniques, neural networks have some disadvantages.

First and foremost, neural nets are notorious for producing output that is almost completely opaque (they are frequently referred to as a "black-box" method). Unlike regressions, neural nets don't make it easy to tell a story about the relation between the inputs and the output. It is possible with JMP to look at the weights or coefficients which make up the model, but these do not admit of easy interpretation. We thus encounter the same trade-off between predictive accuracy and interpretability as occurred with large partition trees. By comparison with a neural net, though, a large partition tree is a model of easy readability. It is, after all, possible to read any branch of a tree and understand it. But neural nodes give us the iteratively generated weights for a large number of interactive parameters. And the meaning, for instance, of the weight of a first level hidden node's contribution to a given second-layer hidden node is not very easy to grasp.

Second, because they are based on an iterative learning process which builds on initial random guesses, neural nets are somewhat inconsistent. Running a neural net program in JMP twice, on the same data, using the same variables, with the same parameter settings, and validating on the same cases will produce two different models, with fit statistics which vary not insubstantially. This instability of the neural platform is reduced when we use larger datasets and less complex models, but it remains regardless.

Thirdly, neural nets, since they specialize in prediction, have a strong tendency to overfit data. However, this can be counteracted by using cross-validation. If the fit statistics in your test set are significantly worse than in your training set, it means that you have built a model that is too complex and specific, and you need to dial back the complexity of the models (this is usually accomplished by specifying fewer hidden nodes).

Routines for neural networks exist in SPSS Modeler, R (package neuralnet), SAS (PROC NEURAL), and MATLAB. We will run an example in JMP Pro, because its routine is highly flexible and offers excellent data visualization tools. In our example we again use data from the American Community Survey. These data have been altered to contain only working-age adults who were employed at the time of interview, and we sampled 5% of the cases (to speed up operation of the programs). We will be predicting personal income using a set of covariates.

To begin to build the model, open the initial variable selection platform for neural networks (Analyze Modeling Neural). In this window we can specify the independent and dependent variables in the neural model. We set the Y variable to be the natural log of personal total income. Predictor variables chosen are region of the country, age, educational attainment, a dummy flagging those who are enrolled as students anywhere, citizenship and nativity, gender, race, number of weeks the respondent worked in the previous year, and usual hours worked per week in the previous year. We could also set a validation variable here if we wanted; this is often good to do if you want to compare how different tunings of the neural network on the same training and validation sets.

We click OK and get the Neural launch platform (figure 11.3), and we encounter a large set of controls and parameters that we need to set. The top panel of this platform lets us specify the validation procedure. We can choose between a holdback portion, excluded rows (if we have previously excluded rows; this is equivalent to using a holdback validation variable), or k-fold cross-validation. We choose to hold back a third of the data to validate.

The next panel lets us choose how many hidden layers we want, how many nodes per layer, and what kind of transformations (or *activations*) we want to occur in each node. Only two layers are available here. Using more layers and more nodes per layer exponentially increases the complexity of the model. This will tend to produce more accurate prediction in the training set, but also increase the likelihood of overfitting in the test set.

JMP uses the hyperbolic tangent (tanh) function as the default here. This is a sigmoidal (S-shaped) function, similar to the logistic function but centered and scaled. The "linear" activation uses the simple linear identity link function that OLS regression uses. Finally, there is the Gaussian transformation, which uses the function e^{-x^2} to transform the linear combination of the x's. The tanh and Gaussian activations both enable the model to capture complex nonlinearities in the data; if we used only the linear activation function, we would in effect be performing a complicated linear regression.

The next panel permits us to employ additive boosting to the neural net. This works much like boosted trees: we fit a series of smaller neural nets one after another, each on the scaled residuals from the previous model. This process should in theory improve prediction. The learning rate tells the model to what degree it should adjust weights on the basis of newer information from the last model. Lower learning rates down-weight new information and integrate it more with older estimates; higher learning rates (closer

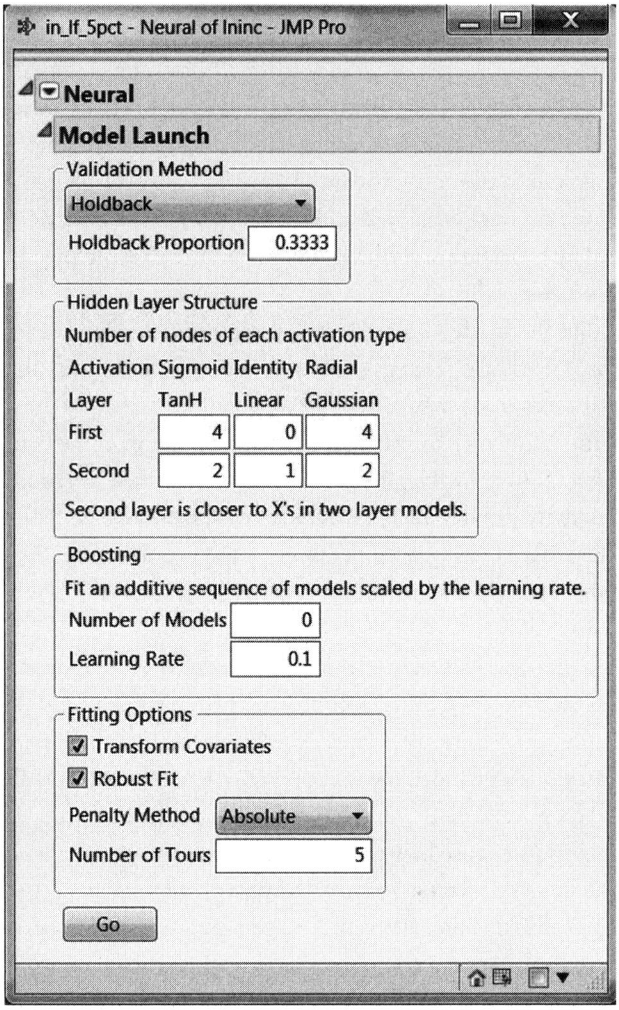

Neural

Model Launch

Validation Method

Holdback

Holdback Proportion | 0.3333

Hidden Layer Structure

Number of nodes of each activation type

Activation Sigmoid Identity Radial

Layer	TanH	Linear	Gaussian
First	4	0	4
Second	2	1	2

Second layer is closer to X's in two layer models.

Boosting

Fit an additive sequence of models scaled by the learning rate.

Number of Models | 0

Learning Rate | 0.1

Fitting Options

☑ Transform Covariates
☑ Robust Fit

Penalty Method | Absolute

Number of Tours | 5

Go

FIGURE 11.3

The Neural launch platform in JMP Pro.

to 1) result in higher weighting of newer data. There is here a trade-off here between speed of convergence and tendency to overfit. Higher learning rates permit faster convergence but more likely to fit specifically to the particular data one is working with.

Next, there are a series of fine-tuning options. "Transform Covariates" refers to an automatic transformation that JMP can make to the input variables which corrects for skewing, and thus work to "normalize" the variables. This can make neural nets more accurate, and is recommended. Second, for continuous outcomes a "Robust Fit" option is offered. This reduces the impact of outliers in the data. We have already logged income, which should rein in this problem, but we enable the option just in case. The "Penalty Method" is yet another way of guarding against overfitting to the data by imposing a "penalty parameter" on the estimates. Here we specify the functional form of this parameter (the value of the parameter itself is arrived at by validation). The default is the square of the penalty parameter; use this unless (a) there are a large number of predictors and (b) you think that some of them are far more influential than others on the model. In that situation it is recommended to use either the Absolute or the Weight Decay form.

Neural nets use randomly generated starting values to begin fitting the data, and adjust these over time. The "Number of Tours" setting instructs the program to create a number of *separate neural nets,* using different random starting values for weights. From these it will choose the model that best fits the validation data. Because of the instability of neural models mentioned above, this is a good option to take; even though it increases running time, multiple models should always be run in order to achieve good fit.

After running a neural net, the default output from JMP is rather sparse (figure 11.4). It consists simply of fit statistics. An R^2 from a neural net with continuous outcomes is precisely equivalent to an R^2 from an OLS regression: it is the proportion of the variance in the outcome accounted for by the model. Likewise, the R^2 produced for neural nets with dichotomous or categorical outcomes are identical to the pseudo-R^2 calculated for probit or logit models (in this case, McFadden's pseudo-R^2). Validation statistics are provided for both the training and test models; one should in particular inspect the differences in fit between these two in order to determine whether the model has been substantially overfit. If a model is overfit, typically this means that a sparer model will fit better on the validation set.

JMP excels in data visualization, and neural nets are no exception to this. One of the menu options (in the menu triangle next to Model) is Diagram, which will give a visual representation of the neural net you just ran. Note that there are three different symbols that appear in hidden layer nodes; these indicate the three separate activation functions we used in this neural net model.

Clicking the red triangle at the top left of the output window (figure 11.4, next to Model) and selecting Show Estimates will display the equivalent of coefficient estimates for all the parameters in the model. Doing this demonstrates the famed *opacity* of the neural net referenced above. Despite the iterative learning process that goes into building it, the resulting neural net can, like a regression, be represented as a single complex equation, and in the end what it has done is to estimate a set of parameters. However, this is a very large set of parameters; the neural net above, for instance, has estimated around 200 of them. Many of these represent quantities like the connection between the third hidden node in the first layer and the fifth hidden node in the second layer. These of course are the result of transformed summations of prior weighted inputs, and so cannot be interpreted in isolation. Such a parameter is combined with other parameters and subjected to a mathematical transformation, so that its effect on the outcome variable is even more obscure. And this is true of *all* the parameters in the model. None has real meaning outside of its particular appearance in the full architecture of the neural net. For this reason, though neural nets are, in a mathematical sense, *completely transparent* (in that they can be expressed as an equation), the relations they sketch are quite impervious to interpretation.

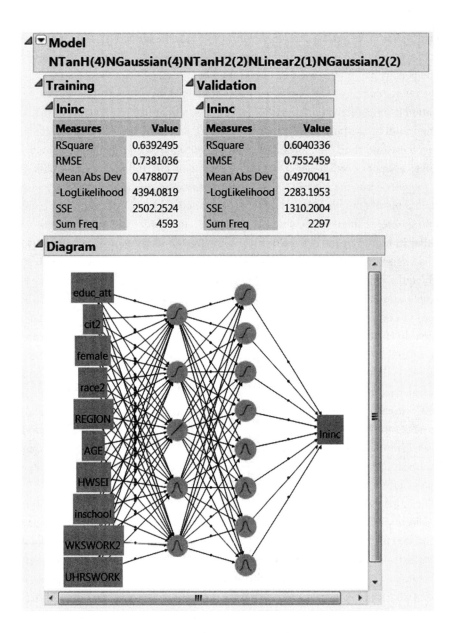

FIGURE 11.4
Output from a neural network in JMP Pro (with a visualization of the network).

JMP, however, has included a feature which helps to address this drawback. As it does with regression models, it provides a set of "profiler" features which allow the researcher to explore the marginal relations between the various inputs and the output.

The Surface Profiler lets us look at a three-dimensional representation of the data (figure 11.5). One axis, of course (Z), will always be the outcome variable. The other two

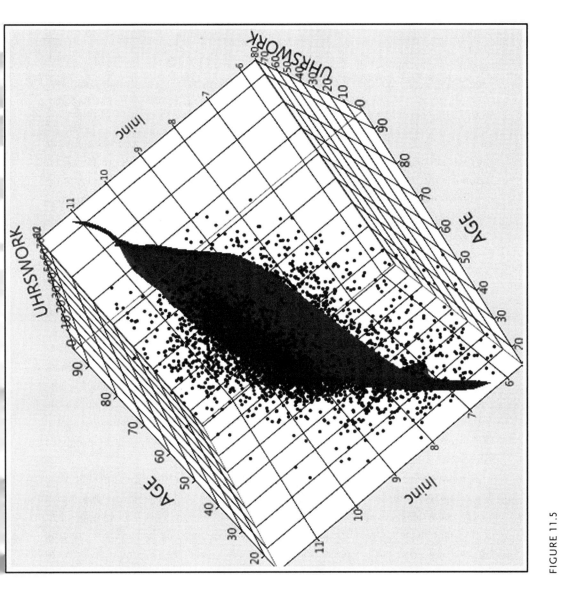

FIGURE 11.5

Three-dimensional depiction of the data using JMP Pro's Surface Profiler.

TABLE II.I   Predicted Income by Race and Gender Calculated Using a JMP Profiler
Feature

	Men	Women	Difference
White	$43,480	$35,950	$7,530
Black	$41,360	$29,143	$12,217
Latino	$38,560	$32,532	$6,028
Asian	$46,630	$34,540	$12,090

axes we can set, and this permits us to examine the three-way relation between any two variables and the response variable, for various settings of all of the other variables. We can move this box around three-dimensionally so that we can see various angles of the nonlinear relations. These are smoothed representations of the predicted relations from the model; to get an idea of how the real data fits to this, choose the Actual option under Appearance. This will plot the actual data points in three-dimensional space along with the predicted relation.

The profiler lets us look at how each variable, when moved along its range, affects the relation between all the other variables and the outcome. This option lets us see exactly how good neural nets are at mapping complex nonlinearities in the data. It also lets us observe marginal effects very clearly. The researcher can set all other variables at quantities of interest, and then toggle an individual variable along its range. This lets us see, for example, the effect of race and gender on personal income, letting us look at gender differences in income by race. Among 35-year-olds in the South Atlantic region (the largest) who work full-time (40 hours per week, 50–52 weeks per year), were born in the U.S., and are of middling occupational prestige (40) and in the median category of educational attainment for the population (some college, no degree), we calculated the predicted values of income by race and gender (table II.I).

Remember, we are holding constant most of the really robust determinants of income (hours and weeks worked, age, occupation, and education)—through which labor-market disadvantage typically expresses itself. This, combined with the fact that we have an R^2 of .60 in the *validation* data, gives us good reason to be confident that we are witnessing real race and gender differences rather than specification error. JMP has allowed us to see a clearly complex pattern of joint determination of income by race and gender, all without explicitly specifying it in the model. Interactions like this are automatically generated by neural net models.

Neural networks are extremely popular and flexible algorithms for prediction. They can be used to predict continuous, dichotomous, or multicategory outcomes, and they do so with substantial accuracy. They are notoriously resistant to interpretation, even though they do produce quantities which are directly analogous to regression coefficients. Nonetheless, in combination with features like JMP Pro's profiler, they can be used to examine interesting marginal relations, though at present *average* marginal effects cannot be produced.

In the next couple of sections, we move to examine a series of unsupervised methods for studying relations in data.

12

CLUSTERING

Cluster analysis is designed to address a very common situation in research. You may think that cases in your data—cities, students, children, or labor unions—do not represent a simple random smattering of individual observations, but are better described as *groups* of observations. What we want to do is to separate our cases into categories or *clusters* of cases—to do what is in some sense the simplest, most natural kind of social modeling, the kind everyone does constantly on an ad hoc basis in regular social life. But we want to do it with more precision, theoretical sophistication, and empirical support than is normally done.

How, then, are we to form our clusters? And how are we to confirm that the clusters we stipulate are actually the best, or even a decent, way of classifying our data? Typically we are guided by theory and some degree of observation—think of Paul Willis's (1977) types of students in *Learning to Labour* or of Esping-Andersen's (1990) taxonomy of welfare regimes in *The Three Worlds of Welfare Capitalism*. Or, if we are more quantitatively inclined, perhaps we propose some method of grouping our cases which makes use of two or three variables, and then we look for confirmation that cases within a cluster are indeed similar in terms of some outcome variable of interest (using ANOVA or regression with dummy variables, for instance).

Cluster analysis can be thought of as a more powerful, sophisticated manner of going about both creating categories and confirming the existence of categories. But it does so by leveraging not merely one or two dimensions of characteristics but as many as you have in your data which you think are relevant. And it "confirms" the existence of these categories through the use of all of the variables specified, not merely by using one privileged target or outcome variable. Finally, it permits empirical data to play a sizeable role in the generation of categories, rather than being dominated by theory (though theory, as always, plays a role).

SIMILARITY AND DISTANCE

We generate categories in cluster analysis by grouping cases together which are similar, according to a prespecified set of relevant characteristics which form *input variables* for the clustering routine. Now, what constitutes "similarity"? Mathematically, two observations will be more similar if they have similar *values* for many or all of the input variables specified. This is obvious if we have only one variable, but becomes harder to think about when we have a large set of variables. This gets into the matter of defining *distance in multidimensional space.*

Mathematicians have many ways of describing distance, but thankfully one of the most common ways distance is calculated in cluster analysis is familiar to all of us from high school geometry: Euclidean distance. Let's say you have two dimensions, and two points in those dimensions, and we want to know the distance between these points. The easy answer is that this distance is given by the shortest straight line between these points. In high school geometry, we plotted both points on a Cartesian plane, and then employed the Pythagorean theorem to find the length of the shortest line that connected them. That is, between two points A and B, each defined by two coordinates (x, y), we find the distance by

$$d_{EUC}(A, B) = \sqrt{(x_A - x_B)^2 + (y_A - y_B)^2}$$

But what if we have more than two dimensions? The great thing is that it does not matter—this method generalizes to three, ten, n dimensions. Cases which are similar will have relatively small Euclidean distances separating them, regardless of the number of dimensions specified. If we want to know the distance between two points A and B in a space defined by four coordinates (x, y, z, d), this is accomplished by:

$$d_{EUC}(A, B) = \sqrt{(x_A - x_B)^2 + (y_A - y_B)^2 + (z_A - z_B)^2 + (d_A - d_B)^2}$$

Other types of distances can also be used. We might use Manhattan (or "city-block") distance, which is the sum of the absolute values of the differences between input values. Or we could use Minkowski distance, which is a generalization of both Euclidean and Manhattan distance to higher powers. Or we could take variable correlations into account by using Mahalanobis distance.

GENERAL STRENGTHS OF CLUSTERING

Cluster analysis can be highly fruitful for both exploratory and confirmatory purposes. In the former case, it may be that we do not yet have a firm idea of the subgroups into which observations might fall, or even if they could be profitably so divided. Clustering lets us search for latent groups in the data, given important characteristics. It can tell us, after a fashion, whether our data are clustered at all, and if so how these underlying clusters differ. On the other hand, perhaps we have a *theory* about existing subgroups. In that case, we can use clustering to determine whether, and to what extent, our theory is empirically supported by our data. Perhaps it is, or perhaps we will discover that there is some better way of sorting our cases into categories.

Another possible use of clustering is the exploration of different covariance structures in different parts of the data. Typically, when we analyze relations between variables—in linear regression, for instance—we look for linear relations that obtain in all of the data. Or, at most, we generate a few interaction terms to allow for the possibility that these relations might depend on other variables. Clustering allows us to go beyond this. Through clustering, we can find subspaces of the data in which relations between variables vary dramatically. We might find that the correlation between two variables is .78 in cluster A, for instance, and −.24 in cluster B. This means that the relation between variables is different in different chunks of our data, and we can use clusters to generate complex sets of interaction terms for later inclusion in regression models. This use of clustering is quite similar to mixture modeling, which we discuss later.

THEORY DEPENDENCE

It is important, though, to emphasize the importance of the choice of inputs in the determination of categories. Cluster analysis is not a magic formula for uncovering latent groupings in the world. Rather, what it yields is entirely a function of what the researcher puts into it. Whether two cases are "similar" or "different" in terms of their Euclidean distances depends on the variables specified. Change those variables, and you change both the distances between cases and, ultimately, the shape of the clusters which emerge at the end. So it is essential to choose carefully the dimensions you think are important to your research question, and to represent them well in the set of input variables. Cluster analysis is in this way similar to factor analysis and to principal component analysis, in which the choice of inputs determines the specific components or factors that result.

It is important to note that in cluster analyses *each variable has equal influence* in the formation of clusters. This is important to consider for two reasons. First, it may be that you don't think that each variable should be equally important, for theoretical reasons. You might want some variables to be more heavily weighted than others. Secondly, sometimes you have to use more than one variable to capture a given dimension or social reality. The racial makeup of a city, for example, can really only be expressed through a group of variables (percentage black, percentage white, percent Asian, etc.). This racial dimension will have as much weight in the determination of clusters as the number of variables used, and because it is represented by three or more variables it might overwhelm other measures (like population size) which can be captured with only one variable.

There are a number of different subspecies of cluster analysis, but we will focus here on four which are available in JMP: *hierarchical clustering, k-means clustering, normal mixtures,* and *self-organizing maps.* Each of these has strengths and weaknesses which we will discuss below.

HIERARCHICAL CLUSTERING

In this method, we start with all of our cases separated out individually—think of each being its own little single-member cluster. Of these clusters, we find the two which are the most proximate, and we aggregate them into a larger cluster. We repeat, joining the closest two clusters at each step, until finally we have one single, large cluster with all cases in it. Thus, hierarchal clustering is an agglomerative procedure, which generates, throughout the process, any possible number of clusters between one and the number of cases in the data. Smaller clusters from earlier in the process are, in a sense, nested within larger clusters formed later. How the cases are aggregated is shown after the fact in a graph known as a *dendrogram.*

We discussed earlier how to determine how proximate or similar two individual cases or observations are, but hierarchical clustering usually joins not just two cases but two clusters, each of which contains multiple cases. How is the distance between two *clusters* determined? In JMP, there are four methods of calculating this. (One must be chosen by the user at the outset.) *Single-linkage* clustering defines the distance between two clusters as the *minimum* distance between any member of the first cluster and any member of the second cluster. In contrast, *complete-linkage* clustering defines it as the *maximum* distance between any two members of these two clusters. These two methods of determining distance are both highly sensitive to outliers. The compromise between them is *average-linkage* clustering, which uses the *average* distance between all members of the two clusters. *Ward linkage* is more complex; it combines the two clusters whose union would result in the smallest increase in total within-cluster variance, as defined by some function (usually the error sum of squares).

At the end of hierarchical clustering, as mentioned above, we have not a number of separate groups but rather a big ball of cases cumulatively joined together. But the point of clustering is to create discrete groups. How do we divide the big ball of cases into the discrete clusters we were looking for? And how do we determine how many groups there ought to be?

The answer to the second question will help us to answer the first. Remember that hierarchal clustering generates any number of clusters between 1 and *n*, the latter being the number of cases in our dataset. It is ultimately up to us to decide how many clusters we ought to have. But we have guidance in this decision by inspecting the dendrogram and the clustering history. In JMP, after running a hierarchical clustering routine, a dendrogram will be produced. If you change the dendrogram scale to Distance Scale (red triangle Dendrogram Scale Distance Scale), it will show how much relative distance is crossed to join two clusters. Under this, a rectangular scree plot will be generated, which plots the sequential order of the clustering by the distance between joined clusters. In both the scree plot and the dendrogram we are looking to identify a "natural breakpoint" at which the distance between clusters increases rapidly (this is analogous to using a scree plot to determine the number of factors to use in factor analysis). This can also be done numerically by examining the clustering history.

Answering the question "How many clusters?" in turn answers the question "Which cases go in each cluster?" For cases are joined sequentially according to the distance separating them; we are simply, by choosing the number of clusters, deciding where in the agglomeration process it is optimal to stop. Cases will be in whatever cluster they were in at this stage.

Hierarchical clustering is recommended principally for small datasets with 200 or fewer cases. In fact, it is ideal for data of this size, for it is less sensitive to the influence of outliers in small datasets than are other methods discussed below, especially *k*-means clustering. With large numbers of cases, it tends to be computationally intensive, and other methods are preferred.

HIERARCHICAL CLUSTERING IN JMP

We are going to use hierarchical clustering to group together U.S. counties in the 2012 election dataset. Now, to use hierarchical clustering in the most appropriate setting, we have randomly selected only a small number of counties (75, to be exact).

We open the Clustering dialog box (Analyze > Multivariate Methods > Cluster). In this window (figure 12.1), hierarchical clustering is set as the default (under Options at lower left). The program allows a choice of linkage functions, and we select Ward. The Standardize Data option is checked; this is a nice feature, because we want the inputs to be on the same scale.

We select as input variables percentage of the county identifying as non-Hispanic white, percentage with a bachelor's degree or higher, poverty rate, and natural log of population density. Clicking OK launches the analysis.

A dendrogram, scree plot, and clustering history are automatically produced. We will use these charts, along with the clustering history, to choose our clusters. We adjust the dendrogram to reflect distances (red triangle > Dendrogram > Scale > Distance) and to make clusters visually distinct (red triangle > Color Clusters; red triangle > Mark Clusters). The dendrogram and scree plot are shown in figure 12.2.

This visualization will assist us in choosing the number of clusters we will retain. There is a small diamond-shaped marker at both the top and the bottom of the dendrogram; by scrolling this right and left, it is possible to change the number of clusters. We can also look to where, on the scree plot, the distance between clusters begins to rise precipitously—toward the very end, five combinations from the far right. This would be a good number of final clusters. That this is a good choice can be verified by looking at the clustering history, which in JMP appears under the dendrogram (but is not shown

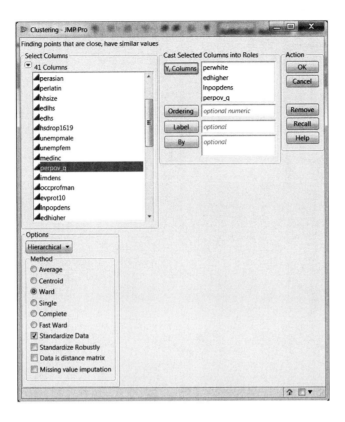

FIGURE 12.1
Clustering launch platform in JMP Pro.

here). We look for a point where the distance between clusters begins to rise more rapidly than previously. Here, to go from five to four clusters requires crossing a distance of 1.85, while going from six to five crosses a distance of only 0.07. We therefore settle upon five clusters as a good solution.

Once you have the number of clusters you want, it is possible to save the clusters (red triangle > Save Clusters). This will create a new variable in the data, called "cluster." You may also want to Save Display Order, which saves the order of the cases in the present dendrogram, from top to bottom.

You can then explore how variables differ by cluster, which shows the meaning of the clusters (table 12.1). In these data, among our 75-case sample, cluster 1 has the lowest proportion of the population which is non-Hispanic white, the highest poverty rate, and the lowest population density. Cluster 2 has a relatively high percentage of whites and population density and middling rates of both poverty and college-educated adults. Cluster 3 has the lowest percentage of the population with a college degree, a relatively high poverty rate, and a fairly high density of whites. Cluster 4 is the most heavily white and the most sparsely populated, and has a relatively low poverty rate. Finally, cluster 5 contains counties which

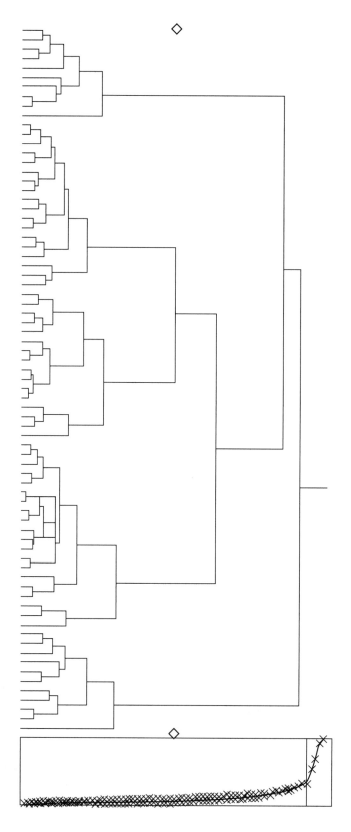

FIGURE 12.2
A dendrogram depicting clustering of cases from JMP
Pro's hierarchical clustering routine.

TABLE 12.1   Characteristics of Clusters Produced by Hierarchical Clustering

	Cluster 1	Cluster 2	Cluster 3	Cluster 4	Cluster 5
% white	52.05	85.65	88.47	91.22	79.81
% higher ed.	16.85	21.27	11.95	18.53	35.97
Poverty rate	20.45	11.21	17.12	9.15	6.58
Population density (log)	2.97	4.85	3.76	2.01	5.66
% Obama	41.78	38.32	31.62	29.22	46.71
N	10	18	16	20	11

on average have highly educated adult populations, high population density, and low poverty. The average vote for Obama was highest in clusters 1 and 5, which corresponds to results we have shown previously, that county Democratic vote share tended to be higher in more racially diverse counties and in counties with high levels of education. However, recall that the counties we included here are a small random subset (about a 2.5% sample), so generalizing on the basis of these findings should be done with caution. In the next section, we use techniques which permit the inclusion of all counties.

K-MEANS CLUSTERING

K-means clustering, the most popular clustering procedure, is quite a bit different from hierarchical clustering. Most importantly, in k-means the clusters are not nested—in no sense are smaller clusters subsumed by larger clusters. Rather, k-means clustering (and in fact this is true of the other two forms of clustering we will discuss) creates a given number of *discrete* clusters, separating the data into discontinuous parts rather than agglomerating it all. Also, the number of clusters is not determined as an outcome of the clustering operation but must be stipulated by the researcher in advance. Finally, k-means clustering is more likely than hierarchical clustering to stumble into less-than-optimal solutions, necessitating quite a bit of supervisory work on the part of the researcher.

At the outset of k-means clustering, the researcher specifies k, which is the number of clusters to be found in the data, along with a set of input variables. The program proceeds to choose k points *at random* in multivariate space; frequently it does so by choosing a set of actual data points or cases. These points become the centers (or "centroids") of clusters. K-means clustering then calculates the (Euclidean) distance between each case and each centroid, and "assigns" a case to the centroid to which it is most proximate. We thus get k centroids, each surrounded by a misshapen "cloud" of cases. Next, k-means clustering finds the *mean* or *center* of each of these point-clouds (it is unlikely that the mean will be the initially chosen point), and makes these points the new centroids. It repeats the same steps as above—calculating distances, assigning cases to centroids, finding mean points and shifting centroids—over and over until the program converges to a stable solution. At this point we have a set of k clusters, each made up of a given number of cases.

The first obvious question to sort out is how we go about choosing the number of clusters we want. There are two possible answers to this question. We could choose our value for k according to some theory; we might choose three welfare-state regimes, for example, if we are guided by Esping-Andersen's typology. This may or may not be the optimal number of clusters empirically, however, leading us to the second approach. In this solution, we proceed like a proper data miner, and try a number of different values for k (usually over a range), selecting the one in which the solution is best.

But how do we know which solution is "best"? There are in fact a couple of fit statistics we can use to help us determine this. The most useful in this case is the *dissimilarity ratio*: the ratio of the distance between clusters to the distance within clusters. We should choose the number of clusters which maximizes this ratio. The great thing about this measure is that, unlike in other measures of fit (such as the sum of squared errors), the dissimilarity ratio does not automatically decrease when we add clusters. Adding clusters may reduce within-cluster distance (more clusters means each cluster will take up a smaller space and include fewer cases), but it will also probably reduce between-cluster distance (more clusters in the same multidimensional space means the clusters themselves are packed more tightly). Therefore, there is likely to be an "optimal" solution to the number-of-clusters question identifiable using the dissimilarity ratio. Unfortunately, JMP does not produce this ratio automatically (as it ought to); users need to calculate it themselves. How to do this will be described below.

Using the dissimilarity ratio can help us choose k, but this in no way ensures that we will find an optimal solution. To understand why this is, remember how initial cluster starting-points are chosen: at random. Leveraging randomness helps remove subjective bias from the procedure, but it has the unfortunate quality of rarely finding the perfect solution to a problem. Iterating through the algorithm to move the center-point certainly helps somewhat in correcting this, but the final solution remains unfortunately influenced by the randomly chosen initial starting values.

Consider the following. Let's say that our data contain k "real" clusters. And let's say we get lucky and choose the same value of k for the number of clusters to find with our k-means clustering program. The program chooses k central points at random and begins to iterate. But the likelihood that randomness enables us to choose central points in such a way that each "real" cluster has one and only one central point chosen within it is very, very low. It is rather like knowing that there are eight dartboards on a wall; if we throw eight darts randomly at the wall, most likely some boards will have multiple darts in them, and some will have none.

If all real clusters are the same size (which is best for our purposes, but is of course unlikely), then the number of ways we could choose one point per cluster is $k!$ ($1 \times 2 \times 3 \times \ldots \times k$). But the number of ways we could choose k points is k^k (assuming that all of our multivariate space is "in the territory of" one or another real cluster). This means

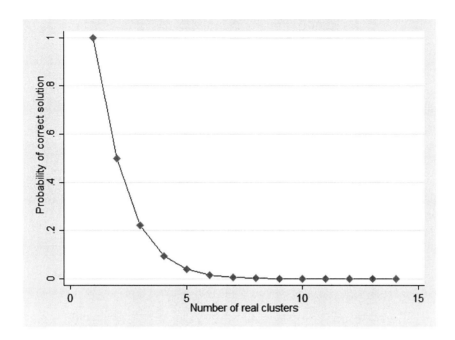

FIGURE 12.3

The probability of selecting one centroid per "real" cluster, by number of "real" clusters.

that in general our probability of choosing one point per cluster ($P = k!/k^k$) is low, and it plummets when the number of clusters increases (see figure 12.3). By the time we have just five clusters, the probability of initially choosing one centroid per cluster has fallen to .038. By the time we are at 11 clusters, our odds are about one in 10,000.

As previously noted, iteratively moving the central point will help somewhat, but does not guarantee that we converge to an optimal solution. The odds are even lower if the clusters are not of equal size, or are not of equal density, or are not "spherical"—and chances are, in real data, at least one of these problems will be encountered. The ways of dealing with this problem with k-means clustering are threefold. First, within any given value of k we can try to both minimize the sum of squared errors and maximize the dissimilarity ratio. This involves rerunning the algorithm a number of times, looking for which solution is "best" but also for solutions which recur—the same cases ending up in one cluster together time and time again. Second, we can use methods of visualization, looking for outlying cases which could be skewing findings, and inspecting the clusters themselves to see whether we think the solution is feasible (JMP permits looking at the clustering solution with two- and three-dimensional principal component plots). Finally, we should remember that the existence in our data of any number of "true" clusters is pretty unlikely; clustering solutions are best regarded as heuristics for helping us simplify data and search for interesting patterns, rather than to uncover hidden layers of reality. Therefore, if it is true that the degree to which a clustering solution is "right" will always be relative; similarly, it can only be so "wrong."

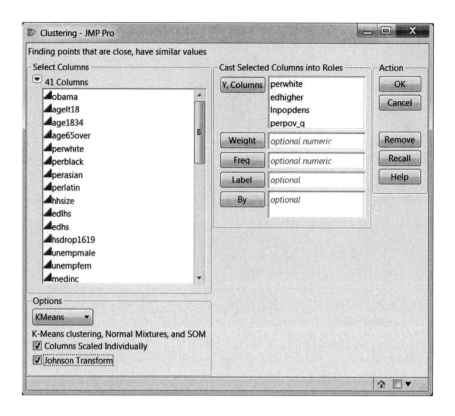

FIGURE 12.4
Choosing *k*-means clustering in JMP Pro's Cluster launch platform.

K-MEANS CLUSTERING IN JMP

We are going to use the 2012 county-level election data (which we just used for hierarchical clustering) to carry out *k*-means clustering, but this time we will use all 3,114 counties rather than a small sample of them. This is done by opening the data and finding the initial Clustering dialog box (figure 12.4). In the menu under Options in the lower-left-hand corner, we change the setting from Hierarchical to KMeans. We also choose to "Johnson Transform" the input variables, which normalizes skewed variables and reins in outlying cases. We make use of the same set of input variables that we used for hierarchical clustering, but we add Obama vote share, percentage of the population that is black, and median income. The Iterative Clustering launch platform opens (for its general appearance, see figure 12.7, later in the chapter).

We select a number of clusters, or alternatively, a range for *k*. We allow the program to give us results for 3–5 clusters (not shown). It is also a good idea to use within-cluster standard deviations; this will help in calculating fit statistics later.[1]

We have used the full population of 3,441 counties, and we see in figure 12.5 that most have ended up in a single cluster (cluster 2). Many of the other generated clusters

K Means NCluster=3

Columns Scaled Individually, Use within-cluster std deviations

Cluster Summary

Cluster	Count	Step	Criterion
1	136	24	0
2	2890		
3	88		

Cluster Means

Cluster	perwhite	edhigher	lnpopdens	perpov_q	obama	medinc	perblack
1	0.97505188	0.24401959	-1.7185925	-0.6253437	-1.2323663	-0.1389045	-1.7367295
2	-0.0868893	0.03458119	0.08513217	-0.0041018	0.07714976	0.05269747	0.10880101
3	1.34662458	-1.5127989	-0.1398114	1.10114552	-0.6291022	-1.515962	-0.8890874

FIGURE 12.5

K-means clustering output in JMP Pro.

have small numbers of cases. This could mean that (a) our data aren't very amenable to clustering, (2) we chose the wrong number of clusters, (3) we have found a nonoptimal "local solution," or (4) our actual data consist of a whole lot of similar cases with various groups of outliers. We can check for this by rerunning the analysis; but note that if we simply "Relaunch Analysis" the same seed values will be used and we will get an identical solution. We would need to start over from scratch to get a differing cluster solution.

To produce the sum of squared errors for the model, we click the red triangle next to "K Means NCluster=3" and choose Save Clusters. This will create two new columns: the cluster assignment and a column called Distance, which is each individual case's distance to its centroid. We create a third column that squares these distances. Next, we calculate the mean of this squared-distance variable and multiply it by the number of cases in the analysis. This is the sum of squared errors.

To produce a dissimilarity ratio (table 12.2), we first obtain basic descriptive statistics (mean and SD) for each input variable. Next, using these descriptive statistics, together with the results listed under "Cluster Centers Original Scale" for each variable,[2] we compute a z-scored cluster center. This will be different from Johnson-transformed cluster means. We compute the Euclidean distance between each set of z-scored cluster centers, and take the smallest of these distances as the measure of between-cluster distance. Next, for each cluster we find the maximum distance of a case to the centroid, and take the average of these maximum distances as our measure of within-cluster distance. To get the dissimilarity ratio, we divide between-cluster distance by within-cluster distance.

This analysis suggests that the four-cluster solution is slightly superior to the three- and five-cluster solutions. The high numbers for average maximum within-cluster distance could be driven by the presence of outliers in the data; mean distances within clusters are much smaller. We can investigate this possibility by examining a three-dimensional biplot; this will show how the cases and clusters are arranged in the

TABLE 12.2   Fit Statistic for *K*-Means Clustering

	Sum of squared errors	Smallest between-cluster distance	Avg. max. within-cluster distance	Dissimilarity ratio
3	253,043.64	1.52	36.13	0.041453
4	252,981.36	2.07	49.93667	0.041453
5	250,739.28	1.64	31.49333	0.052075

three-dimensional space defined by the first three principal components of the input variables. We can generate this by opening the menu next to the clustering solution we are interested in investigating and choosing Biplot 3D. We display the 3D biplot for this analysis in figure 12.6. The plot reveals the structure of our data. Cases are not clumped in very disparate regions but are gathered toward the center of the overall space (in our experience, this is much more common than clearly "clustered" data). Each cluster also has numerous cases assigned to it which are clearly outliers.

The four-cluster solution in these data identifies counties whose profiles are somewhat different (table 12.3). In the first cluster we have a small group of counties which are heavily Caucasian and quite poor on average. These counties had the lowest rate of support for Obama in 2012 out of all the clusters. The second cluster is also overwhelmingly white, but is less densely populated, with a higher median income and a lower poverty rate. The Obama vote share in these counties was slightly higher than in cluster 1. The third cluster is the modal cluster. It is much more ethnically diverse than either cluster 1 or 2, and has a poverty rate near the national average. Finally, in cluster 4 we find counties which are ethnically diverse, have many college graduates and high median incomes, and are relatively densely populated (about 375 people per square mile).

NORMAL MIXTURES

Normal mixtures and its sibling *robust normal mixtures* are very similar to *K*-means clustering. The principal difference is in the assignment of cases to clusters. In *K*-means clustering, each case is assigned to a single cluster. Instead, normal mixtures calculates a *probability* that a given case is in each cluster. Essentially, the model first maps the space with a set of multivariate normal distributions which act as "clusters." Each case will have a given value in each cluster's multivariate normal distribution. As in *k*-means, the central points of these clusters are iterated until a stable, but quite possibly local, solution is found.

One nice thing about normal mixtures is that it produces, as part of its baseline output, a variance-covariance matrix of the input variables *for each cluster*. This allows us to look at how the correlations between variables differ between clusters, and can help if we

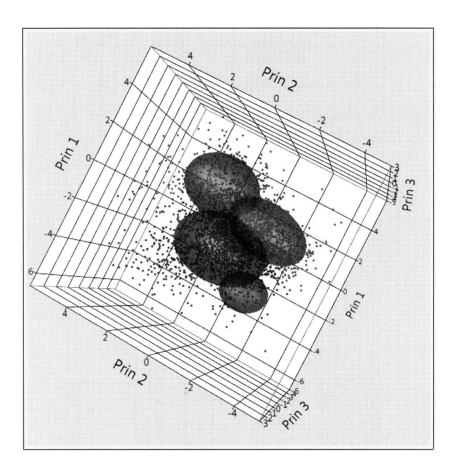

FIGURE 12.6
Three-dimensional biplot showing the clusters produced by *k*-means clustering.

TABLE 12.3   Characteristics of Clusters Produced by *K*-Means Clustering

	Cluster 1	Cluster 2	Cluster 3	Cluster 4
% white	97.46	92.51	74.25	74.43
% higher ed.	9.22	19.70	15.09	30.21
Poverty rate	22.22	9.34	17.49	10.23
Population density (log)	3.45	2.63	3.59	5.92
% Obama	28.18	33.24	37.83	47.49
% black	0.19	0.51	12.35	10.14
Median income	29,300	47,570	37800	59000
N	46	749	1721	598

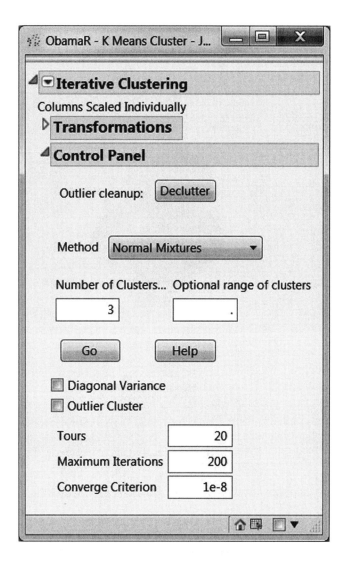

FIGURE 12.7

Choosing normal mixtures clustering in the Iterative Clustering
launch platform.

want to transfer a clustering solution to regression with interaction terms. Additionally, the fact that probabilities are estimates for each case–cluster pair lets us identify cases which are on the borderline of being in multiple clusters.

In JMP, normal mixtures clustering is performed largely in the same manner as *k*-means. Once you get to the Iterative Clustering platform, simply change "K-means" to either "Normal Mixtures" or "Robust Normal Mixtures." The platform will appear as in figure 12.7 or 12.8.

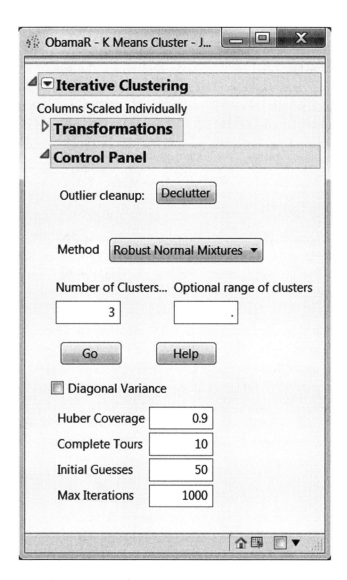

FIGURE 12.8
Choosing robust normal mixtures clustering in the
Iterative Clustering launch platform.

Some differences here emerge from *k*-means clustering. Note that both of these programs allow for different numbers of "tours." This is to guard against finding a local clustering solution, by running the program repeatedly with different starting values. The Max. Iterations setting constrains the optimization algorithm to a given number of iterations, to quicken processing. The Convergence Criterion (available in Normal Mixtures, but not Robust Normal Mixtures) tells JMP the difference in the log-likelihood at which it should consider the model converged and stop iterating.

There are a few differences between these two windows. Robust Normal Mixtures has a setting for Huber Coverage. This is an estimator similar to the Huber-White "sandwich" estimators used for robust standard errors; the setting tells JMP what proportion of the cases should *not* be considered "outliers" and thus down-weighted. Normal Mixtures permits the creation of an extra "outlier cluster," which will capture cases which fall too far outside the region of any of the user-designated clusters; this will prevent outliers from exercising too much influence over where the clusters are located.

SELF-ORGANIZING MAPS

Most *self-organizing maps* (SOMs) are, like neural nets, learning algorithms. But the SOM program in JMP is not; it is quite similar to k-means clustering. The whole benefit of SOMs in JMP is their interpretability. They are made so that the clusters appear in a two-dimensional, grid-like structure (the axes of which correspond to the first two principal components of the variable variance-covariance matrix). Clusters which are closer to each other are more similar, and those which are further apart are more different.

What occurs under the hood is that a two-dimensional axis is drawn using the first two principal components, this space is cut up into a researcher-specified number of equal-sized regions, and seed values are assigned to each region. K-means is used to assign cases to seeds, and the mean for each cluster is found. Regressions are then run to predict means, resulting in the selection of new centroids, and then new regressions, until the process has converged.

To build an SOM, we first open the Iterative Clustering platform, and change "K-means" to "Self Organizing Map" (figure 12.9). Instead of picking the number of clusters, we must instead select the number of rows and columns we want in our grid (the number of clusters will be the product of these two). Next, we set the Bandwidth parameter, which affects the degree of impact that neighboring clusters have on centroid estimates. We choose a 2 × 3 set-up, with a bandwidth of just below 0.5.

The initial printout is quite similar to that for k-means and normal mixtures (figure 12.10). We can examine it for patterns in the data as it is, but we should treat initial outcomes from SOMs much as we have treated outcomes from k-means and normal mixtures. We should inspect fit statistics, try other numbers of cases, rerun to guard against local solutions, and so on.

A self-organizing map is designed to be reducible to two dimensions. We reproduce the biplot, with the variable "rays" overlaid (figure 12.11). This helps illustrate the two-dimensional nature of the SOM, but also brings out the close relation between clustering and principal component analysis. The first principal component (horizontal axis) is closely related to the percentage of the population with higher education and median

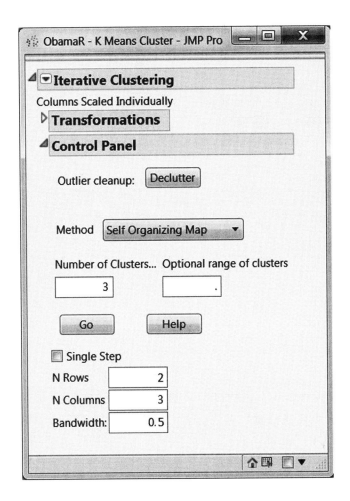

FIGURE 12.9
Choosing self-organizing map in the Iterative Clustering
launch platform.

income (positively), as well as to the poverty rate (negatively). The measures of Obama
vote share, percentage black, and population density are highly interrelated and correlated positively with the second principal component (vertical axis); percentage white
correlates negatively with this component. We also see that the various clusters fall into
different regions of the space defined by the principal components. The biplot is thus
telling us that the first cluster describes counties which are both dense and diverse as
well as relatively wealthy, and the second describes those which are wealthier but less
dense and less diverse (and less likely to support Obama). The third cluster contains poor
urban counties; the fourth contains counties which are poor, but less dense and whiter
than cluster 3.

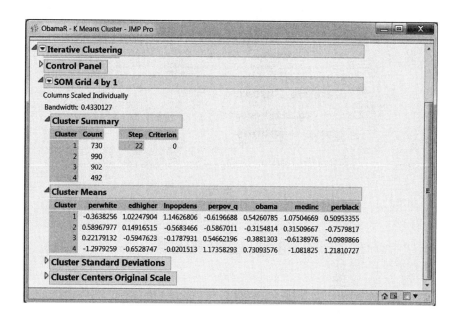

FIGURE 12.10

Output from self-organizing map in JMP Pro.

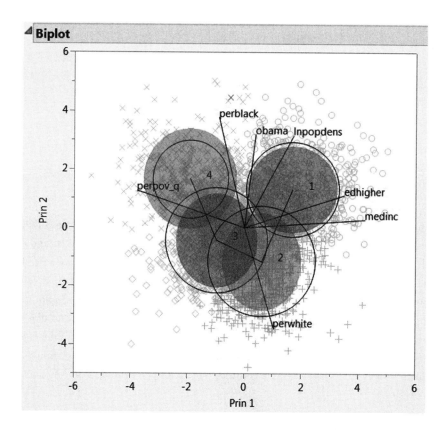

FIGURE 12.11

Biplot depicting the relation of clusters to variables in self-organizing map
(JMP Pro).

This demonstrates the usefulness of using SOMs together with principal components and variable rays to characterize finalized cluster analyses in terms of positioning along continua of interrelated variables in multidimensional space. Our analysis of voting patterns is not a perfect demonstration, but in our experience social science data are rarely clearly clustered. Nonetheless, cluster analysis can be used to identify patterns of similarity among cases in terms of theoretically interesting inputs.

13

LATENT CLASS ANALYSIS AND MIXTURE MODELS

LATENT CLASS ANALYSIS

First prominently used in the social sciences by Lazarsfeld and Henry (1968), latent class analysis (LCA) is another statistical technique in the broader family of latent variable models which includes principal component analysis, factor analysis, and clustering. It can be thought of as a model in which only one latent variable is estimated, and in which this latent variable has a categorical distribution. This assumption about the number and distribution of latent variables sets it apart from principal component analysis, which presumes that there are multiple latent variables and that these have a normal distribution. LCA is in some ways more similar to clustering in that it works to detect latent groups; but it differs in that the input variables used to find the groups must be categorical in the case of LCA and (mostly) continuous in the case of clustering. Still, LCA is a very close relative of normal mixtures clustering in that it assumes that the observed distribution of responses is made up of a mixture of multiple simpler distributions. Finally, since it handles categorical input data and estimates the probability of a categorical latent variable, it is also closely related to log-linear modeling.

Latent class analysis is often used in the analysis of attitudinal response data from surveys. Let's imagine that we've asked a set of people whether they approve of school prayer, abortion, and gay marriage. This gives us a set of three variables, each of which takes on two possible values, giving us eight potential response patterns. We want to sort people into classes based on these response patterns, but we think that eight classes are too many. With LCA we sort response patterns into a smaller number of latent classes, specifying that number ahead of time. This allows us to estimate two sets of parameters. First, we estimate the prevalence of each of the latent classes. Secondly, we estimate the probability of a given response given membership in a latent class. With our attitudinal example, we might presume that there are two groups—"social liberals" and "social conservatives." Based on our response data, we can estimate the proportions of individuals who are socially liberal versus those who are socially conservative. And we can estimate the likelihood that one supports, say, gay marriage given that they are socially liberal.

It is important to stress, though, that LCA is an unsupervised technique. The researcher stipulates the number of classes the model will estimate, but the solution which will be found cannot be determined from the start. There is no guarantee, then, in our example above, that we would find groups that match up to our conceptions of social liberals and social conservatives. Instead, as with factor analysis, it is up to the researcher to interpret what the latent groups signify on the basis of the distribution of their responses to the various inputs.

The LCA model presumes that the latent class structure accounts for any associations among responses in the data. That means that within latent classes, responses to various inputs are presumed to be independent. As we previously stated, the researcher must specify the number of classes prior to analysis. But how are we to know that we have chosen the "right" number? Typically, researchers try different numbers of classes and see which has the best fit to the model (in terms of log-likelihood, Akaike information criterion, Bayesian information criterion, G^2, or some other fit statistic).

Often, however, given a prespecified number of latent classes and a number of response patterns in the data, the LCA model cannot be fully identified. This means that multiple parameter estimates will yield the same maximum likelihood, or, in other words, there are multiple solutions to the LCA problem that fit equally well. This means that LCA is often unstable. Given different starting values, it can reach very different solutions. For this reason, the number of latent classes which can be identified given input data is restricted. In general, the LCA model is better able to uniquely identify smaller numbers of latent classes. In order to determine whether a model is fully identified, it is often necessary to try multiple starting values and see whether the results converge to the same solution. And frequently the LCA model with the best fit is not fully identified. One solution to this could be to perform many LCAs using the same data, and average the solutions. As of now, however, this remains a problematic issue with latent class analysis.

It is also important to note that the LCA model is prone to converging at local rather than global maxima. Attempting different starting values and inspecting the log-likelihood statistic can resolve this issue. This issue is more readily addressed than that of identifiability.

Since LCA has been around for some time, a number of statistical software packages contain LCA routines. SAS has a program called PROC LCA which performs it quite easily. Stata does not have LCA built in, but there is a user-generated program—which, unfortunately, can be run only on Stata's SE or MP versions, not IC. It is also possible to use the user-generated gllamm package to perform LCA. The statistical software package Latent GOLD is specifically designed for LCA and other latent variable models and is user-friendly.

R has a number of packages which can perform LCA, including lca and gllm. Here, we demonstrate how to perform a latent class analysis in R using the package poLCA (Linzer and Lewis, 2011). We will use this to analyze response data from the 2012 General Social Survey (http://www3.norc.org/Gss+website/).

The data were prepared ahead of time. We selected six questions in which survey respondents were asked how they felt about government spending on various items: the environment, the military, welfare, cities, crime, and science. An answer of 1 on each item means that the respondent thinks that the government doesn't spend enough; 2, it spends just about the right amount; and 3, it spends too much. We also included an item in which two questions are combined—who the respondent voted for in 2008, or, if they did not vote, who they would have voted for. The responses were coded 1 for Obama, 2 for McCain, and 3 for other or no opinion.

We load the data and then download and activate the poLCA package in R as follows:

```
library(foreign)
gssdata<-read.dta("gss_s12.dta")
attach(gssdata)
install.packages("poLCA")
library(poLCA)
```

Next, we need to bind the terms which we are going to use to create the latent classes, and save them in an object called xs2. The model is regressed on an intercept term, for reasons that will become clearer below in our discussion of latent class regression.

```
xs2<-cbind(envir,urban,welfare,army,crime,science,vote08)~1
```

Once this is done, the researcher can run the program with the following single line of code:

```
lca1<-poLCA(xs2, gssdata, nclass = 2, maxiter = 1000,
    graphs = FALSE)
```

As we stated above, xs2 is the object in which the latent class model is saved. The data are specified by gssdata, and we are estimating a two-class model (nclass = 2). The maxiter option sets the maximum number of iterations for maximizing the likelihood,

TABLE 13.1   Selecting Number of Classes for Latent Class Analysis by
Examining Fit Statistic

No. of classes	Log-likelihood	AIC	BIC	G^2
2	–13,945.89	27,953.77	28,126.92	2,483.06
3	–13,876.40	27,846.80	28,109.31	2,344.08
4	–13,821.94	27,769.88	28,121.75	2,235.16
5	–13,779.99	27,717.98	28,159.22	2,151.26
6	–13,751.00	27,692.01	28,222.61	2,093.29
7	–13,725.87	27,673.74	28,293.71	2,043.04
8	–13,714.06	27,682.12	28,391.45	2,019.40

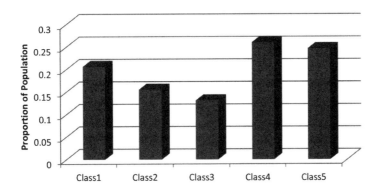

FIGURE 13.1
Distribution of cases to latent classes in latent class analysis.

and `graphs = FALSE` turns off a graphing function. A thousand iterations will be plenty to find the maximum-likelihood solution for a two-class model; when we increase the number of classes we will have to raise the number of iterations. We ran this model a number of times with different numbers of latent classes to find the best fit to the data (table 13.1).

Notice that the fit statistics do not unambiguously point to an optimal number of classes. The BIC trends back upward after five classes, but the AIC takes a bit more time (after seven). Which fit statistic you choose to listen to is something of a judgment call, and there are surely partisans of both sides. For purposes of parsimony, we choose the five-class model.

The five-class solution has a class prevalence indicated by the bar graph in figure 13.1. Classes 4, 5 and 1 are most commonly encountered, with between 20% and 25% of the population. Classes 2 and 3 are somewhat less common.

TABLE 13.2   Conditional Response Probabilities by Class from Latent Class Analysis

		Class 1	Class 2	Class 3	Class 4	Class 5
Environment	Increase	0.2382	0.3196	**0.6771**	**0.8043**	**0.7438**
	Just right	0.3520	**0.6307**	0.2222	0.1830	0.2299
	Decrease	**0.4098**	0.0497	0.1007	0.0127	0.0263
Cities	Increase	0.1536	0.1181	0.0000	**0.4829**	**0.3666**
	Just right	0.2786	**0.6188**	0.0429	0.4402	0.2815
	Decrease	**0.4678**	0.1415	**0.6046**	0.0362	0.1457
	Unsure	0.0999	0.1216	0.3525	0.0407	0.2062
Welfare	Increase	0.2137	0.2264	**0.7250**	**0.4738**	**0.5738**
	Just right	0.2106	**0.6541**	0.1169	0.3097	0.2106
	Decrease	**0.5757**	0.1196	0.1580	0.2165	0.2156
Military	Increase	**0.4894**	0.0866	0.1026	0.0438	0.4320
	Just right	0.3951	**0.7151**	0.3231	0.2609	**0.5587**
	Decrease	0.1155	0.1983	**0.5744**	**0.6953**	0.0093
Crime	Increase	**0.5378**	0.3179	**0.4800**	**0.4805**	**0.8441**
	Just right	0.3512	**0.6175**	0.3176	0.4250	0.1387
	Decrease	0.1111	0.0646	0.2024	0.0945	0.0171
Science	Increase	0.2945	0.2203	0.3384	**0.4735**	0.4033
	Just right	**0.4606**	**0.7028**	**0.5091**	0.4165	**0.5347**
	Decrease	0.2449	0.0770	0.1526	0.1100	0.0620
Election 2008	Obama	0.0643	**0.6295**	**0.6204**	**0.8872**	**0.6015**
	McCain	**0.8062**	0.1952	0.1295	0.0646	0.2887
	Other/unsure	0.1294	0.1753	0.2502	0.0482	0.1098

Conditional response probabilities are given in table 13.2. As stated above, the "meaning" of the classes needs to be interpreted by the researcher, and we endeavor to do so here. Class 1's meaning is rather clear—these are, simply put, *conservatives*. They favor cutting spending on the environment, cities, and welfare, and spending more on the military and crime-fighting, and they supported McCain over Obama by a margin of more than 12 to 1. The other groups are all Obama supporters—not entirely surprising, given that Obama supporters make up about 57% of all the cases. (Obama won by about 54%, and this item includes the support of nonvoters.) But these are Obama supporters with differing priorities. Class 2 can be described as *satisfied centrists*. They think that government spending is just about at the right level in all six areas (though they are more likely to favor spending more on the environment or crime than on other things). Class 3 members are, interestingly, *anti-urban liberals*. These folks are in favor of spending more money on the environment, poverty, and crime, but respond very negatively to the question about spending money on the problems faced by cities. They also favor cutting money to the military, and are more likely than other classes to support third parties or be undecided. Class 4 consists of *progressives*. They supported Obama at the highest rate, and are strongly in favor of increasing money for environmental issues. They are the only ones who think funding ought to be increased for science, and they favor increasing funding for just about everything *but* the military, which they are strongly in favor of cutting funding to. Finally, class 5 seems to consist of people who favor spending more on crime-fighting, cleaning the environment, and on welfare; we might think of them as *state-oriented liberals*. They lean toward increasing funding to the military as well, whereas most Obama supporters do not.

This is a rather quick-and-dirty analysis; of course we could have gotten different classes by including different variables. And the results are probabilistic and more suggestive than definitive; within most classes there were people who took positions different from the modal position on any given item. Moreover, these results are not particularly stable; when we ran more five-class models with different starting values, we got somewhat different solutions. In each solution, there was a clear conservative group with response probabilities very similar to those above (though it was not always class 1), but the Obama-preferring groups varied in their specific profiles.

LATENT CLASS REGRESSION

Latent class regression (LCR) is an extension of latent class analysis (LCA). LCR not only categorizes cases into a likely number of prespecified classes but also uses covariates to predict class membership. This makes it quite similar to a structural equation model, and it functions essentially as an LCA with a multinomial regression attached to it.

In R, it is very easy to turn an LCA into an LCR. We do this using the GSS data from above, but here, for the sake of parsimony, we presume the existence of only three latent classes.

```
xs2<-cbind(envir,urban,welfare,army,crime,science,vote08)~
  AGE+conserv+pared+inc
lca1<-poLCA(xs2, gssdata, nclass = 3, maxiter = 5000, graphs
  = FALSE)
```

Note that the only difference in code from the LCA performed earlier is that there the column-bound attitudinal variables are simply regressed on an intercept term. The 'poLCA' program interprets this code as specifying a null regression model. When covariates are added, the column-bound variables are used to generate probability of class membership, and then class membership is regressed on the predictor variables. LCR gives us a picture not only of the distribution of political attitudes but also of what the correlates of each group might be (table 13.3).

A three-class solution gives us groups which make up 36%, 31%, and 33% of the population, respectively. The makeup of these groups is somewhat different from that of the groups discussed in the five-class LCA solution above. Class 1 consists of more conservative

TABLE 13.3 Conditional Response Probabilities by Class from
Latent Class Regression

		Class 1	Class 2	Class 3
Environment	Increase	0.3130	**0.8401**	**0.6301**
	Just right	**0.3935**	0.1497	0.3521
	Decrease	0.2935	0.0101	0.0177
Cities	Increase	0.1677	**0.3645**	0.2757
	Just right	0.3058	0.2165	**0.5166**
	Decrease	**0.3972**	0.2071	0.1215
	Unsure	0.1293	0.2119	0.0861
Welfare	Increase	0.2771	**0.6846**	0.3689
	Just right	0.2619	0.1292	**0.4828**
	Decrease	**0.4609**	0.1862	0.1483
Military	Increase	0.4281	0.2521	0.0366
	Just right	**0.4394**	**0.3930**	0.4800
	Decrease	0.1325	0.3549	**0.4834**
Crime	Increase	**0.5621**	**0.7459**	0.3599
	Just right	0.3362	0.1726	**0.5606**
	Decrease	0.1017	0.0815	0.0795
Science	Increase	0.2914	0.4492	0.3710
	Just right	**0.5098**	**0.4619**	0.5464
	Decrease	0.1988	0.0888	0.0827
Election 2008	Obama	0.1547	**0.7401**	**0.8600**
	McCain	**0.6808**	0.1375	0.0574
	Other/unsure	0.1645	0.1224	0.0826

individuals, who favor cutting back on welfare and "urban problems" but want to beef up crime-fighting. Their support for the military is strong, but not as strong as that of Class 1 in the five-class solution. They supported McCain at about 68%, but 15% backed Obama. Classes 2 and 3 are more progressive voters and more centrist voters, respectively. Class 2 favors increasing spending on the environment, cities, welfare, and stopping crime, and three-quarters of this group are Obama supporters. Class 3 is more lukewarm about increasing spending, and wants to cut spending on the military. But this group, which appears to be more centrist in its views, is actually a bit more likely to support Obama.

We regressed class membership on income, age, parental education (years), and a measure of political conservatism. All of the predictors are measured continuously. The political-conservatism scale derives from responses to a question asking people to state their political ideology, and is coded to range from 0 (very liberal) to 5 (very conservative). Results of the LCR (table 13.4) should be read similarly to results from a multinomial logit regression. That is, LCR makes one class a reference group, and estimates the rela-

TABLE 13.4   Parameter Estimates Predicting Class Membership in
Latent Class Regression Model

	Class 2 (vs. 1)		Class 3 (vs. 1)	
	Coeff. (SE)	p	Coeff. (SE)	p
Age	0.002 (0.002)	.339	−0.008 (.002)	<.001
Conservatism	0.020 (0.001)	.151	−0.058 (0.014)	<.001
Parental education	0.001 (0.001)	.902	−0.017 (0.036)	<.001
Income ($1000s)	−0.015 (0.001)	.001	0.011 (0.000)	.004
Constant	0.002 (0.003)	.565	0.001 (0.000)	<0.001

tion between predictor variables and the log-odds of being in each of the other latent classes rather than in class 1.

It is interesting to note that though those in class 2 have the most progressive profile of all groups, they are quite similar to class 1 (conservatives) in terms of age, parental education, and self-reported political orientation. The principal difference is that those in class 2 are on average lower-earning than those in class 1. Individuals in class 3, on the other hand, are very different from the conservatives in class 1 in numerous ways—they are younger, have less well-educated parents, appear to be somewhat better-off on average, and identify as less conservative. It is also interesting that this group supports Obama at particularly high rates. This would seem to indicate that those in class 3 are something like "party" Democrats, and many are upwardly mobile. Class 2, by contrast, could be something like blue-collar progressives.

Confirming these patterns would take a much more intensive analysis than we can engage in here. In particular, we would have to tinker with different attitudinal questions, and make sure that the latent class model was stable in its solution. But this exercise points to how LCR could be used instead of clustering in the presence of mostly binary or categorical input data.

MIXTURE MODELS

Somewhat related to both LCA and LCR is a class of techniques called mixture models. First developed conceptually in the 1800s, mixture models were not put into practice substantially until the rise of modern computing. They have substantial applications in speaker identification, genetics, and image analysis. Mixture models have also found application in the social sciences, especially since the development of techniques to apply mixture models to growth trajectories (see e.g. Laub, Nagin, and Sampson 1998).

Unlike latent class or cluster analysis, finite mixture models are oriented toward an outcome variable of interest. This outcome is typically continuously distributed—either as normal, log-normal, Poisson, gamma, or negative binomial. The assumption is that the continuous distribution being witnessed in the dependent variable is in fact a "mixture" of two separate distributions from different populations. A classic example of this would be height among a sample of both men and women where gender is unobserved. If we looked at a histogram, the distribution would be either normal or slightly bimodal, but if we could separately identify the genders we would see that what we were looking at was in reality two overlapping normal distributions.

The key to the mixture model, though, is that we cannot see—or in any event have not measured—the underlying heterogeneity in question. But we have reason, usually theoretical, to believe that the relation between the predictor variables and the outcome differs across latent groups within a population. That is, we expect to see the coefficients in our regression model vary substantially between different classes. Mixture models can also model class membership, making it quite similar to latent class regression.

Mixture routines exist for many statistical systems. SPSS Modeler has a Generalized Linear Mixed Models node. Various packages in R have been written for mixture models, including flexmix and bgmm. Latent GOLD is a commercially available software package designed specifically for latent variable models, including mixture models. Stata has a user-generated program called fmm, and the user-generated gllamm program can also be used.

We demonstrate mixture models using the fmm program in Stata (Deb 2012). Since the program is user-generated—that is, it is not built into Stata's main architecture—it needs to be located online first. This is accomplished easily by typing:

```
findit fmm
```

This will take you to a search screen on which the program is easily locatable. Simply follow the instructions to download it. The program's syntax takes the basic form:

```
fmm depvar indvars [if] [in] [weight], components(integer)
   mixtureof(distribution) probability(model2) vce(type)
```

In this syntax we are telling Stata to estimate a finite mixture model, regressing the dependent variable on a set of predictors. We specify the number of latent groups we think are represented in the data (**components**), and the **mixtureof** option allows us to specify how the dependent variable is distributed (normal, log-normal, Poisson, negative binomial, or gamma). We can also specify forms of the standard error (**vce**), for example robust, bootstrap, or jackknife. The **probability** option enables the user to specify predictors to model the probability of class membership.

We analyze our 2012 General Social Survey data again, using as our dependent variable a composite scale of religiosity, which consists of responses to questions in which individuals say how important their religion is to them, how often they pray, and how often they attend church. We combine these items into a summated rating scale which has a Chronbach's α of .81, suggesting that the items are indeed closely related. We

TABLE 13.5   Parameter Estimates for Modeling Dependent Variable (Religiosity) Using OLS and Mixture Model (Three Latent Groups)

| | OLS | | Finite mixture model | | | | | |
| | | | Group 1 | | Group 2 | | Group 3 | |
	Coeff. (SE)	p	Coeff. (SE)	p	Coeff. (SE)	p	Coeff. (SE)	p
Income	0.001 (.011)	0.997	−0.012 (.008)	0.146	−0.013 (.012)	0.228	0.005 (.005)	0.291
Female	0.282 (.037)	<0.001	0.035 (.022)	0.114	0.263 (.042)	<0.001	0.054 (.021)	0.011
Age	0.010 (.001)	<0.001	0.0007 (.0006)	0.244	0.0060 (.0013)	<0.001	0.0001 (.0007)	0.867
Parental education	−0.015 (.005)	0.003	−0.005 (.003)	0.115	−0.010 (.005)	0.055	−0.005 (.003)	0.084
Black (vs. white)	0.471 (.054)	<0.001	−1.893 (.052)	<0.001	0.538 (.064)	<0.001	2.514 (.041)	<0.001
Other (vs. white)	0.180 (.065)	0.006	0.060 (.048)	0.207	0.263 (.063)	<0.001	0.046 (.035)	0.178
Constant	−0.547 (.143)	<0.001	1.184 (.104)	<0.001	−0.359 (.154)	0.020	−1.412 (.072)	<0.001

model religiosity using income, gender, age, parental education, and race (which the GSS codes as white, black or other; we make white the reference group).

Our specific model has the syntax:

```
xi:fmm religiosity lninc female AGE par_ed i.RACE, compo-
   nents(3) mix(normal) probability(EDUC AGE lninc female)
```

We are specifying a model in which the outcome is a mixture of three normal distributions. As with LCA, the number of components is typically chosen either because of prior knowledge or theory, or by choosing the number of components which has the best fit statistics. We opt for the latter strategy.

We also model group membership using own education, age, income, and gender. For comparison, we also show the results of an OLS regression model, which will show average outcomes for the three latent classes (table 13.5).

The OLS regression model tells us that greater religiosity is unrelated to income, but is higher (on average) among females than males, and higher among blacks and "other"-race individuals than whites. There is a negative relation between parental education and religiosity, suggesting that better-educated parents tend to raise less religious offspring. Interestingly, we ran models which included own education, which was unrelated to religiosity whether or not parental education was controlled for. Finally, there is a positive relation between religiosity and age.

The mixture model sorts the population into three underlying groups across which these relations differ. Income remains unrelated to religiosity in all latent groups. Age is a positive predictor of religiosity, but is statistically significant only for group 2. Parental

	Class 2 (vs. 1)		Class 3 (vs. 1)	
	Coeff. (SE)	*p*	*Coeff. (SE)*	*p*
Age	.037 (.007)	<.001	.018 (.006)	.002
Female	.412 (.216)	.056	.352 (.188)	.062
Education	−.073 (.038)	.051	−.111 (.033)	.001
Income	.102 (.076)	.177	.015 (.056)	.790
Constant	−1.659 (.894)	.063	2.153 (.680)	.002

education is related to lower religiosity, but these results are only significant at $p < .10$ in groups 2 and 3. Females in groups 2 and 3 are more religious on average, but the difference doesn't attain significance in group 1. Racial differences in religiosity are most striking. In group 1, blacks are substantially *less* religious than whites, and the difference between whites and "others" is nonsignificant. But in groups 2 and 3, blacks are more religious on average, and this difference is particularly large in group 3. Individuals from "other" racial groups are slightly more religious than whites only in group 2.

Table 13.6 shows the results of our models of the probability of class membership. Once again, this should be read in the same manner as a multinomial logistic regression. It seems that there is an increased probability of being in group 2 or 3 (rather than group 1) if one is older, and this relation is stronger for group 2 than for group 3. Education is negatively related to membership in either group relative to group 1, but this relation is only significant at $p < .05$ for group 3. Finally, there appears to be a positive relation between being female and the probability of being in group 2 or 3, but this is only significant at $p < .10$.

SUMMARY

We have examined, in this section, three parametric techniques for examining the presence of latent groups in data. These methods—latent class analysis, latent class regression, and mixture modeling—can be seen as parametric alternatives to clustering. The choice of technique depends for the most part on the type of input data we have (continuous or categorical) and on whether we want to estimate group membership in relation to a particular outcome variable. We have shown that latent class analysis can be used to investigate political response data and sort respondents into latent like-minded groups, and that mixture models can investigate underlying heterogeneity in religiosity. We counsel, though, against the interpretation that these models find "real" latent classes or groups. Rather, they are ways in which we can statistically model patterning in data, which can be fruitful for the advancement of theory and inquiry.

14

ASSOCIATION RULES

Assocation rule mining is one of the most widely used data mining techniques. In its classical form, as first developed by Agrawal, Imieliński, and Swami (1993), it was used to examine market-basket data in commercial settings. This practical application was designed to be of use to retailers who may be interested in patterns of purchasing engaged in by customers. Stores have a given set of items for sale at a point in time, and customers purchase sets of these items when they come to the store. A retailer may wish to know what else customers tend to buy when they buy milk, or eggs, or dog biscuits. Understanding such patterns can help retailers sell more merchandise by suggesting, for example, that items which are frequently bought together be stocked near each other. The problem is that stores like supermarkets handle a very large number of transactions, and carry a lot of different products, and in each transaction a fairly large number of items can be bought.

Clearly, then, this is *a big data problem,* in that it is a problem whose sheer scope makes it forbidding to human analysts. After all, if a store sells just 20 separate items, and we are simply interested in associations between just 2 items, there are 190 possible combinations. If we look at *all* possible associations (not just two-way) among these items, the number of possible associations is $2^{20} - 1 = 1,048,575$. Of course, *most* of these potential combinations of purchases will not occur. However, even among the combinations which do occur, the data problem is of such immensity that it demands automation.

In order to discuss which associations are important and which can be ignored, we need first to introduce two terms. The first is *support.* The support of a given item combination is equal to the number of all transactions which contain this combination, divided by the total number of all transactions. So if the support for the item set {milk, cookies} is 10%, this means that both milk and cookies were bought in 10% of all transactions (transactions which could include any number of other items). The next measure is *confidence*. The confidence of a rule is the probability that we see one item given that we see the other item. However, this measure requires that we consider a subset of the items in our item set to be the *consequent*, which is the counterpart to the dependent variable, and the remainder to be the *antecedent*. A confidence of 75% in the relation (milk → cookies) implies that 75% of the time that a customer buys milk they also buy cookies. Note, though, that reversing the arrow could give a very different confidence. That is, the probability that we have milk given that we have cookies is unlikely to be equal to the probability that we have cookies given that we have milk. Also, it is important to note that both consequents and antecedents can be multi-item subsets. So it is possible to have a rule like (hot dogs, buns → ketchup, mustard)—the probability that we have both ketchup *and* mustard given that we have hot dogs *and* buns.

This brings us to something important for making association rules useful for social science research. It is possible to designate an item as a *target*—that is, to set it as a consequent. The mining algorithm will then find rules which indicate the probability of that consequent given the appearance of antecedent items.

Given the immense number of combinations in a dataset, some rule for distinguishing noteworthy from irrelevant rules must be implemented. This is done somewhat arbitrarily by the researcher before running the rule mining algorithm. Researchers choose minimum values of support, or confidence, or both, and discard combinations as uninteresting if they fail to meet the minimum criteria. Another way to limit the number of rules is to set an upper (or lower) limit to the size of both consequent and antecedent item sets. Finally, we note that the very act of designating an item as a consequent has the effect of shrinking the rule set returned.

One issue that arises in transaction data is that some items are bought frequently (milk) and others, rarely (spatulas). Any minimum support and confidence rules will of necessity include lots of rules that contain milk but very few that contain spatulas. One can think about this as a counterpart, in association rules, to the problem of rare outcomes. One solution to this is to allow minimum support to vary across items—to require high minimum support for item sets that contain milk, for instance, and low support for those that contain spatulas.

Now, we have spent most of the time so far talking about supermarkets and groceries and milk and cookies, and this no doubt could be quite useful to supermarket proprietors. But of what use is it to social scientists and other researchers? Why should researchers be interested in association rules? How would we use association rule mining to support our research?

We believe that association rules can be powerful exploratory tools for research when we have data with many independent variables (features). One can use association rule mining in its unsupervised form (i.e. without a target variable) to get an idea of how things work with each other, but we think that for many researchers it is more useful to have a dependent or outcome variable of interest. Once this is specified, one can use association rule mining to search through many independent variables to find out which ones tend to be associated with the outcome. This can be done more quickly and efficiently than producing a correlation matrix. But more interestingly, association rule mining can find novel *combinations of conditions* which are associated with the target. Such combinations can point to the existence of interesting interaction-type effects (Ragin 2008).

ASSOCIATION RULE MINING IN SPSS MODELER

Association rule mining has been around for over 20 years at this point and is heavily used in commercial settings. As a result, there are a number of applications which are able to do it, but it is not incorporated into the software most commonly used by social researchers (SAS, Stata, SPSS). However, there is a large, complex package for R called arules; SPSS Modeler is also able to perform association rule mining. We demonstrate the use of association rules in SPSS Modeler below using data from the American Community Survey and focusing on individuals lacking health insurance coverage.

It is important to prepare your data prior to rule mining. Rule mining typically assumes that your data are in *transaction form*, where each row represents a customer–item combination (or, more accurately, a transaction–item combination). Multiple items bought together will appear not in the same row but in sequential rows. The dataset will be very long and narrow, with one column designating the transaction ID and another column identifying an individual product. However, it is also possible to enter data in *tabular form*. Here, rows represent individual transactions or purchases, and each column refers to an item which could be purchased. Tabular data contains, then, dummy variables equal to 1 if the item was purchased in a given transaction, 0 otherwise.

For social scientists, this means that association rule mining needs dummy variables, or at least categorical variables. In particular, it cannot handle continuous variables for antecedents or for consequents. Continuous variables need to be rendered categorical by some method of discretization prior to running an association rule routine. Also, association rule mining doesn't do that well with multicategory variables with many categories. These categories will have very low support rates almost by definition, so one ought to consider aggregating these categories into larger categories. For how to do this, see our earlier sections on discretizing continuous variables (pp. 95–99) and grouping multicategory variables (pp. 105–108).

In general, we prefer to have data in which only dummy variables appear. But dummy variables can be created in interesting and novel ways. Remember, you are not building a regression model, so there is no reason to make sure that categories are mutually exclusive and exhaustive, because you will not need to interpret effect coefficients. The dummies should be thought of as flag variables for conditions of interest. So one can enter a flag for combinations of conditions—being over 30 and enrolled as an undergraduate in college, for instance—without having to worry about what the reference group for this indicator is. In an association rule mining routine, this does not matter. One can also enter dummy variables for combinations of categories which overlap. If we have five ethic groups in our data, for instance, one can enter dummy variables for each group separately (entering them all, *not* excluding the reference), but one can also enter combinations of the groups, or all groups exclusive of one (for instance). These can all be entered simultaneously into an association rule mining dataset, and the routine will simply churn through all of the flag variables indicated in search of what we can think of as predictive rules for our target (outcome) variable.

So, we created a dataset from the American Community Survey in which we discretized age and household income into a number of categories, and created a number of flags for combinations of states of interest (like being a working-age adult who is not in the labor force). Our antecedent condition is "nohealthins"—a flag for not having any health insurance. We are looking for attributes and combinations of attributes which are frequent antecedents (predictors) of not having health insurance. Now, it is important to reiterate that we will find rules for predicting not having insurance, rather than attributes of conditions that often accompany being uninsured. This is an important distinction. In more mathematical terms, the confidence measures we will be finding will tell us, for instance, the probability that one lacks health insurance given that one is a poor and from a racial minority, *not* the probability that one is poor and from a racial minority given that one has no health insurance.

It is important to note the baseline probability of your target or outcome variable when setting minimum support. If your target variable occurs rarely in the data, you will need to set the minimum support rule quite low indeed. You will always need to set your minimum support to lower than the baseline frequency of a positive value on your outcome, otherwise you will find no rules. Minimum confidence measures can be set more at your discretion—according to what you think is interesting as a conditional probability.

The screenshot above indicates how we set up this analysis. The node furthest to the left is our Source node, where we selected our data. Next is a Derive node (Fields palette), where we transformed some of our variables. Finally, the Apriori node[1] is selected from the Modeling palette (figure 14.1). Modeler has three separate association rule routines; we chose Apriori because it allows the researcher to designate a flag variable. (The Carma routine generates all possible rules without a flag being specifiable, and Sequence makes the order in which items occur important.)

Next, we set parameters. In this case it is advisable to set minimum antecedent support relatively low (at 0.5%) because our outcome only appears 14% of the time, but to set minimum rule confidence fairly high (at 70%). In the Expert tab, we can enter alternative settings to sort out rules. We can choose to exclude on the basis of the absolute

FIGURE 14.1

Association rule stream and Apriori node in SPSS Modeler.

difference between confidence given the rule and prior confidence (e.g., the probability of observing the consequent regardless of antecedent). On the other hand, we could choose on the basis of the ratio of these two confidence measures. In Modeler these are called Confidence Difference and Confidence Ratio, respectively. These settings are particularly appropriate when our outcome is relatively rare, as in this case. Other methods are possible as well. "Information Difference" tells us to what degree the appearance of the consequent is given by the appearance of the antecedents. It takes support into account, such that more frequently occurring rules are preferred. However, it is less helpful with rare outcomes like ours. "Normalized Chi-Square" is also dependent on support.

Our data and the settings we chose generated 16 separate association rules, indicated in table 14.1. In reading and interpreting this list, it is important to remember what association rules can and can't do. The way to read rule no. 1, for example, is "80% of those who are noncitizens, age 30–39, Latino, *and* with less than a high school degree also lack health insurance." Association rules are entirely nonparametric, and they do not involve

Rule no.	Antecedent	Support %	Confidence %	Lift
1	Noncitizen + Age 30–39 + Latino + Edu. < HS	0.6	80.0	5.87
2	WS Central Region + Noncitizen + Latino + Edu. < HS	0.5	78.0	5.72
3	Noncitizen + Age 30–39 + Edu. < HS	0.7	77.14	5.66
4	Unemployed + Age 19–29 + Never married + Male + Citizen at birth	0.65	76.92	5.64
5	Latino + Age 19–29 + Edu. < HS + Never married	0.51	76.47	5.61
6	Unemployed + Age 19–29 + Never Married + Male	0.71	76.06	5.58
7	Noncitizen + Latino + Edu. < HS + Never married + Male	0.58	74.14	5.44
8	Latino + Age 19–29 + Edu. < HS	0.73	73.97	5.43
9	Age 19–29 + Edu. < HS + Never married + Male	0.78	73.08	5.36
10	Age 19–29 + Edu. < HS + Male	0.95	72.63	5.33
11	Unemployed + Age 19–29 + Male + Citizen at birth	0.73	72.60	5.33
12	Unemployed + Age 19–29 + Male	0.82	71.95	5.28
13	Age 30–39 + Latino + Edu. < HS	0.74	71.62	5.25
14	WS Central Region + Noncitizen + Edu. <HS	0.56	71.43	5.24
15	Not in labor force + Noncitizen + Latino + Edu. < HS	0.52	71.15	5.22
16	Age 19–29 + Edu. < HS + Never married + Male + Citizen at birth	0.61	70.49	5.17

anything like statistical control. *Association* rules, as their name suggests, do not let us infer *causality*—we don't know which, if any, of the antecedent factors in rule no. 1 lead people to not have insurance. They also don't tell us about comparison groups (such as citizens age 40–49 who are white and have college degrees.)

They are very good at telling us *who* lacks health insurance, however. Moreover, they do so in an interesting multivariate manner. And this output does let us make some local comparisons. For instance, compare rules 1 and 3. The only difference is that no. 1 is slightly more refined in that it includes "and Latino"; the other indicators are identical. Also, though, the rule confidence for no. 1 is higher than for no. 3. Among those who are 30–39, are noncitizens, and have less than a high school degree, it would seem that Latinos are somewhat less likely than average to have health insurance. To figure out whether or not this last difference is "significant" one would have to perform a separate formal statistical test, of course. The value of association rules, in this case, is that they can suggest to us which formal tests among subgroups might be interesting.

The table includes a few statistical measures. In the third column is *support*. All of these subgroups amount to a small, small portion of the total population—less than 1% in all cases. Lacking health insurance is a "rare event" (though surely not as rare as it ought to be), and the union of the set "lacking health insurance" and of a number of other sets is of course very small indeed. The next column is *confidence*, which is the conditional probability of no insurance given the antecedent conditions. Finally, we have *lift*. Lift is the improvement in prediction of the outcome that we get by knowing the antecedents—the "posterior probability divided by the prior probability." In English, this is simply the probability of having no insurance given a set of antecedents (e.g. Latino, age 30–39, noncitizen, less than a high school education) divided by the simple probability of having no insurance in the total population. A lift of 5.87 tells us that the subgroup of interest is 5.87 times more likely to lack health insurance than the population average. It is a function of the confidence and the baseline probability of the outcome. Because we set minimum confidence to 70 and our baseline rate of lacking insurance is 13.63%, we only see subgroups with lifts of 5.13 or higher.

In this table we see indicators appearing over and over. Sometimes this is because the indicator is simply common (like buying milk or bread, in grocery-store data). But this is clearly not what is happening for the most part here. Majority, and even modal, categories are not prevalent. In a situation like this, the results are more interesting and helpful. The table makes it clear that the current system of health insurance is most likely to fail to insure more marginal populations—especially noncitizens, those with little formal education, young adults, and the unemployed. Where a few of these markers coincide, rates of noncoverage are strikingly high.

Note that we have set the minimum rule confidence quite high; we could set it much lower, but then we would get more association rules. In these data, if we set minimum confidence to 90 we find no rules at all. We have to drop it to 80 before we find a single rule. But after this, further decreases in confidence increase the number of rules found exponentially. At 70, we find (as above) 16 rules. At 60 this increases to 94; at 50, it is 301; at 40, it is 815; and so on. Finally, if minimum confidence is set at 15, just above the population average for lacking health insurance, we find 6,729 rules. Thus, lowering the confidence casts a larger net, allowing more meaningful information to be collected about potentially interesting subgroups, but at the cost of overloading us with information (figure 14.2). At this point, the purpose of the data mining exercise would be defeated. Rather than using computational power to highlight meaningful patterns within a huge amount of data, we would have organized this massive amount of data differently but accomplished little in the way of simplification.

Association rule mining is a data mining technique used often in commercial settings, but we have demonstrated above that it can be used profitably by researchers for exploratory purposes. Association rules can help researchers discover states and

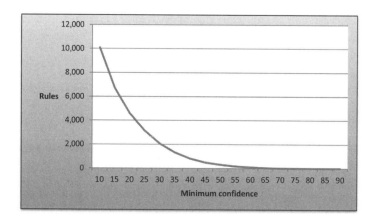

FIGURE 14.2

Number of association rules generated at different levels of minimum confidence.

combinations of states which occur frequently along with a given target outcome. And while the rules thus generated give us no information on the causal nature of the relation between the antecedents and the consequents, they are quite suggestive. Used in combination with other exploratory methods, they can be fruitful in suggesting interesting avenues for research.

CONCLUSION
Where Next?

It is over half a century since computerization started spreading through society, and by now its impacts are evident in many aspects of our lives. When businesses began installing computers in the 1960s and 1970s, they had very limited and practical goals in mind: automating various kinds of transactional records, reducing the costs of preparing bills and invoices, helping with accounts and balance sheets. Few realized that an important by-product would be a flood of business data that enabled managers to access the details of sales or cash flow at that very moment, instead of waiting for accounts to be closed out at month's or year's end. Firms soon realized that thousands of transactional details could be analyzed to identify high- and low-performing parts of the company, to slim down inventory, to shift to just-in-time production, or to more finely target sales and advertising. Transactional data changed from being a paperwork burden to being an valuable source of information and insight into business processes and performance. The era of Big Data had begun.

Entirely new sources of information and new possibilities for analysis have become available as so much communication has gone digital or moved online. We can follow epidemics through online queries about symptoms; discover public sentiments by analyzing word counts in social media; track changes in language use through Google documents; examine social networks and the spread of ideas; and (if we are the National Security Agency) snoop on digital phone conversations and search for terrorists or other "needles in haystacks" by looking for patterns in mountains of data.

Machine-learning and pattern-recognition methods were initially developed by computer scientists and applied mathematicians for practical goals such as handwriting recognition, automated sorting of mail, machine translation, and robotic vision. But these methods have quickly spilled over into the ways we analyze quantitative data of all kinds. As a result, analytics and data mining are burgeoning fields. Data mining is a rapidly expanding enterprise, spawning a new discipline, "data science," and new occupational specialties.

The purpose of this book has been to provide an accessible introduction to some of these methods, and given the mushrooming of courses on data mining and business analytics, we expect that many people will decide to learn about these new methods for analyzing data. This field is in its infancy, however, and there are already some barriers to future progress. These do not come from the computer science or applied mathematics communities, who are clearly innovating at an extraordinary rate, producing new algorithms and methods. But software remains a problem. Technically savvy data miners often write their own programs in MATLAB or Python, but most aspiring data miners will be unwilling or unable to create programs from scratch. As readers will have noticed, in this book we resorted instead to a palette of reasonably user-friendly and widely available software products to provide our overview of data mining methods, sometimes using JMP Pro, sometimes SPSS Modeler, sometimes R, and so on. This fragmentation of accessible software tools—because no single package currently covers all the tools one needs—creates a serious burden for would-be data miners; there is a steep learning curve in gaining familiarity with so many different types of software.

Although we use all these products, in some cases we are far from impressed with their quality. All too often, programs crash, or run forever. These problems tend to occur when datasets are large: more than a thousand cases. It seems absurd to write a book rhapsodizing about Big Data, and then provide examples using less than a hundred cases, yet that is what one finds in several books on this subject. We have tried to avoid doing that, and in this book we have used data of considerable size whenever possible, but readers should be aware that they may encounter similar frustrations when they try to apply data mining to their own large datasets. We hope that these problems will soon recede as software products become more comprehensive in the tools they include, and as their developers make sure that the software can handle sizable datasets. At the moment, however, they remain a hazard.

Although data mining provides automated tools, in our experience analyzing data still requires a lot of insight and expertise on the part of the analyst. One cannot simply enter raw data into these programs and expect to obtain anything useful. The analyst's expertise is crucial in defining the problem or question to be addressed. Preprocessing the data—deciding what variables to include, and how to measure or scale them—is a time- and thought-consuming phase. Exploratory analyses of the data, looking for what features or variables matter, and puzzling through unexpected findings or lack of findings, are critical. In many cases, even the choice of technique is complicated; there are many alternatives, and one probably wants to try out or perhaps combine several alternatives. In our experience, models improve considerably with fine-tuning, through trial and error and adjustment of parameters. Finally, translating the findings from analyses to something that clients or customers can understand is not a trivial undertaking.

So, the next step in becoming a data miner, beyond mastering the content of this book, involves developing these strategies and skills through extensive engagement with data and projects.

BIBLIOGRAPHY

Abbott, Andrew. 2001. *Time Matters: On Theory and Method*. Chicago, IL: University of Chicago Press.

Agrawal, Rakesh, Tomasz Imieliński, and Arun Swami. 1993. "Mining Association Rules between Sets of Items in Large Databases." *Association for Computing Machinery (AMC) SIGMOD Record* 22(2):207–16.

Aiken, Leona S., and Stephen G. West. 1991. *Multiple Regression: Testing and Interpreting Interactions*. Newbury Park, CA: Sage.

Altman, Naomi S. 1992. "An Introduction to Kernel and Nearest-Neighbor Nonparametric Regression." *American Statistician* 46(3):175–85.

Armstrong, J. Scott. "Significance Tests Harm Progress in Forecasting." *International Journal of Forecasting* 23(2):321–27.

Attewell, Paul, Scott Heil, and Liza Reisel. 2011. "Competing Explanations of Undergraduate Noncompletion." *American Educational Research Journal* 48(3):536–59.

Benjamini, Yoav. 2010. "Simultaneous and Selective Inference: Current Successes and Future Challenges." *Biometrical Journal* 52(6):708–21.

Berk, Richard A. 2006. "An Introduction to Ensemble Methods for Data Analysis." *Sociological Methods & Research* 34(3):263–95.

Berry, William D. 1993. *Understanding Regression Assumptions*. Newbury Park, CA: Sage.

Blyth, Colin R. 1972. "On Simpson's Paradox and the Sure-Thing Principle." *Journal of the American Statistical Association* 67(338):364–66.

Boser, Bernhard E., Isabelle M. Guyon, and Vladimir N. Vapnik. 1992. "A Training Algorithm for Optimal Margin Classifiers." In *Proceedings of the Fifth Annual Workshop on Computational Learning Theory*, 144–52. ACM.

Brambor, Thomas, William Roberts Clark, and Matt Golder. 2006. "Understanding Interaction Models: Improving Empirical Analyses." *Political Analysis* 14(1):63–82.

Breiman, Leo. "Statistical Modeling: The Two Cultures." 2001. *Statistical Science* 16(3): 199–231.

Breiman, Leo, Jerome Friedman, Charles J. Stone, and Richard A. Olshen. 1984. *CART: Classification and Regression Trees*. Belmont, CA: Wadsworth.

Canty, Angelo, and Brian Ripley. 2012. *boot: Bootstrap R (S-Plus) Functions, Version 1.2–42* (R package). http://cran.r-project.org/package=boot.

Coleman, James S., Thomas F. Pettigrew, William H. Sewell, and Thomas W. Pullum. 1973. "Inequality: A Reassessment of the Effect of Family and Schooling in America." *American Journal of Sociology* 78(6):1523–44.

Collins, Linda M., and Stephanie T. Lanza. 2010. *Latent Class and Latent Transition Analysis: With Applications in the Social, Behavioral, and Health Sciences*. Hoboken, NJ: John Wiley & Sons.

Comon, Pierre. 1994. "Independent Component Analysis: A New Concept?" *Signal Processing* 36(3):287–314.

Cortes, Corinna, and Vladimir Vapnik. 1995. "Support-Vector Networks." *Machine Learning* 20(3):273–97.

Cover, Thomas, and Peter Hart. 1967. "Nearest Neighbor Pattern Classification." *IEEE Transactions on Information Theory* 13(1):21–27.

Cui, Dapeng, and David Curry. 2005. "Prediction in Marketing Using the Support Vector Machine." *Marketing Science* 24(4):595–615.

Daniels, Ben. 2012. *CROSSFOLD: Stata Module to Perform K-fold Cross-Validation* (user-generated Stata program). http://ideas.repec.org/c/boc/bocode/s457426.html.

Davison, Anthony Christopher, and David Hinckley. 1997. *Bootstrap Methods and their Application*. Cambridge: Cambridge University Press.

Deb, Partha. 2012. *FMM: Stata Module to Estimate Finite Mixture Models* (user-generated Stata program). http://ideas.repec.org/c/boc/bocode/s456895.html.

Dudani, Sahibsingh A. 1976. "The Distance-Weighted K-Nearest-Neighbor Rule." *IEEE Transactions on Systems, Man and Cybernetics* 4:325–27.

Dunteman, George H. 1989. *Principal Components Analysis*. Newbury Park, CA: Sage.

Dupuis, Debbie J., and Maria-Pia Victoria-Feser. 2013. "Robust VIF Regression with Application to Variable Selection in Large Data Sets." *Annals of Applied Statistics* 7(1):319–41.

Efron, Bradley. 1979. "Bootstrap Methods: Another Look at the Jackknife." *Annals of Statistics* 7(1):1–26.

Efron, Bradley, and Gail Gong. 1983. "A Leisurely Look at the Bootstrap, the Jackknife, and Cross-Validation." *American Statistician* 37(1):36–48.

Elwert, Felix, and Christopher Winship. 2010. "Effect Heterogeneity and Bias in Main-Effects-Only Regression Models." In *Heuristics, Probability and Causality: A Tribute to Judea Pearl*, edited by Felix Elwert and Christopher Winship, 327–36. London: College Publications.

Esping-Andersen, Gosta. 1990. *The Three Worlds of Welfare Capitalism*. Cambridge: Polity.

Fawcett, Tom. 2006. "An Introduction to ROC Analysis." *Pattern Recognition Letters* 27(8): 861–74.

Foster, Dean P., and Robert A. Stine. 2004. "Variable Selection in Data Mining: Building a Predictive Model for Bankruptcy." *Journal of the American Statistical Society* 99(461): 303–313.

Foster, Dean P., and Robert A. Stine. 2008. "α–investing: a Procedure for Sequential Control of Expected False Discoveries." *Journal of the Royal Statistical Society: Series B (Statistical Methodology)* 70(2):429–44.

Freedman, David A. 2006. "On the So-Called 'Huber Sandwich Estimator' and 'Robust Standard Errors'." *American Statistician* 60(4):299–302.

Gavrishchaka, Valeriy V., and Supriya Banerjee. 2006. "Support Vector Machine as an Efficient Framework for Stock Market Volatility Forecasting." *Computational Management Science* 3(2):147–60.

Goeman, Jelle J. 2010. "L1 Penalized Estimation in the Cox Proportional Hazards Model." *Biometrical Journal* 52(1): 70–84.

Goeman, Jelle J., Rosa Meijer, and Nimisha Chaturvedi. 2012. *L1 and L2 Penalized Regression Methods* (R package). http://cran.r-project.org/web/packages/penalized/vignettes/penalized.pdf.

Halko, Nathan, Per-Gunnar Martinsson, and Joel A. Tropp. 2011. "Finding Structure with Randomness: Probabilistic Algorithms for Constructing Approximate Matrix Decompositions." *SIAM Review* 53(2):217–88.

Han, Jiawei, Micheline Kamber, and Jian Pei. 2012. *Data Mining: Concepts and Techniques.* 3rd ed. New York: Elsevier.

Haralick, Robert, and Rave Harpaz. 2007. "Linear Manifold Clustering in High Dimensional Spaces by Stochastic Search." *Pattern Recognition* 40(10):2672–84.

Hastie, Trevor, and Robert Tibshirani. 1996. "Discriminant Adaptive Nearest Neighbor Classification." *IEEE Transactions on Pattern Analysis and Machine Intelligence* 18(6): 607–16.

Hastie, Trevor, Robert Tibshirani, Jerome Friedman, and James Franklin. 2009. *The Elements of Statistical Learning: Data Mining, Inference, and Prediction.* 2nd ed. New York: Springer.

Hsu, Jason C. 1996. *Multiple Comparisons: Theory and Methods.* New York: Chapman & Hall.

Hyvärinen, Aapo, Juha Karhunen, and Erkki Oja. 2001. *Independent Component Analysis.* New York: John Wiley & Sons.

Hyvärinen, Aapo, and Erkki Oja. 2000. "Independent Component Analysis: Algorithms and Applications." *Neural Networks* 13(4):411–30.

Ioannidis, John PA. 2005. "Why Most Published Research Findings are False." *PLoS Medicine* 2(8):e124.

Jaccard, James, and Robert Turrisi. 2003. Interaction Effects in Multiple Regression. 2nd ed. Thousand Oaks, CA: Sage.

Jencks, Christopher, Marshall Smith, Henry Acland, Mary Jo Bane, David Cohen, Herbert Gintis, Barbara Heyns, and Stephan Michelson. 1972. *Inequality: A Reassessment of the Effects of Family and Schooling in America.* New York: Basic Books.

Kostaki, Anastasia, Javier M. Moguerza, Alberto Olivares, and Stelios Psarakis. 2012. "Support Vector Machines as Tools for Mortality Graduation." *Canadian Studies in Population* 38(3–4):37–58.

Kuhn, Max, and Kjell Johnson. 2013. *Applied Predictive Modeling.* New York: Springer.

Kuhn, Thomas S. 1962. *The Structure of Scientific Revolutions.* Chicago: University of Chicago Press.

Larose, Daniel T. 2005. *Discovering Knowledge in Data: An Introduction to Data Mining.* New York: Wiley.

Larson, Selmer C. 1931. "The Shrinkage of the Coefficient of Multiple Correlation." *Journal of Educational Psychology* 22(1):45.

Larzelere, Robert E., and Stanley A. Mulaik. 1997. "Single-Sample Tests for Many Correlations." *Psychological Bulletin* 84(3):557.

Laub, John H., Daniel S. Nagin, and Robert J. Sampson. 1998. "Trajectories of Change in Criminal Offending: Good Marriages and the Desistance Process." *American Sociological Review* 63(2):225–38.

Lazarsfeld, Paul Felix, and Neil W. Henry. 1968. *Latent Structure Analysis.* New York: Houghton Mifflin.

Lewis, David D. 1998. "Naive (Bayes) at Forty: The Independence Assumption in Information Retrieval." In *Machine Learning: ECML-98,* 4–15. Berlin: Springer.

Lin, Dongyu. 2011. *VIF Regression: A Fast Regression Algorithm for Large Data* (R package). http://cran.r-project.org/web/packages/VIF/VIF.pdf.

Lin, Dongyu, Dean P. Foster, and Lyle H. Ungar. 2011. "VIF Regression: A Fast Regression Algorithm for Large Data." *Journal of the American Statistical Association* 106(493):232–47.

Linzer, Drew A., and Jeffrey B. Lewis. 2011. "poLCA: An R Package for Polytomous Variable Latent Class Analysis." *Journal of Statistical Software* 42(10):1–29.

Marchini, Jonathan L., Christopher Heaton, and Brian D. Ripley. 2012. *FastICA Algorithms to Perform ICA and Projection Pursuit* (R package). http://cran.r-project.org/web/packages/fastICA/fastICA.pdf.

Martinsson, Per-Gunnar, Vladimir Rokhlin, and Mark Tygert. 2011. "A Randomized Algorithm for the Decomposition of Matrices." *Applied and Computational Harmonic Analysis* 30(1): 47–68.

McKinsey Global Institute. 2011. *Big Data: the Next Frontier for Innovation, Competition, and Productivity.* http://www.mckinsey.com/insights/business_technology/big_data_the_next_frontier_for_innovation.

Melamed, David, Ronald L. Breiger, and Eric Schoon. 2013. "The Duality of Clusters and Statistical Interactions." *Sociological Methods & Research* 42(1):41–59.

Miller, Alan. 2002. *Subset Selection in Regression.* 2nd Edition. Boca Raton, FL: Chapman & Hall/CRC.

Mooney, Christopher Z., and Robert D. Duval. 1993. *Bootstrapping: A Nonparametric Approach to Statistical Inference.* Newbury Park, CA: Sage.

Morrison, Denton E., and Ramon E. Henkel. 1970. *The Significance Test Controversy: A Reader.* New Brunswick, NJ: Transaction.

Murphy, Kevin. 2012. *Machine Learning: A Probabilistic Perspective.* Cambridge, MA: MIT Press.

Nickerson, Raymond S. 2000. "Null Hypothesis Significance Testing: A Review of an Old and Continuing Controversy." *Psychological Methods* 5(2): 241.

Nisbet, Robert, John Elder IV, and Gary Miner. 2009. *Handbook of Statistical Analysis and Data Mining Applications.* New York: Academic.

North, Matthew. 2012. *Data Mining for the Masses.* [United States:] Global Text Project.

Pearl, Judea. 2000. *Causality: Models, Reasoning, and Inference.* New York: Cambridge University Press.

Qian, Bo, and Khaled Rasheed. 2010. "Foreign Exchange Market Prediction with Multiple Classifiers." *Journal of Forecasting* 29(3):271–84.

Ragin, Charles C. 2008. *Redesigning Social Inquiry: Fuzzy Sets and Beyond*. Chicago: University of Chicago Press.

Ridgeway, Greg. 1999. "The State of Boosting." *Computing Science and Statistics* 31:172–81.

Rish, Irina. 2001. "An Empirical Study of the Naive Bayes Classifier." In *IJCAI 2001 Workshop on Empirical Methods in Artificial Intelligence*, 41–46.

Rubin, Donald B. 1978. "Bayesian Inference for Causal Effects: The Role of Randomization." *Annals of Statistics* 6(1):34–58.

Ruger, T. W., Kim, P. T., Martin, A. D., & Quinn, K. M. 2004. "The Supreme Court Forecasting Project: Legal and Political Science Approaches to Predicting Supreme Court Decision-making." *Columbia Law Review* 104(4):1150–1210.

Saville, Dave J. 1990. "Multiple Comparison Procedures: The Practical Solution." *American Statistician* 44(2):174–80.

Schonlau, Matthias. 2005. "Boosted Regression (Boosting): An Introductory Tutorial and a Stata Plugin." *Stata Journal* 5(3):330.

Shaffer, Juliet Popper. 1995. "Multiple Hypothesis Testing." *Annual Review of Psychology* 46(1):561–84.

Silver, Nate. 2012. *The Signal and the Noise: Why So Many Predictions Fail—But Some Don't*. New York: Penguin.

Tan, Pang-Ning, Michael Steinbach, and Vipin Kumar. 2005. *Introduction to Data Mining*. Boston: Addison-Wesley.

Taleb, Nassim N. 2005. *Fooled by Randomness: The Hidden Role of Chance in Life and in the Markets*. New York: Random House.

———. 2007. *The Black Swan: The Impact of the Highly Improbable*. New York: Random House.

Thomas, Scott L., and Ronald H. Heck. 2001. "Analysis of Large-Scale Secondary Data in Higher Education Research: Potential Perils Associated with Complex Sampling Designs." *Research in Higher Education* 42(5):517–40.

Tibshirani, Robert. "Regression Shrinkage and Selection via the LASSO." 1996. *Journal of the Royal Statistical Society, Series B (Methodological)* 58(1):267–88.

Tukey, John W. 1991. "The Philosophy of Multiple Comparisons." *Statistical Science* 6(1):100–16.

Vempala, Santosh S. 2004. *The Random Projection Method*. Providence, RI: American Mathematical Society.

Weerts, David J., and Justin M. Ronca. 2009. "Using Classification Trees to Predict Alumni Giving for Higher Education." *Education Economics* 17(1):95–122.

Williams, Graham. 2011. *Data Mining with Rattle and R: The Art of Excavating Data for Knowledge Discovery*. New York: Springer.

Williams, Richard. 2010. *Estimating Heterogeneous Choice Models with oglm*. Department of Sociology, University of Notre Dame. http://www3.nd.edu/~rwilliam/oglm/oglm_Stata.pdf.

Willis, Paul. 1977. *Learning to Labour: How Working-Class Kids Get Working-Class Jobs*. Farnborough: Saxon House.

Witten, Ian H., Eibe Frank, and Mark Hall. *Data Mining: Practical Machine Learning Tools and Techniques*. 3rd ed. New York: Morgan Kaufmann.

Xu, Lei, Adam Krzyzak, and Ching Y. Suen. 1992. "Methods of Combining Multiple Classi-fiers and their Applications to Handwriting Recognition." *IEEE Transactions on Systems, Man and Cybernetics* 22(3):418–35.

Zhang, Harry. 2004. "The Optimality of Naive Bayes." In *Proceedings of the Seventeenth International FLAIRS Conference*, 562–67.

NOTES

CHAPTER 5

1. The error rate is equal to the number of cases misclassified by the model divided by the total number of cases. Through bootstrapping, we can generate a distribution of error rates which is approximately normal. This distribution's mean will typically be larger than the naive estimate of the error rate from the training data, and will constitute the bootstrap estimate of the error rate. It is also possible to calculate the bootstrap standard error of this estimated error rate, which is equal to the standard deviation of error rates in the set of bootstrapped resamples divided by the square root of the sample size.

2. In leave-one-out CV, for a dataset consisting of n observations, a model is built on $n-1$ observations and then tested on the remaining observation. This is repeated n times. In essence, leave-one-out CV is a special case of k-fold CV where k is equal to n.

CHAPTER 7

1. Since we balanced these data on the outcome, the conditional probability of having insurance given age summarized in table 7.2 does not correspond to real population quantities. But since the insured and uninsured groups were randomly sampled (at differing rates), the relative differences in probability between age groups are informative.

2. Our additional controls are three measures of age distribution (percentage of the population under 18, percentages ages 18–34, and percentage 65 or older), three of racial distribution (percentages non-Hispanic white, black, and Latino), three of educational distribution (percentage of the adult population with less than a high school degree,

percentage who attended college but left without a degree, and percentage with a bachelor's or higher), the male unemployment rate, the poverty rate, the percentage of the workforce in professional and managerial occupations, and the percentage of the population identifying as evangelical Protestants.

3. Group 1 is the reference group, so it does not appear in the equation. X is a vector of the remaining "component" variables, and Z is a vector of the additional "control" variables.

CHAPTER 10

1. The way to read an ROC curve is as follows. Imagine that cases are arranged from left to right in order of the predicted probability of an outcome, as produced by a model. As we move from left to right, we move systematically downward in predicted probability from the highest percentiles to the lowest. At each point, all cases to the left are classed as positive (on the outcome) and all to the right are classed negative. The curve shows us what percentages of positives and negatives are correctly and incorrectly classified by the model at each centile of predicted probability. The diagonal line down the center represents 50%. This is what would be obtained through random guessing—that is, if the model was useless for helping us sort the cases into categories. Curves further left of and above this line represent improvements on random guessing. An area under the curve greater than 0.5 thus shows that the model is an aid in prediction; this permits comparison across models and with other binary classifiers like logistic regression.

2. The variables appearing in this figure refer to age, educational attainment (educ_att), census region (REGION), citizenship/nativity (cit2), race/ethnicity (race2), gender (female), occupational prestige (HWSEI), and total personal income (INCTOT).

CHAPTER 12

1. On the screen shown in figure 12.7, if Method is changed from "Normal Mixtures" to "K-Means Clustering", three options appear in the window: "Single Step", "Use within-cluster std deviations", and "Shift distances using sampling rates". We recommend choosing the second option.

2. This appears in the Iterative Clustering dialog, which is depicted in figure 12.10 and discussed below.

CHAPTER 14

1. *Apriori* is the name of the particular algorithm for generating classification rules which is used by SPSS Modeler. It is the first association rule algorithm, which was proposed by Agrawal and colleagues in the initial association rule paper cited above. Many other algorithms have been developed since. Interestingly, though they employ slightly varying logic, they all lead to the same set of association rules when applied to the same data.

INDEX

Note: *Page numbers in italics indicate figures and tables.*

bootstrap forests. *See* random (or bootstrap) forests

bootstrapping, 3, 20–23, 29, 65–66, 177–83, 245n1

Breiger, Ronald L., 45

Carma routine, 230

CART. *See* classification and regression trees

Cartesian plane, 197

categorical predictors, binning, 105–8

chi-squared automatic interaction detection (CHAID), 3, 26, 38, 55, 96–98, 97, 98, 115, 162. *See also* classification and regression trees; classification trees; decision trees; partition trees

Chronback's [fix in Word], 224

city-block distance. *See* Manhattan distance

classification and regression trees (CART), 3, 25, 26, 28, 55, 154, 162. *See also* chi-squared automatic interaction detection; classification trees; decision trees; partition trees

classification trees, 95, 99, 105, 162–84, 188. (*See also* chi-squared automatic interaction detection; classification and regression trees; decision trees; partition trees); boosted, 172–77, *175–79*; random forest, 172, 177–84, *180–83*

classifiers, 42, 54, 133–61; *k*-nearest neighbor, 134–41; multiple, 134, 156–61, *160*; naive Bayes, 3, 52, 58, 142–47, *144–46*; support vector machines, 3, 58, 140, 147–56, *149–54*

clustering, 3, 45, 147, 196–216, 223, 226; hierarchical, 199–203; nearest neighbor, 58, 134–41, *137–41*, 156, 158, 159, 203–8; normal mixtures, 208–12; self-organizing maps, 212–15

Collins, Linda M., 45

column contributions, 171, 175–76, 181

Comon, Pierre, 125

confusion matrix, 39–43, *41*, 100, 143, *145*, 154, 181; of logistic regression, 94, 95, 99

continuous predictors, 24, 50, 143; continuous outcomes and, 100–105; discretizing, 95–100

convenience samples, 20

conventional statistical approach, 5–7, 13–29, 45, 50, 66; challenge of complex and nonran-

dom samples in, 20; heteroscedasticity as threat to validity in, 17–20; hypothesis testing in, 15–17; nonlinearity in, 24–25; predictive power in, 13–15; procedures for avoiding pitfalls associated with, 20–23; statistical interactions in, 25–27

correlation matrix, 4, 24, 117, *117*, 229

Cortes, Corrina, 147

Cover, Thomas, 134

Cox's R^2 169

C_p, 74

Crossfold, 67

cross-tabulation, 7

cross-validation (CV), 17, 29–32, 48, 63–71, 106, 172, 245n2; as alternative to significance testing, 20, 23; *k*-fold. *See k*-fold cross-validation; for *k*-nearest neighbor classification, 134–38; logic of, 63–65; methods of, 65–71; overfitting avoided with, 34–35, *35*, 164, 178, 188; stepwise regression and, *69*, 74, 79

data dredging, 17, 30, 79

data mining (DM): basic terminology of, 9; definition of, 3–6; software and hardware for, 7–8 (*see also specific software*)

data partitioning. *See* decision trees

decision trees, 3, 19, 28, 46, 51, 55, 95. *See also* chi-squared automatic interaction detection; classification and regression trees; classification trees; partition trees

"deep learning" methods, 3

DEFF (design effects), 20

dendrograms, 199–201, *202*

dependent variables, 9–10, 14, 22, 26, 108–111, 130–33, 228; binning and, 98–99, 105–6; data mining methods and, 35–39, 50, 52; distribution of, 54, 224, *225*; features and, 54–58, 116; heteroscedasticity and, 17–19; in neural networks, 186, 189; nonlinearity and, 24–25; variance on, 72, 108, 123, 163

design effects, 20

dimensionality, 11–12, 116–17, 121, 123, 132, 135–36, 148

discretization, 19, 25, 94–100, 102–5, *103, 104*, 143, 229–30

DM. *See* data mining

domain experts, 54

Duncan Socioeconomic Index, 101–2, *101–4*, 104